I am really excited about Peyton J[...] personal confrontation, biblical so[...] Peyton sets our eyes on the beautif[...] the lost. I really enjoyed this book, and you will too.

Daniel Fusco, pastor, Crossroads Community Church (Vancouver, Washington and Portland, Oregon); author, *Honestly*

To reach the unreached, we need to get back to basic book-of-Acts principles! Peyton Jones has written a book that will lead the everyday Christian to those basics, and if followed, help to reach the unreached for Christ!

Don Overstreet, president/lead strategist, LA Reaching LA Foundation

Provocative, contemplative, and encouraging. *Reaching the Unreached* inflames the reader's heart, ruminating a quest to drive engagement to reach the lost. Ministry desk-jockeys be warned, this book may lead to radical change!

Matt Fretwell, national director of operations, New Breed Church Planting

If you're dispirited with a toothless twenty-first century version of the New Testament church and are ready to personally engage the intoxicating mission of God, then learn from Peyton's own story. The life-giving journey from sacred consumer to spiritual commando is the path where we connect with the person, presence, and power of God. Highly recommend.

Jeff Christopherson, vice president, Send Network (NAMB); author, Kingdom Matrix

In *Reaching the Unreached* Peyton Jones blends a unique mix of solid biblical foundations, real-life experience, and a fast-paced writing style that packs a punch. You won't be bored reading this book. You'll learn and you'll be inspired to reach the unreached.

Steve Addison, author, *Pioneering Movements: Leadership that Multiplies Disciples and Churches*

Reaching the Unreached is a biblical, transferrable approach creatively designed to motivate and mobilize the church to the front lines of mission. Jones cleverly draws principles directly from the book of Acts, translating them into twenty-first century language and context.

Linda Bergquist, church planting catalyst, North American Mission Board; coauthor, *Church Turned Inside Out*

Peyton has many years of experience in frontline ministry and also training leaders to reach the unreached. Read this book and you'll be sure to flee the office and hit the streets with the gospel.

Alan Briggs, multiplying catalyst, ministry coach, and director, Frontline Church Planting; author, *Guardrails*

People are not merely projects to be fixed. They're image bearers of God in need of the gospel. When it comes to mission and evangelism, there are no short cuts or gimmicks. It is a labor of love. Peyton does a great job of communicating the heart of the Scriptures over and above what "sounds good." Relevant, current, and convicting.

Alex Early, Pastor of Preaching and Theology, Redemption Church

I love Peyton Jones's heart for God and for people who are far from him. I love how he thinks about our mission of seeking and saving the lost, and how he does it in his life. You should read *Reaching the Unreached* and everything else Peyton writes on this topic!

Vince Antonucci, pastor, Verve Church in Las Vegas; author *God for The Rest of Us*

Jones combines the great commission with Acts 1:8 to form a powerful message about reaching the unreached. Put his thoughts into action, and reaching the unreached will no longer be a lost art.

Bill Easum, president, The Effective Church Group

Peyton and I have the same hunger to witness the undeniable, unexplainable, and uncontrollable work of the Spirit empower our church planting enterprises. He might just be the most qualified guy I've ever met to write a book about this subject.

Clint Clifton, author, *Church Planting Thresholds*

Readable and engaging, Peyton Jones's *Reaching the Unreached* puts its finger on precisely where it hurts . . . and where it needs healing. An insightful and challenging meditation on the Great Commission and what it means today.

Dr. Robert E. Logan, author, *The Church Planting Toolkit*

Peyton's direct, no-nonsense message of our need to embed biblical evangelism into the DNA of our churches is spot on. His stories and insights challenge me on nearly every page. I highly recommend *Reaching the Unreached* to anyone involved in church planting and multiplication.

Todd Wilson, founder and director, Exponential

Reaching the Unreached is a much-needed gut punch and a call to return to the first love, and first works of the church: actually reaching lost people with the good news of the gospel. Peyton Jones makes our heritage as Christians come alive as the true adventure it was meant to be.

Caesar Kalinowski, author, *Gospel Primer* and *Bigger Gospel*

Don't be fooled by Peyton's playful style and pop-culture references. There are deep, timeless themes coursing through this compelling book. Winsome and wise, this book calls the church to come out, into the life of mission, to receive our inheritance of adventure and joy.

Brian Sanders, executive director, The Underground Network

If you care about the future of the church, then you should read this book. *Reaching the Unreached* articulates principles that will empower and unleash Jesus followers in the places that they live, work, and play.

Dave Runyon, coauthor, *The Art of Neighboring*

There is a desperate need for ordinary, down-to-earth evangelism to be rediscovered by the American church. Peyton's book is the best apologetic for that rediscovery that I have read in a very long time. This book will winsomely convince you that it's time to get back into the game—back to doing the work of evangelism.

Mike Breen, founder, 3DM

Reaching the Unreached paints a picture of what it looks like to be a twenty-first century missionary and how to mobilize followers of Christ into mission and relationship in the communities God has placed us.

Chris Lagerlof, executive catalyst, Mission OC

Wow! This book could not have come at a better time for our team as we are evaluating all we are doing in trying to reach the unreached. Great writing and power-packed with illustrations and applications. This is going to help our church!

Ron Edmondson, pastor, author, blogger

Read this book, if you dare. Peyton Jones delivers a passionate call to action for the local church. This book will inspire you to change your strategy and reframe your ideas about reaching people far from God.

Brian Bloye, senior pastor, West Ridge Church;
coauthor, *It's Personal*

Peyton Jones is a hard-hitting evangelist with a heart to see people saved. His heart for infiltration is a shared passion, and I am excited to see how this book mobilizes the masses.

Dhati Lewis, lead pastor, Blueprint Church in Atlanta, Georgia; director of BLVD, NAMB

In *Reaching the Unreached*, Peyton Jones combines his knowledge of Scripture with his passion for today's church. The result is a practical, biblical, and missional approach that any church of any size will be able to use.

Karl Vaters, author, *The Grasshopper Myth*; director, newsmallchurch.com

Time to transform church from weekly performance to daily mission. No more spectators! Reaching the Unreached is thoroughly biblical and intensely practical. Jones's stories are real, hopeful, and as gutsy and dangerous as the Great Commission he calls us back to.

Kris Langham, pastor, Refuge Long Beach; founder, Through the Word app

Let Peyton guide you back to Jesus's original adventure of mission on a path that is creative and biblical, provocative and practical. Peyton turns Acts 1:8 into Axe 1:8— cutting to truth, chopping dead branches, and clearing the way to Jesus's original adventure that we often call the church's mission.

Will Mancini, founder and team leader, Auxano

Biblical, honest, transparent, provocative, and challenging! These are the words I use to describe *Reaching the Unreached*. Filled with numerous stories, humor, and wisdom, Jones's book is a raw look at what we are all called to do, but few do: make disciples. Read and heed!

J. D. Payne, pastor, missiologist; author, *Evangelism* and *Apostolic Church Planting*

REACHING THE UNREACHED

BECOMING RAIDERS OF THE LOST ART

PEYTON JONES

FOREWORD BY ALAN HIRCH | AFTERWORD BY CAREY NIEUWHOF

ZONDERVAN®

ZONDERVAN

Reaching the Unreached
Copyright © 2017 by Peyton Jones

This title is also available as a Zondervan ebook.

Requests for information should be addressed to:
Zondervan, *3900 Sparks Dr. SE, Grand Rapids, Michigan 49546*

ISBN 978-0-310-53110-4

Cover design: David Welch
Cover photo: David Welch
Interior design: Kait Lamphere
Interior photos: bsd555/123RF, pandavector/123RF, pandavector/123RF, Alexandr Pintyuk/123RF, Ecelop/istock, Oleh Markov/Shutterstock, Dn Br/Shutterstock, grmarc/Shutterstock, miceking/123RF

Printed in the United States of America

17 18 19 20 21 22 23 24 25 /DHV/ 15 14 13 12 11 10 9 8 7 6 5 4 3 2 1

CONTENTS

To Refuge Long Beach, who taught me more about
being on mission than I ever taught you

FOREWORD

The present is theirs. The future from where
I've primarily worked, is mine.

TESLA

There are those in every field who seem to be working from the future. It may take years for their colleagues to catch up to their ideologies or principles. Even today, Tesla's ideas are largely revolutionary. Scientists look back and scratch their heads, wondering how he could fathom such mysteries years ahead of his time. As the founder of forward-thinking ministries such as Forge International, and Future Travelers, I've dedicated much of my writing career and ministry to preparing the church for the future that is coming. Many of the ideas may seem new and ahead of their time, but as I pointed out in *The Forgotten Ways*, these truths, when uncovered and restored to the church, will cause a *Permanent Revolution*. After all, the great scientist Newton claimed that he was only "thinking God's thoughts after him." How much more so with those of us who write about the church. If it's true genius, it belongs to him. We've merely tapped into what he was already saying. God himself is the ultimate innovator.

Personally, it has been refreshing for me to see a generation of leaders being raised up who are voices crying in the wilderness for everyday believers to become empowered by the Holy Spirit, as they have the gifts awakened within them. Peyton Jones is one of those leaders. Those of us who subscribe to the APEST model realize that leadership is not the point of Paul's message. Rather, it is the equipping of the saints that will fill the earth with the presence of Christ, as each part does its share. *Reaching the Unreached* takes that next necessary step that such conversations need to take.

Reaching the Unreached will serve the church for years to come in the principles that are laid down. Similarly, the New Testament continues to be the ultimate source that the church goes back to repeatedly to ask a collective, "How shall we then live?" Ultimately, how we respond to Jesus's words and the response of the apostles will determine the church's place in the world. Jones believes, like I do, that the kingdom of God is big enough for even the birds to perch in, and that we ourselves have limited it by thinking small.

Here's to the visionaries. Those who, like Tesla, Einstein, and Newton, seem to be tapping into God's thoughts and thereby taking us further than we thought possible. As in the realm of God's universe, so in the realm of mission. There are new frontiers to cross. God is waiting for us to rediscover his thoughts.

ALAN HIRSCH
Founder of 100Movements, Forge International,
The 5Q Collective. Author of numerous books including
The Forgotten Ways, The Permanent Revolution, *and* 5Q.

ACKNOWLEDGMENTS

First, I thank God, who took a spiritual hobbit and made him a burglar. Took a bookworm, and made him a raider. It's been quite a journey.

To my wife, Andrea, my coadventurer in everything written in these pages, the number one Inkling, best friend, favorite theologian, and funniest comedian. Without your heart for missions, I'd still be in the lecture halls and would have never learned to crack a whip.

To my Inklings group (in particular Andy Froiland, Dan Samms, Matt Frettwell, Joel Hughes, Ty Petersen, and Beau Moffat). You've saved this book from being a bigger mess than it is.

To the team at Zondervan, Ryan Pazdur, Paul Pastor, Kim Tanner, and Nathan Kroeze.

To my agent, Steve Laube, who has given me many a beating to make me a better author.

To everyone else who has had the guts to accompany me on some harebrained scheme . . .

Thank you.

CHAPTER 1

A BUTT-KICKING IS A TERRIBLE THING TO WASTE

Reaching the Unreached Isn't a New Thing... It's a New Testament Thing

Fight the good fight of the faith.

1 TIM. 6:12

I keep telling you, you listen to me more, you live longer!

SHORT ROUND

The morning of the epic beatdown of my life, I was a missionary in Port Talbot, a rough steel-working town in Wales, United Kingdom.

I was to be welcomed as the evangelist at Dr. Martyn Lloyd-Jones's legendary church, Sandfields. To this day, I don't know what I did to anger him—not Lloyd-Jones, he was dead, but the 300-plus pound rugby player on the Juice. I was new to driving on the "wrong" side of the road, so maybe I triggered his 'roid-fueled rage by doing something stupid. I may never know. In any case, as he pulled alongside us, he flipped us off, British style, gesturing with a backward peace sign and shouting through the rolled-up window. Like a bad kung-fu film, his mouth was moving, but nothing intelligible could be heard through the glass of his car window.

I thought no more of it, pulling over to park in front of the church. But as I made my way around the building, he was across the street, beckoning me to come over to the entrance of an alley, postured like he wanted to tell me a secret.

The secret was that he was going to beat a hole into the street with my head. Unaware of his intentions, I crossed the street to explain myself. Since I was going into a church building, I didn't want him to associate my stupidity with Jesus.

Rounding the corner, I approached him, attempting to explain myself with the universal blanket statement for stupidity in the UK.

"I'm a yank."

That usually did the trick.

As I got within reach, he lunged at me, screaming. I'm a short guy—five feet, seven inches. He hefted me effortlessly off of the ground, my feet dangling inches above terra firma. For a half second it was as if my childhood dream of being an astronaut was being fulfilled.

Then the shaking started.

He simultaneously shook me and bellowed obscenities into my face. He shook so hard that the next day, bruises formed in the shapes of his fists from where he'd bunched my sweater in his hands.

Then the throwing started.

Depending on your point of view, the brick wall that stopped the throwing could have been a bad or good thing. But before I had time to get back to my feet, he utilized a rugby move, flipping me facedown.

Then the hitting started.

All five hundred pounds of pressure per square inch of haymaker barreled down on the back of my skull, only the asphalt getting between me and oblivion. As he hammered me into unconsciousness, my forehead split open, crunching the front of my skull into the pavement. The solitary eyewitness—a woman parking her car across from the alleyway—later reported to police that he appeared to have no intention of stopping. She shouted repeatedly, "He's killing him!"

as he rained down blows on my limp form. Her panicked screams probably saved my life. The scar just above my left eye reminds me of the valuable lesson I learned that day . . . next time, run.

But running would have caused me to miss another lesson about not walking down dark alleys in the UK. Nobody likes a beatdown, but beatdowns can reimburse with wisdom what they cost in pain.

IN THE CAGE WITH JESUS

That wasn't the first time I had my butt kicked.

Being five feet, seven inches tall doesn't give many martial advantages other than providing a bit of a fighting spirit. Some call it "short man syndrome." When I was a teenager, my high school coach called it being a "punk."

I guess he was right. I am a punk, and I owe a lot of that to my short stature. I might need to climb a tree Zacchaeus-like to see Jesus walking past, but looking up at the world from my low-to-the-ground vantage point gives a man an interesting perspective. Being a punk with short man syndrome has taught me that a butt-kicking is a terrible thing to waste. A knee to the crotch, a boot to the head, a fist to the nose—getting wailed on from time to time offers an even more unique angle. Right now, the church seems small, acts a bit like a punk, and seems to be facedown on the street, spitting blood. I'm just not sure that it's learned its lesson or gained any new perspective. Throughout history, when the church has been in that place, Jesus has used the experience to flip us on our back, so that all we can do is look up.

I can't picture Jesus kicking anyone when they are down, but there are some things Jesus said to the seven churches of Asia to give them a new perspective despite being painful to hear. Sometimes I confess wanting to run from those passages myself. Probably because I see myself in them so much. Nevertheless, when you love somebody, you sometimes have to say some things that might inflict necessary pain . . . and I hear that Jesus loves us quite a bit.

That's why in Revelation 2 and 3, he says some very encouraging things to his church, but also says things that must have hurt:

- I have a few things against you.
- There are some among you who hold to the teaching of Balaam.
- You have a reputation of being alive, but you are dead.
- If you do not wake up, I will come like a thief.
- Because you are lukewarm—neither hot nor cold—I am about to spit you out of my mouth.
- You do not realize that you are wretched, pitiful, poor, blind and naked.
- You have forsaken the love you had at first.

The PJV (Peyton Jones Version) translates that last one, "You don't love me like you used to" or as Bill Medley sang, "You've lost that lovin' feelin' . . . now it's gone, gone, gone." Undoubtedly hard to hear, yet necessary for the relationship to return to full health. No matter how many times I've read those words in Revelation 2 and 3, I stagger away—dazed, with a ringing in my ears—but my soul is refocused and righted. There's nothing like getting your rear end lovingly handed to you by Jesus. Unlike a beating from a rugby player, it heals as much as it hurts. Indiana Jones's inspiration was a treasure hunter named Fedora, who tells Indy after he loses his first fight, "You lost today, kid, but that doesn't mean you have to like it." Not being crazy about confrontation, even with a good God, we usually avoid it like the plague. We run.

Why? Because although we're redeemed, the church is still a pooled amalgam of fallen humanity. We sew fig leaves for a living, trying to cover our nakedness. Over time, we've improved our skill at covering our naughty bits, but haven't improved upon Adam and Eve's lack of ability to humbly admit when we're wrong.

Perhaps the hardest jabs to the face in the letters to the seven churches is, "You have a reputation of being alive, but you are dead"

(Rev. 3:1). I imagine many people parking in the pews Sunday after Sunday can feel the deadness, despite attempts to put on a grand show up front. Like a WWE wrestler, we swagger across the stage, swinging at the air, faking clotheslines, stomping our feet in thunderclaps full of bravado, and talking tough. At some point, we stopped being the underground, countercultural dynamic force that we were during the first century. If our goal was to become a giant, then we may have reached our goal, at the cost of being a sleeping one. So the sleeping giant slumbers on . . . and dreams about how awesome it is.

When we lose our ability to collectively examine ourselves, we miss out on the necessary reexaminations, re-dresses, and rectifying work that would ensure the Church stays the dynamic, radical, cutting-edge movement it was designed to be. Is it any wonder that God occasionally has to raise his voice to rouse us from our slumber? Jesus's perpetual marching orders of mission echo down through the centuries because we still haven't accomplished the goal of reaching the ends of the earth.

Before I took that beatdown, I was sure I could take care of myself. I imagined I was tougher than I was. Like the seven churches of Asia, the church today imagines the same.

And we're still getting our butt kicked.

And with that butt-kicking comes a choice; stop and spar with Jesus's words and stand a fighting chance, or keep taking the pounding that has kept us pinned and knocked senseless. In *Raiders of the Lost Ark*, after Indy had five Nazis test him out as a human punching bag, his old flame Marion asks him where it hurts. Each cut, bruise, or scrape that he points to gets a kiss. Jesus's words rough us up a bit, but are an invitation to vulnerability, so he can heal those areas with a kiss.

CHASING THE CHICKEN

I'm not any crazier about taking a beating than anybody else, but I hold to the Proverb "blows and wounds scrub away evil" (Prov. 20:30).

In the movie *Rocky,* nobody wanted the big lug to win like Mickey did. "Mick" was the cranky shriveled little Irish guy who served as Rocky's coach. Rocky could stay the bum that boasted of beating Spider Rico, or he could become a real champion. And because Mickey saw that Rocky could be a contender, he ran him hard, gave him grief, and made him chase the chicken. He was willing to give Rocky the kick up the backside that a champion needs, but nobody wants. Because that's what coaches do. They discipline those that they love (Heb. 12:1–11).

In the same way, Jesus saw the unreached potential of the seven churches of Asia and jumped into the octagon for a sparring match, knowing the value of a good kicking to toughen them up for the real fight. Nobody loves the church as much as Jesus, who bled for it, but he'll confront it if they climb into bed with the stuff he hates, and tell it, "No Boom Boom!" When we're flat on our backs, he'll get down on his knees and yell at us to get up again . . . because he loves us . . . and he loves the lost around us. If we really are God's heavyweight contender in the fight of the ages, taking an occasional beating should be an expected occupational hazard of being a damage dealer for the Kingdom.

If our eyes swell up so bad we can't see, Jesus will be like Mickey cutting the eye, to help return our clear vision to keep us in the fight. Jesus seems to hold to the proverb "Faithful are the wounds of a friend" (Prov. 27:6).

Jesus wasn't afraid to ask Peter if he loved him that third time on the beach, knowing it would hurt Peter (John 21:17). Christ was unafraid to put his finger on the sensitive broken place, pin-pointing exactly where Peter needed healing. The letters to the seven churches help us to see how Jesus responds to churches that don't have it all together. Churches like ours. Am I alone in wondering what Jesus might say to the church today? Churches who have failed to fulfill the mission mandate to reach the unreached? Would he diagnose our vision as myopic? Would he pronounce the same painful verdict on our churches that he proclaimed regarding the church in Jerusalem, as swapping a house of prayer for a den of thieves?

Churches who have lost their way?

Churches who are starting to go down for the count?

Churches who don't know what hit them?

Churches like ours?

This isn't the first time the church has gotten its butt kicked by the world. Nor is it the first time it had to hear some tough guy stuff from Jesus. Throughout church history, God has raised up prophets and reformers like Martin Luther, William Tyndale, John Wycliffe, John Calvin, and Jon Huss who loved the church enough to jump into the cage and give all they got. God sends men like A. W. Tozer, John Wesley, J. Hudson Taylor, or Keith Green to deliver some kidney punches that bring us to our knees again; and we're better for it. Like the prophets of old, these men served as the metaphorical spiritual cage fighters of their day and were equally hated by the establishment because they stood for Jesus and raged against the machine. More often than not, however, we let our prophets go to waste. Has our perspective needed as much correction as the church in Jerusalem, the church prior to the reformation, or the church at other critical times before revival? Generally, the church throughout history has not been aware of its condition any more than when the letters to the seven churches were written, and has often ignored what Jesus has to say. Jesus remarked that if people didn't listen to him, they probably hadn't listened to his prophets either.

I'm no prophet. I'm just a knucklehead who can't shut up, like Martin Luther whose love for the church compelled him to "squawk as a goose among the swans."[1] I love the church. A lot. And writing this book has been like wrestling the angel, but my prayer is that you inherit the blessing. I may walk with a limp, have some scars, and have experienced my fair share of bare-knuckled beatdowns in order to be a temple raider.

But that's all an occupational hazard for those who were meant to make a dent in this world . . . and there I go talking about myself again. I'll do a little bit of that in this book, but I'm really talking about you and how you fit into Jesus's plan to reach the unreached. Therefore I intend to draw your attention to Jesus as he lays out his strategy for a church wired for impact. It may sometimes feel like the world is spinning, and you can barely focus, but if you can get up on your feet, you'll be the champion that Jesus knew you could be. Jesus wants the world to see the marks of his own fighting style in us as we swing like the heavyweights he died to make us. Like Mickey, Jesus has some words that will hurt, but ultimately reverse the decline that we find ourselves in, get our backs off the ropes, and help turn this fight around.

As demonstrated by the letters to the seven churches, the early church was far from perfect. They got a lot of things wrong. They invented a lot of heresy. They stalled out and moved in fits and starts, but when they were refocused and righted back on mission, they were masters at reaching their generation. I believe that's what Jesus was trying to do in the letters to the seven churches. He was trying to refocus them back on the original mandate in Acts 1:8, "But you will receive power when the Holy Spirit comes on you; and you will be my witnesses in Jerusalem, and in all Judea and Samaria, and to the ends of the earth." That had been the last thing he'd spoken about to the church at large before his ascension. It is still his last word to all of us. If we take an honest look at ourselves, let Jesus speak to us, and refocus back on that original mandate, I believe we'll take less butt-kicking and start kicking more butt. Just like they did in Acts.

KICKING BUTT FIRST-CENTURY STYLE

Have you ever read the book of Acts? It all started out so well. Pentecost was only one generation before John's letters to the seven churches, demonstrating how quickly the fight turns around. In Acts, the church was doing the butt-kicking. In the letters to the seven churches of Asia, it's hard to tell who's doing the lion's share of kicking—the world, the church, or Jesus. In Acts 1:7–8 Jesus lays out the mission strategy, "It is not for you to know the times or dates the Father has set by his own authority. But you will receive power when the Holy Spirit comes on you; and you will be my witnesses in Jerusalem, and in all Judea and Samaria, and to the ends of the earth." These words were a response to the disciples lined up in front of Jesus, ready for the end of the world to be served up just after breakfast. They had asked if now was the time for Jesus to restore the kingdom of the world to Israel. Jesus politely told them that kingdom restoration was none of their business, but from that moment on, they would be in the business of kingdom expansion.

Let's reword that conversation slightly.

"Lord, are you at this time going to restore the kingdom to Israel?" (Translation: Jesus, can we finish breakfast before you smite our enemies, and then we all go to heaven like bosses?)

Jesus replied, "It's not for you to know the times or dates that the Father has set by his own authority." (Translation: Guys, that's none of your business . . .) "But you will receive power . . . and you will be my witnesses . . . to the ends of the earth." (Translation: All this time you thought that the Father was in the restoration business, but first he's going to be expanding his business to the four corners of the globe, and you are a part of it at the ground level!)

The book of Acts unfolds in terms of the geographical expansion of the gospel from the epicenter of Jerusalem: "in Jerusalem, and in all Judea and Samaria, and to the ends of the earth." You could literally pull out a map of the Mediterranean and trace the entire structure of the book of Acts following Jesus's outline in Acts 1:8.

Here, I'll prove it:

- In Acts 1–7: We see them waiting in Jerusalem for the power to accomplish the mission of expanding the kingdom. "You will receive power . . . and you will be my witnesses in Jerusalem . . ."

- In Acts 8: Thanks to the persecution of Saul, the kingdom expands throughout Judea, even spreading to Samaria. "In all Judea and Samaria . . ."
- In Acts 9–28: The kingdom breaks beyond the Jewish barrier into "the ends of the earth." Paul, the apostle to the Gentiles, is converted in chapter nine. Peter has a vision, and finally accepts his mission to the Gentile world starting with Cornelius in chapter 10. From chapter 11 to the end of the book, Luke chronicles the expansion of the kingdom, eventually to Rome, the epicenter of the known world.

The rest is literally history.

From Jerusalem, the church spreads to the borders of the known world, or to the ends of the earth. Even though kingdom expansion is clearly in focus, we can easily be mistaken as the early disciples were, believing that kingdom restoration is the name of the game. We demonstrate this by opting to establish rather than multiply, or by building upward instead of spreading outward. We try to keep people in, instead of sending them out. We make Christianity about a show of force. Taking over. Being a presence. Getting big. Showing them all. Like the disciples in the first chapter of Acts, we obsess over the second coming when the majority of the world still hasn't heard of the first. In the nineties all we talked about was getting raptured, in an echo of the disciples' first order of business, "Can't we just go home now, Lord?"[2]

Nope.

There was work to do after breakfast that morning, and I'm not talking about dish duty. Acts reveals how the disciples reached the unreached in a pagan world. If we stand a fighting chance to impact our world, reaching the unreached, we're going to need to unpack what got the job done in the first century.

WHERE IS THE GOD OUR FATHERS TOLD US ABOUT?

Acts is the story of Jesus working powerfully through frail and broken humanity to aggressively expand his Church. But Acts wasn't written to show us how to do church. It was written to show us how to advance the Church in an unreached world. Talk about reaching the unreached! Nobody has had the challenge that the early church did. As the world's first Christians, they were the only Christians in the world. All the vast unconverted pagan empires lay before that small pack of Jewish boys and girls that Jesus commissioned. If anybody should be counted experts at reaching the unreached, it was they. Because to them, everybody they came into contact with was unreached.

But they took Acts 1:8 seriously, and lived that verse out to fulfillment. If we want to witness kingdom expansion like the apostles did, it's not enough to know what they knew. *We need to do what they did.* Two thousand years later, we flatter ourselves over and above our first-century counterparts, imagining we have the advantage of superior knowledge. Mission theorists traffic speaking circuits and endless conferences about "How to Reach the Unchurched" while failing to "get out there" themselves. The film *Raiders of the Lost Ark* contrasts Indiana Jones's swashbuckling adventures with his day job as an archaeology professor in the lecture halls of Princeton. But we never seem to graduate beyond making profound statements, to actually raiding sunken temples. Now is not the time in church history to wax lyrical. Ours is a day for living out, not sounding smart. Besides, the church has fewer answers than it realizes, or it would demonstrate more impact. We should be asking the right questions instead of providing wrong answers. As a rabbi, Jesus's method of teaching involved asking searching questions. In the gospels, Jesus asks 307 questions but only answered two. Why? Because Jesus knew that when we start asking questions, we begin to experience breakthroughs and gain deeper insight into our situations.

During the days of the Judges, bandits and enemies had the Israelites' backs to the ropes, beating their self-dependency out of them. There are eerie parallels between the days when "everyone did what was right in their own eyes" (Judg. 21:25 ESV) and our gimmicks, antics, and over-confidence today. Gideon may have been a coward, hiding in the bottom of a winepress against the onslaught of what was befalling his culture, but he turned the tide when he started asking the right questions.

"If the Lord is with us, why has all this happened to us?" (Judg. 6:13).

"Where are all his wonders that our ancestors told us about?" (Judg. 6:13).

I have a sneaking suspicion God's been waiting quite a while for us to ask the right questions. But the important questions don't sell books. The right questions are seldom popular. Asking them often guarantees that you won't be asked back to speak again. I don't have the corner market on the right questions, but some of them sound like:

- Why does the church seem to be losing when we're on the winning team?
- Why does the average Christian seem bored when Jesus is supposed to provide life more abundant?
- Why do most of the stories we hear about God working powerfully, like he did in Acts, tend to come from missionaries?
- Has the dynamic faith we read about in Acts been tamed into an impotent ghost of its former self?
- Have we replaced the power of the Holy Spirit with automation, processes, systems, money, and crowds?
- Why have we stripped mission of risk and faith, and opted for security instead of dependence upon God?
- What's the way back to becoming the dynamic force that Jesus unleashed on the world two thousand years ago?

- Does the church even know it has lost its way, or is it like the Laodiceans, blind, poor, and wretched without realizing it?

Perhaps you've asked some of those questions yourself but are coming up empty. In the famous brawl scene in the Cairo bazaar, Indiana Jones takes on a handful of thugs until a twirling sword master donned in black, steps into the clearing. Indy simply reaches for his trusty revolver, abruptly ending the fight.

I always wonder why he didn't lay hold of the more powerful weapon in the first place. It would have saved so much time and trouble. It's time the church asked that same question. We've got the invitation to receive the arsenal in Acts, and still we attempt to outsource what can only come from an eternal source. Incessantly firing blanks, the church appears to always be looking for another silver bullet. Perhaps we've ignored the real firepower at our disposal simply because what's not working is more convenient, comfortable, and familiar than what would actually work.

WHAT'S BEHIND DOOR NUMBER TWO?

I train a lot of church planters. You'd think that ministers planting a church would be able to strip it all back to the essentials, but it's at this level that I often see how we're tempted to reproduce newer versions of what's not working. We replace the power of an unpredictable God, wild to the core, with what is secure, manageable, and predictable. We opt for what's behind door number two. "I'll take critical mass, 100,000 dollars, and fail-safe formulas, Chuck!" Thus we've eschewed risk that necessitates the kind of faith that results in the unexpected workings of God. Gone are the days where people fell on their faces and cried, wept, and fasted for their communities, asking God to break in and do what he alone could do. Careful, corporate church systems are more predictable than a God who blows like the wind and doesn't feel obligated to explain everything. But if we're not careful, we run the risk of sacrificing true spiritual power—the only thing that makes accomplishing the mission possible—for the false "power" of numbers, money, and savvy. Western culture tells us to systematize, automate, or medicate away any minor annoyance. Could it be that we've done the same with our spiritual challenges? Have we exchanged rote programs and clever church branding for the work of the Holy Spirit? The answer for the complex issues facing the early church as well as the challenges faced in the Old Testament was simply to return to him.

Last time I read, "Here I am! I stand at the door and knock. If anyone hears my voice and opens the door, I will come in and eat with that person, and they with me." (Rev. 3:20), the message was clear.

Jesus wants his church back.

ACCEPT NO SUBSTITUTES!

Remember Indiana Jones substituting the temple god with a bag of sand at the beginning of *Raiders of the Lost Ark*? Substituting Jesus's words is like substituting your sacred morning coffee with dirty water. "Accept no cheap substitutes" is a misnomer. Cheap substitutes are costly. Ask Indy what the cost was of substituting a golden idol with a bag of sand—it brought the whole temple crashing down around him. Our substitutes have cost us our ability to effectively reach the world around us, and the church has been crumbling as a result.

So just what exactly have we been substituting? Perhaps a better question might be, in substituting one thing for another, what has been sacrificed in the process? If Jesus wrote seven letters to the church today, what might they say?

- You've sacrificed reach for size
- You've sacrificed adventure for security

- You've sacrificed significance for "success"
- You've sacrificed the mission for meetings
- You've sacrificed my power for programs
- You've sacrificed my approval for applause

Jesus told the lukewarm Laodiceans that they were poor, blind, and naked like a cold water contradiction to their self-perception of being rich, successful, and content. True, his word choices would earn Jesus a troll-label in social media circles. But if we've become guilty of building church as a brand, drinking the American "bigger-is-better" success-syndrome Kool-Aid, smacking the cyanide cocktail out of our hands is the most loving thing he could do.

Look, if his love for the church is strong enough to die for it, then that love always tells the truth, even if it hurts. Jesus reminded the Laodiceans that, "those whom I love, I reprove and discipline, so be zealous and repent" (Rev. 3:19 ESV). True to his character, Jesus relentlessly comes after his bride like Hosea, refusing to abandon us to our idolatrous condition. Like the lover he is, he invites himself to dinner so we can talk over the details and get back on track. Although we've abandoned his mission, he's not abandoned the church. He refuses to abandon us, just as he refuses to abandon the world we're called to reach.

Carey Nieuwhof said:

I understand that the idea of the church being imperfect makes some people despair. But rather than making us despair, the fact that Jesus started the church with imperfect people should make us marvel at God's incredible grace. That God would use ordinary, broken human beings as vessels of his grace, and delight in it is awe-inspiring. He's proud of how his grace is beating through your imperfect-but-redeemed life and through the church. The idea that God would use *you* and *me* is pretty amazing. He had other options.[3]

He may have had other options, but he's never made other plans.*

The church doesn't need to be perfect to reach the unreached, and neither do you. God has always planned to win this war against the kingdom of hell with bullet-riddled planes. In the European amphitheater during World War II, too many Allied planes were shot down in flames. They put a statistician named Abraham Wald on the job to research where he should attach extra armor to protect the fly guys. When a plane returned from battle full of holes, he put a mark on every spot that a bullet pierced. When he calculated all of his data, he put the extra armor in the places that had the fewest holes, not the most. He reasoned that the bullet holes in the returned planes were random luck rather than the skill of the enemy pilot. He further reasoned that the planes that were getting shot down were getting shot in places the returning planes were not. Vital places. It was the holes that he wasn't seeing—in the planes that weren't returning—that needed extra protection. The spots that didn't have bullet holes in the returning planes were where the fuselage was, and putting extra armor there turned the tide of the battle for the skies.[4] Today, our church buildings may be shiny new planes, but they don't seem to get airborne anymore. I'd rather be bullet ridden and busted up, yet winning the war. What if, in the church's crisis of today, everybody's patching the bullet holes and putting armor where it's not needed? Here are some of the voices bombarding the leaders of the church:

"Get better marketing."

"Make your website better."

"Buy my course for $39.99 a month."

Our search for success has diverted us from the timeless principles in the book of Acts. We need to patch up the parts of church that

---

* A word of warning however: If you can't handle a little loving fisticuffs from Jesus, you need a different scene. I would suggest something less radical than Christianity. You'd probably like religion. There are rules you can follow to make you feel really good about yourself. Personally, I've got a hunger for what's found in the pages of the book of Acts. That book has created a hunger in me since I was first saved, and I don't want to settle for anything less than the real deal.

people *aren't* talking about because, to be frank, we're not hearing enough about the first century. A return to first-century spirituality will result in first-century results. Francis Chan once asked a room full of Christians, "How many of you read the book of Acts and think, 'Man, I wish I lived in those days'?" He waited while a room full of hands shot up. Then he shocked the room, "Okay, I'm not talking to those of you who raised your hands. I want to spend the next few minutes talking to those of you in here who still believe the stuff in the book of Acts can happen *today*." The same God that moved in the Middle East two thousand years ago is on the move today, proving that reaching the unreached like they did in the first century is still possible in our age. The church of the Global South currently resembles the church of the first century, witnessing explosive growth unlike anything in the West.

AGAINST THE ODDS

In the same way that contemporary painters look back to the old Masters for inspiration, we need to cast our eyes back on the missiological principles of the early church. In one generation, the apostles turned the world upside down and had become a threat to the Roman Empire. Within three hundred years, they'd spread so rapidly, they made up ten percent of the population of that empire.[5] Whenever Indiana Jones traveled the world, a map on the screen traced a trajectory as a red arrow. The first-century church expanded at breakneck speed across the map of the known world at a much faster rate. Paul ran around expanding the kingdom like a chicken with its head cut off, whereas we roll around clucking with our legs cut off. Until we've mastered planting twenty-four churches in eleven years like Paul did, we'd probably better pull up a chair and listen to what Dr. Luke has to say about how the West was won. Because right now, we're not losing the West. We've lost it. C. S. Lewis said, "There is no neutral ground in the universe. Every square inch, every split second, is claimed by

God and counterclaimed by Satan."[6] Like Indiana Jones's arch enemy Belloq, Satan has snatched any ground gained, mocking us, "Once again Jones, what was briefly yours is now mine."[7] I don't know if you've been keeping score, but Western culture has us bowed and cowed, and we haven't won a single culture war in the past few decades. Instead, we've opted to make lesser, fleeting, and insignificant stands of morality at the cost of lasting eternal impact.

Dr. Martin Luther King Jr. wrote his insightful letter from the Birmingham jail cell that still rings true today.

> So often the contemporary church is a weak, ineffectual voice with an uncertain sound. So often it is an arch defender of the status quo. Far from being disturbed by the presence of the church, the power structure of the average community is consoled by the church's silent—and often even vocal—sanction of things as they are. But the judgment of God is upon the church as never before. If today's church does not recapture the sacrificial spirit of the early church, it will lose its authenticity, forfeit the loyalty of millions, and be dismissed as an irrelevant social club with no meaning for the twentieth century.[8]

THE ART OF MOVING CHRISTIANS AROUND

I know what you're thinking. Can it really be that bad? We can't be all that blind, poor, naked, and failing with all the TV and radio stations, big buildings, and bumper stickers.

Ed Stetzer reports that 80–85 percent of American churches are on the downside of their life cycle, thirty-five hundred to four thousand churches close each year, and the number of unchurched has almost doubled from 1990 to 2004.[9]

He reports:

- In 1900, there were 28 churches for every 10,000 Americans.
- In 1950, there were 17 churches for every 10,000 Americans.

- In 2000, there were 12 churches for every 10,000 Americans.
- In 2011, the latest year available, there were 11 churches for every 10,000 Americans.[10]

The research also showed that in the hundred years between 1900 and 2000, "the number of churches increased just over 50 percent while the population of the country has almost quadrupled"[11]

As our congregations have shrunk in recent years, leaders have hired consulting experts to tag and bag the beast that's devouring their churches. Rather than spinning our wheels by asking what's causing the problem, we need to concentrate on the last thing that Jesus told us to do. Go. In the Great Commission, we find answers to the perpetual problem instead of endless surveys and white papers. Jesus saves us from introspectively staring at our navels to gain enlightenment about the problem, and points us to the solution of becoming the answer. Despite what the experts have been selling, the solution isn't slapping a sexier logo on a website, or adding a couple of signs, or remodeling a building to advertise more of what the world's not buying. Perhaps those things can gather a crowd, but heck, P. T. Barnum and Bailey can do that. I thought we were trying to reach the lost, not run a circus. Richard Stearns wrote, "The church that causes the demons to shudder is the church hell-bent on finishing the job that Christ commanded the church to do. Just as Odysseus tied himself to the mast so that he would not be lured off course, so, too, must our churches focus unwaveringly on completing the unfinished mission of the kingdom."[12]

Like Indy replacing the temple god with a bag of sand, we've replaced Spirit-empowered evangelism with marketing—mistaking them for the same thing. Nevermind that our temples seem to be crashing down on our heads. Marketing should supplement evangelism, not substitute it. The difference between the two is that marketing enters the conversation people are already having and cashes in on it. Evangelism creates a new conversation, initiating a thirst for something people don't necessarily want, yet realize they desperately need. In effect, marketing appeals to a desire that's already there. Evangelism creates a desire that wasn't there before. Marketing will draw Christians to "sexier" churches. Evangelism will create Christians out of non-Christians and create a need for new churches once people come to faith.

Marketing and attracting crowds of Christians from other churches is what leaders fall back on when they don't have the nerve to hit the front lines and actually reach lost people. It comes from a lack of faith, and quite frankly, the art of shuffling Christians around in a game of musical churches isn't biblical. When the music stops, we still aren't reaching the lost. There are many books, seminars, and talks that will teach you how to reorganize Christians into shiny new boxes like a Christian Martha Stewart, but unlike Martha's mantra, it's not "a good thing." In *Jurassic Park*, Dr. Ian Malcom noted that the mess they were in was because "the scientists were so preoccupied with whether they could, that they didn't stop to think if they should." When boiled down, the techniques really amount to the science of osmosis between the semi-permeable membranes between two churches. I don't want weird science, I'm hunting for art; the lost art of reaching the unreached.

THE SLIDE INTO DARKNESS

Perhaps our unwillingness to return to first-century principles is because we believe that we face worse odds than our first-century counterparts. The reality is that the spiritual, philosophical, and societal climate that Paul and the apostles stepped into is not all that different from the brave new world the church faces today. On a practical level, our post-Christian world is very much like the apostles' pre-Christian world, and if the challenges are the same, then so are the solutions. Rediscovering the first-century tactics will result in us reaching our own unreached generation just as they did.

Let's briefly examine the intersection of the first and twenty-first centuries to find common ground. Like society today, first-century society in the Roman Empire was a blend of religions in a unified political system that had loosely thrown them together. Faiths, values, and cultural customs blended due to the trade routes connecting the world similar to how the Internet brings us new goods and information. Among the educated was a deep skepticism of religion—in spite of the social norms of public Roman worship and competing world religions complete with the ensuing confusion, cynicism, and distrust of religion in general. Philosophy was elevated above religious dogma among the educated, but masked deep primitive superstitions below the surface among the general populace. Despite intellectual ascension over religious beliefs in Western society, the underlying pervasive belief in aliens, fear of ghosts, and acceptance of karma live in contradiction to the claims of science. Thus the inconsistency of our core beliefs betrays that we still fear what we don't understand, while unconvincingly claiming to understand everything. Superstition remains the underside of our intellectual achievements because our souls intrinsically know something that rationalism cannot prove, and won't be dismissed: the knowledge that we are not alone in the universe.

Decades before America, Europe began to slide back into this all-too-human posture in the early twentieth century. Into this atmosphere of skepticism, C. S. Lewis hit the scene and broadcast *Mere Christianity* over the airwaves to war-torn Britain. War-time Brits listened to an intelligent bare-bones apologetic of *Mere Christianity* because the sheer number of casualties left them in touch with their own mortality. Lewis connected with his post-modern audience through rationalizing the irrational, while also arguing the irrationality of rationalism. Cold rationalism had fallen short, and left the British public with an even greater spiritual longing than they'd known before. Lewis spoke into that spiritual vacuum and gave unflinching, faithful, and reasonable answers to the spiritual questions of the British populace.

What does that have to do with us in America? Have you noticed that as the spiritual climate grows colder in America, C. S. Lewis's writings somehow seem prophetically relevant to our culture nearly one hundred years later? What is the reason if not that America has finally caught up to Britain in the 1940s in its downward spiritual spiral and is now on a spiritual parallel? The reality is that when Lewis writes to war-torn Britain, he speaks to where America is today. Like never before, he hearkens like a prophetic voice from the future. When I immigrated to Europe in the late nineties, I felt like a time traveler, beholding America's future. In the nineties, our megachurches were at the tapering end of their growth spurt and had begun to plateau. We just didn't realize it. There was another growth spurt in 2001 after 9/11 hit, as people came through our doors looking for answers. They quickly dispersed after they discerned we didn't have anything that reached beyond Sunday mornings. After all, most of the emphasis in leadership circles was based on "making your Sunday Service better." The seekers and visitors didn't care for our services because they quickly deduced that our services didn't care for them. We were too excited that our question of getting bigger numbers was answered, but they needed us to answer the questions plaguing them.

A few decades down the road, has much changed? The further we get from the principles of Acts, the more our thought leaders attempt to postulate original ideas like Mars Hill philosophers, pitching profound-sounding theories about life and culture as the reason we're missing the mark, while the church continues to shrink. In an attempt to reverse the downward trend, savvy authors have watered down and undermined Scripture, imagining it will make us look more attractive to the unreached. We could learn a little from history here. The religious leaders in Britain also pandered a more liberal brand of Christianity after World War II, unintentionally emptying the churches in the process. Their approach backfired, and we're witnessing a repeat of history here in America. Once again, the church is out of answers and out of touch. Many Christians are so insulated in their ecclesiastical bubble that they're unaware the world around them moved on ages ago and no longer cares what they're saying. Besides, churches are still born out of a desire to draw a crowd, but the future belongs not to churches that can a draw crowd, but churches that can penetrate one.

Combining Jesus's mission mandates in the Great Commission and Acts 1:8, we find the promise that he'll accompany his church to the ends of the earth, until the end of the age. If Jesus promises to ride shotgun, we'd better let him call dibs. Otherwise, we're the spiritual equivalent of somebody who doesn't understand broadband technology and is still hunting for a faster dial-up modem. My friend, you've got mail. It's the same mail that the Spirit served up to the seven churches of Asia; it's a return to the Christ Himself as the only answer. Tozer said, "The world is perishing for lack of the knowledge of God and the Church is famishing for want of His presence."[13] Besides, the apostles discovered spiritual fiber optics two millennia ago.

The verdict: like the Pharisees, we postulate about the future, but can't discern our own times. In my opinion, the only futurists worth listening to connect the past to the present, and return us to the principles God laid down in the pages of Acts. Lewis himself said, "No man who bothers about originality will ever be original: whereas if you simply try to tell the truth (without caring twopence how often it has been told before) you will, nine times out of ten, become original without ever having noticed it."[14] You can't get more original than Peter, Paul, and Jesus. Despite the fact that we ignore the power of God that Jesus promised to the church on mission, it's still available. Acts remains the constant source of tried and true, timeless principles that show us how to reach the unreached in every culture, in every age, for every generation.

The Great Commission is a perpetual gauntlet that Jesus has thrown down to his church in every age. But he's not waiting to see what *we* can do. He's waiting for *us* to discover what *he* can do *through* us. If we'll trust him. The Book of Acts is a demonstration of what he can do against odds stacked up worse than what faces us today. Besides, it's not the odds that matter, but how we attempt to overcome them.

JUST DO IT

Still with me? I'm sure that hurt a little bit. Don't worry, I took a few hits myself there, but Jesus spars with those he loves. We love the church, right? She's been knocked out before, but she's still his Million Dollar Baby! She's going to win, but we want her to win this round! No matter how bad it looks, she's still the champ, and this fight isn't over yet. So after going a few rounds, I owe you some pep-talk-in-the-corner-time.

If the book of Acts were a video game, the spiritual equivalent of *Space Invaders*, the apostles topped the leader scoreboard in reaching the unreached. Their victory of the game owing to a combo move that pressed two buttons simultaneously—ceaseless action and prayerful dependence. Luke's narrative of a world set on fire by the apostles begins in Acts 1 as they prayed for the evangelistic power they knew they didn't have, but desperately needed. Acts chapter two was the result of possessing it. The outpouring of the Holy Spirit in answer to their powerlessness and dependency resulted in explosive action. It was a polar contrast to the inactivity and self-sufficiency that plagued the seven churches of Asia.

The apostles didn't sit in the upper room endlessly debating about missiology. And sitting around talking isn't going to change things for us either.* Like the apostles, we will have to get our feet moving and our hands dirty. When the seven churches of Asia were flat on their backs, Jesus gave each church its own unique action plan. Let's examine Jesus's action plan for the first church in Ephesus and apply it to our condition in the twenty-first century and see what happens.

To the church at Ephesus he said, "Remember therefore from where you have fallen; repent, and do the works you did at first" (Rev. 2:5 ESV). Boil that down and you've got *Remember, Repent,* and *Return.*

---

* If the apostles had just sat in the upper room having endless debates about theology, we'd have a ready excuse.

Remember from Where You've Fallen

Daredevil stunt motorcyclist Evel Knievel said, "Anyone can jump a motorcycle. The trouble comes when you try to land it."[15] When I was young, I slipped off a ledge while rock climbing, and slid, fell, and thudded back to earth. I was missing the skin off the back of my legs, had a suspected arm fracture, and a punctured side resulting from the rock waiting to catch me at the bottom. The severity of the pain at the end of every fall is measured by the height you fell from. For Ephesus, it fell from the heights recorded by Luke in Acts 19, an outbreak of revival. Luke chronicles Paul's riot-inducing evangelism, Aquila and Priscilla's church-planting skills, Apollos preaching the gospel, Paul baptizing a fresh wave of believers with the Holy Spirit, a massive book burning, the establishing of a church-planting hub, and other things worthy of temple-raiding adventurers (Acts 19:9–10). Not to mention that Timothy, Mary, and the Apostle John all lived in Ephesus for a time. That's a long way to fall! Take heart. Jesus urges us to remember when we were raiding temples instead of bowing to idols. Take a minute and remember how it used to be when you were the most intimate with Jesus. Get it. Got it? Good!

Repent

Here's the good news: the distance you've fallen doesn't equate to the road back. Jesus has traveled that distance for you. All you need to do is turn around.

Using the R word may make the other kids at church think you smell, but Jesus uses it copiously. He used it twice in the letters to the seven churches, first with the Ephesians, and then with the Laodiceans. In this context, *repentance* means to return. Turn around. For the Ephesians, turning around meant looking back to that place in Acts where they were full of revival power and efficiency, turning their city upside down, seeing lives changed from the inside out. For you and me, it will be a look back that returns us to the newness of our faith, when we were wholly consumed with worshipping Jesus and were his witnesses instead of our own. It's looking back to a time when others held you back from mission, rather than needing to urge you on. That look back ensures you don't waste a good butt-kicking and all of this pain turns to gain, to ensure that you get back there again.

Return to the First Works

What were your first works? The things you did when knowing Jesus was brand new? Every reader's experience of that series of new beginnings is different, but Jesus tells us to return to doing what we used to do. Remember it was called the book of *Acts*, not the book of *Thoughts*. Jesus called the Ephesians to action, knowing that a return to the first works will stir up something within us. And if you'll heed the same call, it'll be a return to not caring about what others think. It's a return to the thrill of realizing God can use your frail, flawed, and broken life. It's a return to a time when you were convinced that if you simply told somebody the truth—like letting the genie out of the bottle—their wildest wishes for love, absolution, and redemption would come true. Perhaps you were tapping the power back then. Real power. Because the Holy Spirit had found a willing partner. Or better yet, perhaps your deepest experience with God's power on mission still awaits you.

Discussion Questions

(For Dr. Jones, the Princeton professor in you)

1. What do you think Jesus would say to the church today if he wrote it a letter?
2. What would you like to see happening today that you have read about in Acts?

3. Describe what you used to do when you felt you were at the greatest height of your Christian experience that you don't do now.
4. What action steps could you take to return to the "first works" from that time?
5. What specific things come to mind when you think of the first works of the apostles?

Adventurous Actions

(For Indiana, the Temple Raider in you)

1. Make a list of things that you did when you were first saved and put them into practice this week. Be prepared to report on it next week.
2. D. L. Moody made a promise that he would tell somebody about Jesus every day for the rest of his life (he had to jump out of bed many times). Make that commitment this week alone and journal about the difference it makes.
3. Go on a date with God this week. (Get alone, go to a secluded spot, pray, read scripture, journal, take communion, and worship. Heck, maybe even fast for a day.) Return to the first works.

CHAPTER 2

WAIT

They waited . . . for power . . .
and waiting is the hardest thing to do.

*He ordered them not to depart from
Jerusalem, but to wait . . .*
LUKE (ACTS 1:4 ESV)

Satipo: "Let us hurry, there's nothing to fear here."
Indy: "That's what scares me."
RAIDERS OF THE LOST ARK

The fedora. The whip. The khakis. The revolver. The silhouetted stance of Indiana Jones holding a machete conjures the iconic Spirit of Adventure. But decking yourself out in the aforementioned gear, rushing in where angels fear to tread, hacking and slashing, gets you killed pretty quickly. Despite purchasing the accessories, you're no Indiana Jones. Before Indy's brief vine-slashing jungle adventures, there were years of painstaking research into Mayan archaeology that informed and equipped him once he got to the enshrouded ancient temple. Without the patient years of preparation, Indy would have been quickly impaled on the booby traps that Alfred Molina's character, Satipo, sprung in his haste to escape the temple with his stolen idol. Among his final words to Indy before double crossing him and becoming a human kebob, "You have no choice. Hurry!"

But hurrying to accomplish our mission may be the greatest hindrance to accomplishing it. Over 100 years ago, William Booth, founder of the frontline ministry The Salvation Army, warned that the chief danger confronting the church at the turn of the century would be "religion without the Holy Ghost." A century later, we are more in danger of that being true than it was when he uttered it. In our rush to accomplish the mission that Jesus gave us, we've forsaken the power that propelled our movement into the world. Worse still, our lack of awareness has rendered us as impotent as Samson springing from his chair, shorn of his hair. We rush out to whup up on the Philistines and instead receive yet another kicking. Samson recovered his strength only after getting back to his roots, and it will be no different for us.

What Jesus told his first followers in Acts 1 holds the secret to getting back to our roots. And that starts with the hardest word in the world.

Wait.

GO ON WITHOUT ME . . .

Thousands of years ago, an argument traveled on the back of the hot desert wind, which was blowing sand and scrub in the twilight. The spectacle of Moses' tent pitched in the distance outside the camp appeared all the more bizarre because of the one-sided argument Moses seemed to be having with the night air, his voice atypically desperate and tinged with anguish. God had given Moses the passport for Canaan and given Moses the "Go on without me" line. God would still give them the land. He'd still fulfill the promise to get them there, but God himself wouldn't be going. For Moses, this wasn't good enough.

A plea.

"I'm not going unless you're coming with us!"

A pause.

Silence.

Exasperation. "Show me your glory!"

Once you have basked in the glow of the face of God like Moses had, it is impossible to go through the motions anymore or feign business as usual. After speaking with God face to face as "one speaks to a friend" (Ex. 33:11), the words "normal" or "usual" no longer have any meaning.

Moses had gotten a pure draught of God himself, and that limited taste of God's glory had killed his appetite for anything else. For days his skin cells irradiated celestial after-burn into an atomic tan. To spare people a visible reminder of God's diminishing presence, Moses covered his face with a veil.

For Moses, a veil was sufficient to conceal the fading of God's glory, but in this media-fueled age, we have devised ingenious ways to compensate for our lack of God's presence. We pump up the volume, play faster rhythms, and skillfully smooth the transition between sets. We manipulate the atmosphere, adjust the lights for a sexier ambiance, and make the sermons funnier and more entertaining, believing that if we can produce enough sound and fury, we might be able to drown out the sound of silence. Instead of addressing the silence, we continue pulling all the gears and levers every Sunday for an hour, attempting to convince the crowd that Oz the Great and Powerful is in our midst. But should our elaborate light system burn out, and the sound system short out, we might be confronted with our loss of true power. Radiohead once sang "When the power runs out, we'll just hum." We've been humming for too long.

THE CUTTING EDGE

I trust the irony is not lost on you that the first thing Luke wanted you to know about in Acts is the last thing you're likely to hear about today—the Holy Spirit. It's also the first thing the annals of church history chronicle for us about the golden eras of evangelistic outreach. A. W. Tozer describes the night he was baptized with the Holy Spirit at nineteen years old, "Any tiny work that God has ever done through me and through my ministry for Him dates back to that hour when I was filled with the Spirit. That is why I plead for the spiritual life of the body of Christ and the eternal ministries of the Eternal Spirit through God's children, His instruments."[1] Dwight L. Moody describes a similar experience, "I was all the time tugging and carrying water. But now I have a river that carries me."[2] And the opening of the book of Acts sets up an event at Pentecost where the Holy Spirit fell upon his church and empowered them to become witnesses that would change the world. That same empowerment for mission two thousand years ago gave the church its cutting edge. But it wasn't just a one-time deal. That empowering happened repeatedly throughout the New Testament, and church history.

Paul said that when the gospel came to the Corinthians it didn't come in words only, but in a demonstration of power. As a poor missionary for years, I mastered the art of hand tools until I could afford power tools. You don't appreciate the power of voltage until you've been doing everything by the sweat of your own brow in back breaking work. A church devoid of the Spirit's power is a church that has lost its grip on one of the most powerful evangelistic tools at its disposal. Despite our best efforts, we've neglected the empowerment that Tozer and Moody attest is still available today. Even Peter said, "The promise is for you and your children and for all who are far off—for all whom the Lord our God will call" (Acts 2:39). That's you. If you're called, then Peter says this Bud's for you.

If this generation responded to the promise of the Spirit's power in relation to our mandate of mission, we would be as powerful as Indiana Jones unearthing the ark of the covenant. Yet we think it necessary to don Saul's ill-fitting armor to fell giants, when all we need to reach for is the Spirit of God and a slingshot. The enemy has known this all along and desires these promises to remain hidden away under dust, like the ark of the covenant in *Raiders of the Lost Ark*. But the stakes are too high, and becoming raiders of the lost art of reaching the unreached is a race to save the world before the enemy destroys it.

A. W. Tozer said, "I want the presence of God Himself, or I don't want anything at all to do with religion. . . . I want all that God has, or I don't want any." Moses said, "For how shall it be known that I have found favor in your sight, I and your people? Is it not in your going with us, so that we are distinct, I and your people, from every other people on the face of the earth?" (Ex. 33:16 ESV). As Lloyd-Jones pointed out, "We can have no successes over our enemies without this great realization of God in the midst."[3] We can have our big churches, magazines that praise them, bags of cash, and not the presence of God. Moses didn't want Canaan, with all of its richness, flowing with milk and honey. Moses wanted God himself. And that's what made the difference.

It's time to stop playing church and to get real.

THE KEY TO THEIR SUCCESS

Like Moses, the success of the apostles began with their willingness to "wait."

Wait for what? God himself. He sent us out on a mission, but he never expected us to go it alone. Let's ponder for a minute, exactly *why* the apostles needed to cool their heels in Jerusalem before heading out to the harvest.

The apostles had to be told to wait because, contrary to what you may have been told, they *weren't* scared and hiding in the upper room. You don't need to tell wussies to wait. Besides, Luke doesn't even hint that they were scared. Acts 1:3 tells us they'd spent forty days with the risen Lord as he downloaded the secrets of the universe into their souls. Their hearts were burning, just as the hearts of the disciples on the road to Emmaus were! They were chomping at the bit to get out and take on the world! Nevertheless, despite the preparation of three years with Jesus and forty days with the risen Lord, they still weren't equipped to tackle the world on their own. The best intentions of mice and men often lay to waste, and so would theirs without plugging into the right power outlet.

Years earlier, when the father of the demon-possessed boy turned to the disciples for help, they exerted themselves for hours, "but they were not able" (Mark 9:18 ESV). Doesn't that summarize our current state? The church has been going through the motions, but despite our best efforts, technology, marketing, and antics we lack the power to reverse the downward spiral. As embarrassing as it was for the disciples to be ineffective, we suffer the same incompetence in accomplishing our mission. Perhaps the difference was that the disciples were bothered by it—they wanted to know why they couldn't do it (Mark 9:28–29). After many failures, and abandoning Jesus at the cross, they knew their dependency upon him was a real thing. Similarly, a veteran lifeguard knows to hang back until a swimmer has exhausted their own efforts to struggle. In God's case, we could be waiting a while for the church to give up and surrender. I don't think it even realizes it's drowning yet.

R. A. Torrey said:

> We think that if a man is pious and has had a college and a seminary education and comes out of it reasonably orthodox, he is now ready for our hands to be laid upon him and to be ordained to preach the gospel. But Jesus Christ said, "No." There is another preparation that a man must not undertake this work until he has received it. "Tarry (literally 'sit ye down') until ye be endued with power from on high."[4]

Pause for a moment. This means that many of the preachers and pastors out there aren't ready for what they've been called to . . .

because they haven't waited. Yet ordinary, unschooled men, filled with the Holy Spirit turned the world upside down because they waited in Jerusalem.

I'm about to give you a snapshot of the rest of this book. All the rest of the message, all the rest of this mission flows out of that tiny word—"wait." (*Completely* coincidentally, the reasons below are the outline for the rest of this book, taken from Acts 1:8). I hesitate to do this because I don't want you to think the outline is all you need. For me, this process has been a journey. Perhaps as long and bumpy of a ride as the Indiana Jones Adventure ride at Disneyland. Incidentally, the outline in this chapter is a bit like that ride. It's not at all like the movie, but it gives you a taste. Perhaps a taste of the journey of adventure that awaits you, as you wait on him.

What happened when the apostles waited for God's power instead of moving out on their own? What would happen to believers if they were willing to do the same today?

Waiting empowered them to accomplish eight different aspects of their mission, and it will still do so today.

THEY WOULD BE EMPOWERED
DESPITE THEIR WEAKNESS

"In a few days you will be baptized
with the Holy Spirit" (Acts 1:5).

Jesus tells the disciples that good things happen to those who wait on the Lord. In Acts 1, Jesus acts as M from a James Bond film and tells them that they're going to need some spiritual equipment from Q to accomplish the mission. Therefore he says wait here (Acts 1:4) before you go there (Acts 1:8, Matt. 28:19).

We haven't learned the lesson that not being ready doesn't work against us, but *for* us. In our insufficiency, facing a task unfinished, Jesus supplies us with *his* power. Paul, the Indiana Jones of the New Testament, confesses to being as flawed as Harrison Ford's iconic character. Because Paul knew where true power came from, he had learned to boast of his weakness, that the power of Christ might rest upon him. His weakness became his strength as he allowed his insufficiency to become an opportunity for God's all-sufficiency to channel through him. We try too hard to be street smart and cutting edge, forgetting that in our *weakness* he displays his power. No matter how faithfully Paul sowed, how frequently he watered, or skillfully he reaped, God alone gave the increase. And Paul knew it, even if we don't.

The disciples waited ten days, and their dependence upon God to make the difference made all the difference. We are fond of quoting Acts 2:42 as a template for church, but we forget that you can't become an *Acts chapter two* church unless you've first been an *Acts chapter one* church.* Without a return to first-century dependence, we will never see first-century results. What were they doing those ten days? They were waiting prayerfully in dependence upon him, spreading themselves out upon an altar and asking the fires of heaven to come and consume their weakness with power. That's what prayer is, a practical confession of inadequacy. The exhalation of surrender, and the inhalation of borrowed strength. Those ten days in Acts chapter one were the apostles learning to breathe.

THEY WOULD BECOME FEARLESS RISK TAKERS

"You will receive power" (Acts 1:8).

Don't misunderstand me here. Waiting is not a pass for continued inaction. The apostles waited ten days, not ten years. Waiting is not permission to hide behind theological platitudes like God's sovereignty, or a distraction while we analyze the culture. Paul's conclusion about God's sovereignty was that before the faith comes to others'

---

* I owe this quote to a friend named Brian who had a supernatural experience in prayer where this was driven home to him. He's never been the same since.

ears, movement must first come to our feet. Nor is waiting an excuse to mask a distrustful disobedience stemming from fear.

Unafraid to begin with (since meeting with Jesus after the resurrection), the disciples were further emboldened when the Spirit fell to break new ground, chart new territory, and boldly go where no disciple had gone before. Jesus promised they'd do greater things than he had, and when Peter fearlessly preached his first impromptu sermon about the death and resurrection of Jesus, three thousand were baptized. They defied the Sanhedrin under threats of death. They publicly healed in the temple. Their passion for seeing others liberated set them free from fearing the reprisals of others. Therefore, they risked fearlessly.

Similarly, every period of revival from the Great Awakening to the Jesus Movement can trace its roots to fearless risk-taking as men and women embarked on risky ventures not seen before. George Whitefield hit the fields. William Booth hit the streets. Martin Luther hit the Wittenberg door with a hammer. Bold faith, taking prayerful risks, has always led to a renaissance of reaching the unreached.

Even when the apostles' courage flagged after being beaten, they hunkered down in the bunker to pray for even more boldness. The Spirit empowered them again in what Dr. Walter Martin called "The Baptism of Boldness."[5] They prayed, "'Now, Lord, consider their threats and enable your servants to speak your word with great boldness. Stretch out your hand to heal and perform signs and wonders through the name of your holy servant Jesus.' After they prayed, the place where they were meeting was shaken. And they were all filled with the Holy Spirit and spoke the word of God boldly" (Acts 4:29–31). For our friends that write off the activity of special empowering as a one-time event to the church, it is significant that this filling happened after Pentecost. If the early apostles needed a top up, how much more should we be challenged to seek God for valor in taking the necessary risks for a mission accomplished?

THEY WOULD BE CONTAGIOUSLY CONSUMED WITH HIM

"When the Holy Spirit comes on you" (Acts 1:8)

When the Holy Spirit came upon the apostles, he chose the form of flaming fire instead of a dove. This was no gentle spark. This was a wildfire consuming the apostles, and the wind that blew in the upper room meant that the Holy Spirit intended this fire to spread. If the church is the fire that sets the world ablaze, what is to be done when the coals barely smolder? If the church is God's force for revolution on earth, what can be done when the church itself is in need of a revolution? The church is out to save the world, but who will save the church?

There once lived a generation of men and women who knew the answer to that question. They kept their lamps trimmed and burning for the next generations so that the light of the gospel wouldn't go out. They fell on their faces and cried out to God for him to take back his church. They were too impressed with God to be impressed with themselves or bothered with whether anyone else was. They abhorred spiritual "selfies" and shifted the eyes of the world back onto Jesus. Like prophets of old, they waved the giant foam finger pointing to heaven so that the crowds could celebrate the true champion of the game. They were players, but they knew who had truly won the victory. That generation may be dead, but is the power they knew gone forever?

No. But we must wait for it, long for it, pray for it.

Spurgeon said:

We have in this age but few giants in grace who rise head and shoulders above the common height, men to lead us on in deeds of heroism and efforts of unstaggering faith. After all, the work of the Christian Church, though it must be done by all, often owes its being done to single individuals of remarkable grace. In this degenerate time we are very much as Israel was in the days of the Judges, for there are raised up among us leaders who judge Israel, and are the terror of her foes. Oh, if the Church had in her midst a race of heroes; if our missionary operations could be attended with the holy chivalry which marked the Church in the early days; if we could have back apostles and martyrs, or even such as Carey and Judson, what wonders would be wrought! We have fallen upon a race of dwarfs, and are content, to a great extent, to have it so.[6]

Giants walked the land in those days, the likes of A. W. Tozer and R. A. Torrey. Though they attracted the crowds, it wasn't their goal because it wasn't the game they were playing. More importantly, it wasn't the way they kept score. But the team was winning. We've been winning at the wrong game, our goal to fill a room. But we haven't scored. If the apostles filled a room, it was to turn them out again, so they could create more rooms of people who also got turned out. They didn't spike the ball in the end zone and dance the victory jig after their ministerial touchdowns. Torrey locked himself into his room for three days, determined not to come out until he'd wrestled with the angel and received the blessing of God, the filling of the Holy Spirit. These men sought power. Perhaps if we threw our lifeless corpses onto the bones of these men's lives as the Israelites threw a stiff onto Elisha's bones, and prayed like they prayed, we might spring to life, ready to receive the Spirit's power in these dark days. People who pushed out beyond the camp like Moses did, laid hold of the kingdom of God violently, and witnessed the kingdom come with violent force. The church was revived, reformed, renewed, and revolutionized.

In an age where talk is cheap, and the world is tired of hearing it, actions speak louder than words. The apostles modeled the power of a life consumed with the Holy Spirit, and they fully lived for God, which shouted louder than their words. Lives like that cannot be underestimated, or ignored, like the early church who lived out Acts 2:42, so that they enjoyed "the favor of all the people" (Acts 2:47).

And the Lord added to their number.

Daily.

THEY WOULD BECOME CHANNELS OF THE HOLY SPIRIT

"You will be my witnesses" (Acts 1:8)

When Jesus poured his Spirit out at Pentecost, it was an all or nothing investment of supernatural power mediated through natural humanity. The life of God, manifested as gifts of the Holy Spirit, coursed through every believer as they were empowered to carry out the mission of Jesus. When Peter spoke of the happenings of Pentecost to the crowd, he told them Joel has prophesied that they too were a part of this. They would see visions, have dreams, and experience prophesy. This wasn't a spectator sport, but a participatory one. The promise was that Jesus would pour his power out on all flesh, sons and daughters, wrinkly old men, and prune-skinned women would all receive gifts. Everyone was a participant. Pentecost was an all-inclusive, crowd-swelling revolution that changed the way people were reached. Nobody was excluded. Earthly revolutions chant to restore *power to the people* but when the Holy Spirit is on the move, it's a restoration of power *through the people*. As the Holy Spirit is channeled through people, his outlet is their gifts. When I was a firefighter, we were taught that a person who'd been electrocuted had an exit wound because the energy needed to exit their body. The energy didn't just dissipate; it created an outlet. Your spiritual gifts are an expression of what Jesus's power looks like through you. It's Jesus with you-skin on.

Through our gifts, the world sees Jesus in action. The gifts are what help fill the world with the presence of Christ (Eph. 4:10–13). Unfortunately, we've seen church become about one person's gifts, as the crowds watch and forget they have gifts themselves. As a jealous

Monarchist, the Holy Spirit is consumed with the single aim of bringing worship and glory to Jesus, rather than calling attention to the individual being used. When we merely pay lip service to this, and we focus on running a show, amassing wealth through drawing crowds, and building bigger barns, the Holy Spirit is grieved and withdraws his presence. He's not in the business of glorifying people. Becoming a channel of the Holy Spirit means that you are not the focal point, but God is. You hold treasure, but are a feeble jar of clay. You're God's practical joke to the world, that he can use anybody. He can and does, and we're proof.

THEY WOULD IMPACT THE UNREACHED IN THEIR OWN NEIGHBORHOODS

"In Jerusalem" (Acts 1:8)

When the apostles received the empowering of the Holy Spirit, they got busy in their own backyard—Jerusalem. The missional movement is tapping into nothing short of a rediscovery of what happens when you . . . actually . . . get . . . around . . . people. But with that revelation comes the embarrassing confessional that perhaps we haven't been mixing with the people we talk so much about reaching. Our neighbors. Coworkers. Friends. Jesus didn't talk much about reaching people. He simply modeled it by mixing and mingling with them like a holy cocktail.

We always think of mission "over there," but sometimes it's harder to get us to cross the street than it is to cross an ocean. When God starts moving, he moves in our local surroundings before he moves us anywhere else. We first become witnesses in "Jerusalem" and become driven inevitably outward to the surrounding concentric circles—to our Judeas, Samarias, and eventually, to the ends of the earth. It's often us that need to change as much as our neighborhoods do. Once the Holy Spirit got ahold of the disciples, the mission field started as they stepped out the doorway of the upper room.

When 9/11 hit, I was a missionary evangelist serving in Martyn Lloyd-Jones's legendary Sandfields in Port Talbot, Wales. Charitable giving in America dropped by 50% and our mission took a hit. When that happened, I became a walking statistic and was forced to work in a factory to pay my bills. I worked alongside the rough-necked blue-collar workers I'd been trying to reach in the dockside industrial town where I'd gotten my beatdown. After a year of fruitless laboring as the full-time "evangelist," I saw three conversions within weeks of working at the factory! The recurring pattern in my life has been that I've never really been effective in ministry until I've left full-time vocational ministry. What if our ideas of "ministry" are keeping us from reaching the people right outside our doors?

The key to success for Paul was that he got out there. Paul didn't have the luxury of rolling up to a city with a sexy logo, flashy website, and rented space. He buried himself in the marketplace, immersed in crowds of people, not in a clandestine cell lined with books, cloistered away in a drywall fortress, guarded by receptionists, secretaries, interns, and associates, like ministerial royalty. For over ten years planting churches as an ordained minister, I've worked day jobs as a barista, window cleaner, psychiatric nurse, firefighter, and university lecturer in order to get close to the people I was trying to reach. Sometimes the busyness of our church tasks makes it impossible for us to carry out the one task Jesus asked us to complete. Instead of spending the majority of our time crafting the best sermons on Acts, we need to live the book of Acts.

If you spend the majority of your time in a theological cloister oyster, somebody has sold you bad clams. One of the biggest reasons leaders don't make a dent is because they don't interact with people. My mentor Peter Jeffery used to say that the congregation attending his church on Sunday would interact with more people by lunchtime on a Monday than he would in a week. Have a job working among the people you're trying to reach? You're already one step closer to being as effective as Paul was at reaching lost people.

THEY WOULD STEP OUTSIDE
THEIR COMFORT ZONE

"In all Judea" (Acts 1:8)

Judea represented leaving the place where the apostles were comfortable and getting outside of their church walls. After all, they didn't want to leave. I mean, why would they?

You've got the apostles? Check!

Miracles? Check!

Thousands of people? Check!

Programs?* Check!

Money? Check!

A holy huddle? Um . . . check?

Houston, we have a problem.

The kingdom can't advance when we're in a holy huddle. Enter Saul of Tarsus. He unloaded on the early church like Bruce Lee playing Ping-Pong with nunchucks, scattering the church far and wide. Even the early church found that God had ways of scattering them if they wouldn't move out willingly.

Where are the places you don't want to go with the gospel? Where are the places that take you outside of your comfort zone? Have you ever considered doing an open mic discussion in a gay coffee house? Starting a spiritual reading group in a Starbucks? Throwing down an open-air church service in the projects? What about training prison inmates to disciple others inside the prison walls? Using the church parking lot to build community in the neighborhood through block parties and community yard sales? If you want to reach the ones that nobody is reaching, you need to go where nobody else is going and do what nobody else is doing. Now more than ever, reaching the world requires us to think outside the box to reach those who won't fit inside it.

---

* They had an awesome food closet, and a swap meet collective to die for.

The first-century church was all about expansion. But don't forget that it took God three times to visit Peter in a dream to finally convince him to push beyond his comfort zone and into the Gentile world. Initially, it was persecution that forced the early church to leave the comfortable confines of Jerusalem. Similarly, the current spiritual climate will force us to go to the unreached. In case you haven't noticed, they're not leaping over each other to join our Sunday services. Although culture is described as post-Christian, perhaps people themselves are more aptly described as post-church. They still consider themselves to be spiritual, but Christianity no longer makes sense to them when they come to our churches and then witness our inaction outside of them.

People scratched their heads when Francis Chan traded away his career of megachurch minister, bestselling author, and well-paid circuit speaker for the obscurity of working in the Tenderloin neighborhood in San Francisco. What Francis knew is what the church still fails to grasp. You can have the coolest church building, loaded with a Starbucks and the latest gadgets, while still failing to reach the world around you.

I imagine pastors on their commute to church. As they pull out of the driveway, perhaps none of their neighbors know the gospel. They drive past houses with people that don't know their name, and they drive across a city they never serve. They pull into a neighborhood where their church is nestled, but they don't know how to reach the neighbors. All the while, the community diverts around the church like a stream bypasses a rock. The water wears down the rock over time, but the rock does nothing to affect the water, except divert its course to pass by. Ignored. That's the word to describe how our communities react to us. We've taught them to ignore us. They never hear from us except for strange "It's hell without Jesus" memes and anger expressed on Facebook. When Francis Chan left his big church, it was because he knew we had to do better. He knew that the church wouldn't follow its mission unless it was modeled from the front. A guy standing up on stage and preaching to a room full of Christians isn't the pattern of the New Testament, nor does it model how to reach the unreached. Chan's greatest sermon to Cornerstone church was the day he left to become an urban missionary.

Being witnesses in Judea propels us outward from the safety and confines of our churches. Paul and the apostles preached in the synagogues, but that usually didn't go well. Have you noticed that nearly the entire book of Acts happened *outdoors*? So did the gospels. In fact, the first effect of the Spirit coming in power was, they went outside. They went to the people, instead of waiting for the people to come to them. They went where it's at like they had two turntables and microphone.

Every movement of the Holy Spirit resulted in the church getting turned inside out. Most of what the missional movement has focused on is getting around lost people, but as long as we're still inviting them to come to us, it's just not missional enough for me. The apostles mastered taking the gospel to where the community already was. They found the marketplace. And they penetrated it with the gospel. Where can we go together that we're not currently going?

THEY WOULD REACH THE ONES NOBODY WANTED

"And Samaria" (Acts 1:8)

After Pentecost, the apostles reached the marginalized people on the fringe of society that nobody else was reaching. Just like Jesus. It was a slow burn at first, and took them longer than you would have thought to catch on to what God was up to, but they got there in the end.

It wasn't an accident that Jesus's enemies accused him of being friends with prostitutes, tax collectors, and sinners. What about you? Do your neighbors think you're bringing the neighborhood down? Every movement of the Spirit has hit society around the edges, not the mainstream. When the Spirit moves, the marginalized are reached.

The Samaritans in Acts. The impoverished during the Moravian Movement. The list goes on. The marginalized flocked to Jesus because he was different than the religious leaders of his day. Unlike many of our modern leaders who compromise the truth itself, Jesus didn't alter the truth. True, he was the God who demanded holiness, but how would the one who would fulfill all righteousness on behalf of others treat those who were unholy? He got the balance right, yet still scandalized the religious elite, as did the apostles by receiving Samaritans, women, Romans, and gentiles as equals. A church that doesn't scandalize religious people just isn't reaching the unreached.

THEY WOULD BECOME MEN AND WOMEN OF ACTION

"To the ends of the earth" (Acts 1:8)

Once Jesus thwarted the disciples' immediate after-breakfast-plans to embark on an eternal, all-expense-paid cruise to heaven, they rolled up their sleeves, got their hands dirty, and muddied their boots. The church instantly shifted from being an insular, exclusive club, to the only insider movement on earth that exists for outsiders.

I'm a huge advocate for interaction within the church walls, but I'm an even bigger advocate for *action* outside of it. It's not enough to simply be fascinated by what the disciples said, according to the Bible. Outward expansion won't happen unless we're committed to doing what they did.

There is no other way.

You can read.

You can theorize.

You can preach.

The world was turned upside down in the book of Acts. Not the book of Thoughts. Or the book of Plans. Or the book of Missional Strategies. Acts.

Action.

Here's a commercial to make it simple. If you're over forty and you picture me saying this while cracking an egg into a frying pan, it's a lot more effective.

This is the church.

This is the church in action.

Any questions?

IT'S NOT THE YEARS, IT'S THE MILEAGE

It's not too tall an order to see the church spiritually empowered once again in our time. Each believer has the potential to light a spark that sets the world ablaze. That's why you're dangerous. That's probably why it's easier, less messy, and more convenient to stay packed like lemmings into predictable rows of pews week after week. Acts is the story of the Spirit of God raging like an out-of-control forest fire in a people who have been consumed with what consumes him. As the Spirit rips through communities, it often rips them apart, transforming them into something beautiful, but destroying what was there in the process, like the torn yet beautiful chrysalis after the butterfly emerges. This also applies to churches. What if God moving in our midst is the end of church as we know it?

For this reason, Jesus contrasted the wild dynamic of the Holy Spirit with the rigid, hardened, and inflexible religious system of his day. He used terms like "new wine" and "old wineskins." In Jesus's metaphor, the Holy Spirit must be poured into a new wineskin because it needs to stretch and yield under the expansion. Fermentation is too radical a process for churches that have become old, inflexible, dried up, unyielding containers that are unwilling to expand. As the kingdom expanded throughout Jerusalem, Judea, Samaria, Asia Minor, Macedonia, and Rome, it destroyed as much as it renewed. Old systems were threatened as the new wine of the gospel threatened established centers of power. The Ephesians feared they would lose their temple. The circumcision group feared they would lose the traditions of their fathers. Rome feared it might lose its iron grip of power on subdued people and slaves. The Sanhedrin feared they would lose their credibility. Tragically, churches can resist the Holy Spirit because they are afraid to lose what they have.

Thankfully, God is not interested in preserving our wineskins or maintaining our systems. He's concerned about reaching the lost, even at the cost of our systems, structures, and traditions. John Piper said, "Mission exists because worship doesn't."[7] The Holy Spirit is ruthlessly committed to bringing worship to Jesus, and he has repeatedly caused massive upheaval of the religious status quo in order to bring him glory. Always faithful to his task, the Spirit's power busts loose in different epochs in history, like a solar flare unleashed from the sun, and the church's reach becomes elliptical, thrusting outward beyond its standard borders. These epochs of punctuated equilibrium are marked by things suddenly speeding up, as the kingdom propels itself forward, and the church advances chiefly through individuals desperate enough to take risks as they allow him to take charge.

The church is older than she looks. She's been through a lot, and like Indy said, "It's not the years, honey. It's the mileage." She's seen a lot of changes, renewals, revivals, and reawakenings. During the Great Awakening, The Holy Spirit worked through Whitefield to the shock of the Church of England. Yet ask eighteenth-century Anglicans what they thought of the early Methodist preachers. Ask Rome what they thought of the upstart monk, Martin Luther. Ask any denominational leader during the sixties what they thought of Chuck Smith and the shirtless, blue jean, hippie preachers in Southern California.

When the church was powerless to make a dent in the youth culture during the hippie era, Chuck Smith sparked the Jesus Movement by pitching a tent in a bean field and opening the doors to half-naked, stoned hippies, which led to the creation of Calvary Chapel. Thousands of youth were transformed as they embraced Jesus and flocked to the beaches to be baptized. *Time* magazine dramatically captured the baptism scene on one of its covers! Eventually, Calvary

Chapel morphed from a movement to a denomination. Throughout history, denominations were formed in the wake of the Holy Spirit's moving, but when his presence waned, and the revival flames cooled to embers, the movements calcified, ironically, in an attempt to preserve the forward momentum. Alas, every new wineskin eventually becomes an old wineskin given enough time. That's not to say that denominations can't rekindle the flames, or recapture what made them dynamic, but church history demonstrates that renewals tend to occur outside of the establishment more often than not. Perhaps the lack of complex structures, hierarchies, and infrastructures make it easier, as it was in Jerusalem.

Yet each of these denominations marked renewals throughout the history of the church like tree rings in a bisected log; seasons of fresh life punctuated by the eventual drying out and hardening of the wood over the centuries. Inevitably, over time, the Methodists, Lutherans, Calvary Chapels, and others ran the risk of becoming brittle, rigid, and dry despite once being on the cutting edge of reaching the unreached in new ways.* The church that does not evangelize will fossilize, but God always has a plan.[8] The process begins again as a new movement expands the borders of the kingdom further than before as a new wave of risk takers steps up and steps out. This can happen within any movement when God recaptures the hearts of his children. The Welsh revival of 1904 started when one young man and six teenage girls began to pray for weeks for a fresh outpouring of the Holy Spirit. Welsh Calvinistic Methodism probably wouldn't have been your first pick for a wineskin to hold new wine, but God is faithful to meet anyone where they're at when they're desperate enough.

The rallying cry of Great Britain is "God save the Queen!" but in the kingdom of God we need to cry, "God save the church!"

---

* This is not to suggest in any way that these denominations are not valuable, or that the churches within them are not following God in faithfulness. I personally embrace and love the entire body of Christ and trace God moving in all branches of it. I am merely explaining the process of extraordinary movements.

But we must wait. We cannot control the work and mission of God, although it's in our nature to want to. We simply can't. We never could. But there is a better alternative. What if Jesus was ready to show himself to be the same God of the book of Acts to the church and to you personally? Would you be up for it?

There's something that happens to a person who reads Acts. Who *really* reads Acts. They become like a climber deciding they want to take on all 29,029 feet of Mount Everest. The Everest picture book had always looked good on the coffee table, but now there's that tug to climb it.

That pull . . .

That beckoning to go on that journey, though it might be the hardest thing you ever do.

Feel it? Follow it.

And keep reading.

The greatest adventure beckons.

Discussion Questions

(For Dr. Jones, the Princeton professor in you)

1. Describe a time in your life when God made you wait, trust, and depend on him. What made this difficult? What was the lasting fruit of it?

2. Which of the eight results of waiting on God for his power and help most excites you? Why?

3. Which of the eight results of waiting on God for his power scares you? Why?

4. Which of the eight results of waiting on God for his power challenges you?

Adventurous Actions

(For Indiana, the Temple Raider in you)

1. Make a list of the unreached lost people in your life you would like to reach.
2. Spend five minutes a day in prayer for that person every day.
3. Get around one lost person from your list this week. Take them out to coffee, lunch, or spend time doing a hobby with them.
4. Pray an additional five minutes for that person directly before you meet up with them on the day you meet.

CHAPTER 3

NOT MANY DAYS FROM NOW

We won't wait forever.
God's great adventure calls.

*John baptized with water, but you will be baptized
with the Holy Spirit not many days from now.*
JESUS (ACTS 1:5)

It's like nothing you've ever gone after before.
MARCUS TO INDIANA JONES

I awoke facedown in a pool of my own blood, completely disoriented. Temporarily unaware of who I was, or what had just happened, I stumbled to my feet and staggered back on autopilot toward the 300-pound rugby player who'd just unloaded his haymakers on my head. He was attempting to evade capture by getting into his car. My body was working, but my mind wasn't as I shuffled over to him with a drunken man's swagger, proving that all sense had literally been knocked out of me. By then a crowd had gathered to gawk. The police were called, he went to jail, and it was all over.

Later, in the emergency room, the medical staff stitched up my head. Covered in my own blood, I felt a long way from my safe, cushy, megachurch office insulated with wood-grained shelves packed with volumes of theology books. What was a nice, pasty-white, Reformed, evangelical boy doing halfway around the world getting his head beat in anyway? I certainly didn't have on my Free Punches in the Face shirt. Lying on that gurney, processing events, I finally came clean about something that had been nagging me for some time. I'd been playing it so safe. Cloistered in my monk cell as a sermon factory, churning out homilies for Christians, I'd not known any danger except maybe the risk of a paper-cut from incessant page turning, or possibly spilling coffee on my crotch. I'd devoured plenty of books about risky gospel ventures that I had no intention of living. If I was honest, deep down all I wanted was people to leave me alone to read more books and drink more coffee.

But Jesus loved me way too much to let me stay that way.

A DANGEROUS PRAYER

Rewind the tape back a few years earlier to a day like any other in Huntington Beach, California. I stood gazing out across the city from my second-story office window of the megachurch where I was a pastor. I could see the rooftops of two other church buildings and I suddenly felt . . . unnecessary. In that crucial moment, in a rare moment of honesty, I wondered out loud why my ministry looked nothing like the apostle Paul's or anything that I'd been studying in the book of Acts.

Here were some glaring differences between Paul's ministry and mine at the time:

- I *sat* in a study crammed with books about a Bible I didn't have the faith to live. Paul, on the other hand, *couldn't sit or stand* in a three and a half foot cell lined with urine, had nothing to do except write, and had to beg Timothy to bring him scrolls and parchments.
- I was paid a middle class, median income to compose homilies that entertained rooms packed with Christians (who weren't

going to do much other than read the Bible along with me).
Paul was unpaid, often naked and hungry due to his commitment to reaching the unreached, only finding time to
compose the Bible after prison slowed him down long enough
to stand still.

- I prayed, with my fingers crossed, for doctors to be "given
skill and wisdom," when sick people asked for healing. Paul
laid hands on people and experienced seasons of extraordinary
miracles because "My message and my preaching were not
with wise and persuasive words, but with a demonstration of
the Spirit's power" (1 Cor. 2:4).

- If I'm honest, my ambition was to become well known, lead a
gimongous church, hear my own sermons broadcast over the
airwaves, and speak at pastors' conferences as if I was an expert.
(At what? Reading? Talking? Drinking coffee?) Paul said,
"I make it my ambition to preach the gospel, not where Christ
has already been named, lest I build on someone else's foundation" (Rom. 15:20 ESV). I guess when you plant twenty-four
churches in eleven years and run out of cities in which to plant
churches (Rom. 15:19), this becomes an actual problem.

- I was focused on building my church upwards, increasing
our size by increasing our numbers. Paul was consumed with
expanding the kingdom outwards by increasing its reach.

- I'll let Paul go first this time. Paul wanted to duplicate himself
in others in order to rapidly facilitate a vast number of church
plants that pushed back the darkness, expanded the kingdom,
and reached numerous unreached people. Which in turn
would rapidly duplicate and deploy soul-winning disciples.
I just wanted to preach better and read more books.

Despite my love for the library, I was tired of always reading stories about what other people were doing in church history and never
living any stories of my own. It was on that day that I did something

incredibly dangerous. I prayed a prayer that began to set in motion events that would change the course of my life. "God . . . I'm bored. I don't even know what I'm doing here. Please make me useful, whatever that looks like. I want to experience what the apostles did in Acts."

You see, I'd signed up for ministry in order to change the world, but somewhere along the way, I'd opted for security over adventure. Adventure may result in cuts and bruises, but monotony kills. Deep down, I was afraid to get outside my office and do anything I'd read about in the pages of Acts. The most amazing thing was that no one expected me to. I could keep collecting a paycheck, and never have to do the riskier things the apostles did, or that men and women in church history dissatisfied with the status quo had done to reach their generation. I'd been pursuing ministry, but was somehow getting farther away from it every day that I stayed cooped up in it. But according to John Wesley, "It is the cooping yourselves up in rooms that has dampened the work of God, which never was and never will be carried out to any purpose without going into the highways and hedges and compelling men and women to come in."[1] When I confessed my boredom to God, I was looking for a lifeline. A. W. Tozer said, "We are bored with God but we are too pious to admit it. I think God would love it if some honest soul would begin his or her prayer by admitting, 'God . . . I am bored with the whole thing.'"[2] The Holy Spirit looks down on that individual saying, "Now there's somebody I can do something with. They're finally desperate enough to take me at my word." I'd sat for too long holed up in my office, locked away from the world that desperately needed Jesus, but you can't change the world from behind a desk. Like Indiana said, "If you want to be a good archaeologist you've got to get out of the library!"[3]

If ministry were a game of chutes and ladders, I had nearly reached the top at twenty-three years old. I was close to getting voted in as the senior pastor of the megachurch that had ordained me. But God had other plans. The prayer I prayed looking out that window was like spinning the dial that began my plunge down the chute, breaking some ribs, knocking loose some teeth. The instruction manual to the game of ministry career advancement was clear. According to human rules, I was supposed to progress upwards toward the pinnacle, but sometimes God calls us away on a long walk down the beach, like he did Peter, to speak with us about the plan for our lives. He doesn't promise us stadiums of people, megachurches, or radio ministries. Sometimes, we're handed a call as unglamorous as Peter's: *Love me. And because you love me, feed my sheep. Tend my lambs.* Oh yeah, and there was that last bit . . . "Peter, one day somebody is going to take you by the hand and lead you a way you don't want to go."[4] John sensitively points out that Jesus was referring to Peter's death, but I wonder if it had a wider application. I wonder how many times in Peter's life he felt like somebody was leading him where he didn't want to go. I wonder if he went willingly because the hand that led him to unwanted places had nail prints and had also been led to crucifixion. I've certainly felt led down many paths I didn't want to travel. Without realizing it, I was asking God to take me out from behind my desk to make an impact. I wasn't even sure if he heard me, but in hindsight, God answered by taking me on a journey to undesired destinations, as my life and ministry began to slowly unravel.

GOD'S NOT IN A HURRY

Jesus telling the apostles they would receive power "not many days from now" implies that God isn't in a hurry to prep us for our journey. He's not running in panicked circles like the white rabbit, shouting, "I'm late, I'm late!" God is deliberate and measured in the development of his disciples. If he spent three years preparing the twelve, he's more than willing to take the time to develop you. If he allowed Paul nearly twelve years from the road to Damascus experience to his first missionary journey, he will spend time developing you as well. That's why Jesus told the disciples, "Not many days from now . . ." Why not right then? Why not that day? Why not immediately as he was still standing in front of them? As a results-oriented society, we tend to value arriving at the destination rather than valuing the journey. Yet Jesus put great stock in the journey itself, tacking an additional forty days post-resurrection onto the already three-year pre-mission prep period. If that weren't enough, Jesus gave them ten additional days to stew a bit longer before the power came. Ask the apostles what that ten-day period of prayer and fasting added to their development. It equipped them with a deeply rooted dependency upon the power of the Spirit of God, mirroring Jesus's forty days in the wilderness in reliance upon his Father.

Ask Paul what perspective God forged in his soul during the eleven preparatory years between the Damascus road and his debut in Antioch. Those eleven years of pent-up frustration from an unfulfilled mandate from the Risen Lord on Damascus Road made Paul like a bull out of the gates when he was finally let loose on his mission. "Not many days from now" reveals that God is equally concerned with the spiritual development of those who are sent, as he is with those he sends them to. We can all be on a journey of preparation with the God of the living. Isn't that a major component of the gospels—Jesus revealing himself to the twelve along the way? We expect to jump in feet first, reaching the unreached, but what if the Holy Spirit wants you to experience a transformation in transit?

In hindsight, he led me on a slow journey because that was all I could handle . . . at first. If you'll permit me, I'd like to share my story with you to demonstrate that God didn't throw me into the deep end, but was patient with me, and developed me as patiently as he did the twelve. In the opening to *Indiana Jones and the Last Crusade*, we see Indy's journey to becoming who he was, when he was just a lad on a train. He encounters everything from his first scar to obtaining the fedora, his first artifact, and his fear of snakes. You don't become a temple raider overnight.

I can best describe my reluctant journey from Princeton professor to whip-cracking adventurer if you'll permit me to depart from temple-raiding Indiana Jones for a little bit while I turn to a dragon burglaring hobbit. Like the Tolkien stories, it started off slow, and ramped up from there, because I wouldn't be any more thrilled than Bilbo Baggins about Gandalf knocking on my door asking me on an adventure. Tolkien tells us, "This is a story of how a Baggins had an adventure, and found himself doing and saying things altogether unexpected. He may have lost the neighbors' respect, but he gained—well, you will see whether he gained anything in the end."[5] Reluctant adventurers aren't we all.

At the time, I never would have believed you if you'd told me I'd become a serial church planter,* planting churches in a Starbucks in Europe, running open mic nights in a gay coffee house in Los Angeles, or baptizing Mexican gangsters next to a member of the Aryan brotherhood in Long Beach harbor. I wasn't that guy. You're probably not that person either. That's why I've written this book.

When Gandalf raps on Bilbo's door declaring that he's looking for an adventurer, Bilbo quickly dismisses himself as plain quiet folk with "no use for adventures. Make you late for dinner! I can't see what anybody sees in them."[6] Gandalf had the reputation of being a trouble-maker, who upset the sleepy peacefulness of the shire, responsible for shipping lads and lasses off to the misty mountains on adventures. This is my version of "There and back again," and maybe this book will get the same reputation, upsetting your cozy hobbit hole existence in ministry. Perhaps you're a spiritual dwarf, longing for the kingdom that's rightfully yours, seeking it back from the dragon greedily hoarding everything within the church walls. Perhaps you're hearing the dwarf song of the misty mountains and something is awakening within you. As Bilbo listened to the stirring music of the past, sung by dwarves around his table, a wish "to go and see the great mountains, and hear the pine trees and waterfalls, and explore the caves, and wear a sword instead of a walking-stick"[7] swept over him . . . longing for adventure.

But Bilbo wasn't ready. Nobody ever is. Not even the Twelve. Yet

---

* I prefer the term Ninja Planter. For the reason why, see www.peytonjones.ninja.

what facilitated Bilbo's transformation was *the journey itself.* Gandalf called Bilbo an accomplished burglar before he was one. When childless Abram's name meant Father, God called him Abraham (Father of nations). Jesus called Simon "The rock," despite Peter's crumbling under a little girl's probing questions around a campfire. Who but this same God would call Gideon "Mighty Warrior" as he hid crouching at the bottom of a winepress in fear of his life? God delights to call "those things that do not exist as though they did" (Rom. 4:17 NKJV). We forget that God delights in transforming people. But what facilitates the transformation is the willingness to embark with him on the journey he set out for you. Because the journey is one of faith, God reveals himself, transforming us forever. Jesus promised to transform the disciples, "Follow me, and I will make you fishers of men" (Matt. 4:19 NKJV). But there was a condition attached. The necessary condition of following him first, "follow me," precedes the promise of what he will bring into existence, "fishers of men." Because it's a conditional invitation, if we don't accompany him on this journey, like Bilbo, we won't be changed. We won't become burglars, raiders of a lost art.

What about you? Has God started to take you on a journey to places you haven't wanted to go? A place where there's no read-along-storybook guide? No magical chimes telling you it's time to turn the page? No guarantee that there's not a scary monster at the end of the book? That's called risk, and it's what makes an adventure worth living. It was a risky endeavor when Jesus took twelve men and called them to leave the security of their nets. And he's still in the business of rapping on your door like Gandalf. Don't worry. He'll supply the fabulous fireworks and dreaded dragons.

Besides, Bilbo didn't gain any confidence until he encountered danger and overcame his fears in the form of three stone trolls. What is it you fear most? For me, the scariest part of Paul's life was how much time he spent behind bars. Maybe that's why when God began calling me out of the hobbit hole of my comfort zone and onto the road to adventure, I kept narrowly avoiding landing in jail.

YOU'RE GOING TO JAIL, PUNK!

There I was, holed up in my office, minding my own business. But the Holy Spirit kept knocking and beckoning me out onto the open road, flinging the door wide open so I could glimpse the road before me. I caught a whiff of adventure on the morning air, before predictably turning back to the pages whose intoxicating smells of newly-printed paper and glue beckoned me, siren-like, begging me to never leave. Yet God's envoys were sent to me like missionaries in disguise. My sending pastor would stand in the doorway to my office, rap his knuckles on my doorjamb, and ask what I was doing that particular day. I'd usually list off studies, books, sermons, and theological problems I imagined I'd been working to solve. His brows would furrow, and he'd pause before asking, "So, you're not going to be meeting anybody, or getting out onto any campuses doing any outreach?" He can't remember such conversations to this day, but I'll never forget them because, in the silence that would follow his departures, the Holy Spirit would speak loudly.

Although the promptings were gentle at first, it was only a matter of time until God resorted to using a metaphoric crowbar to pry me out of my comfortable ministerial burrow. With the force of twelve dwarves bursting through Bilbo's door, the Holy Spirit crashed my long awaited party to get the journey started with a single phone call. That single phone call commenced a game of peek-a-boo with the God of the first century who wanted me to know that he was still in the business of transforming hobbits into burglars and fishermen into world changers.

On the other end of the phone line was a hysterical mother of two kids from my church's youth group, one of them future Navy Seal, Chad Williams, author of *Seal of God*. Chad's sister had invited a friend to church that had recently been converted to Christianity. Unfortunately, around the same time, that same friend became pregnant. The girl's shocked parents had confined her to the house until she agreed to abort the baby against her will. Chad's mom had taken her daughter to go see the pregnant girl, but the girl's distraught parents refused to let anyone speak with her, so they locked her in the solitary confinement of her bedroom until she had the abortion. Because this behavior sounded abusive, if not illegal, I told Chad's mom that I'd come down and speak with the parents. Chad's mom said she'd pray for a miracle until I got there. When I arrived on the scene twenty minutes later, Chad's mom was hysterically laughing through her tears, excitedly gesticulating, and talking loudly. I confess to thinking she may have cracked under the pressure, but after she slowed down a bit, I pieced together an amazing story as she caught her breath. In frustration and helplessness, Chad's mom had sat on the curb with her daughter to pray for the friend, "If only we had a megaphone, God, I could yell some encouragement to that scared girl and she could hear me."

One minute later, a man with a megaphone hopped over the brick wall nearly landing on them both! (This is where the story seems as unbelievable as an angel opening the prison doors so Peter could briskly walk out a free man.)* Shocked, Chad's mom asked where he had come from. (It had all the makings of the setup of a prank show, except that God did the punking!) Mysterious Megaphone Guy (MMG) said he'd been on the nearby major intersection yelling Scriptures at passing cars through his megaphone when God suddenly told him he had to walk a block, go behind the supermarket, and hop over the wall, and into the residential tract. A few minutes before I pulled up in my car, MMG suddenly jerked up, grabbed his megaphone, and said softly, "I have to go now. I'll need my megaphone back." (You can't make this stuff up). With that, he hopped back over the wall and was gone in a poof of smoke like Kaiser Soze from *The Usual Suspects*. By the time I arrived, the cops were on their way to arrest some nut with a megaphone. The first officer on the scene approached me with hand outstretched, saying, "Hand over the

---

* Even Peter didn't believe it at first (Acts 12:9)! Neither did the rest of the crew (Acts 12:15).

megaphone." When I tried telling the story I'd just heard, the cop told me I was lying, and pulled out his cuffs to arrest me. Luckily for me, his partner was a Christian and interceded. I narrowly avoided the slammer. Heaven had invaded earth.

Nonetheless, God's will was being done on earth as it was in heaven, and nobody could stop him. We were all spectators that day, and I began to ask the same question as the disciples did after Jesus had calmed the storm on the Sea of Galilee, "Who is this that even crazy mysterious megaphone men obey him?" When it was all over, I drove back to my office, my hands shaking as they gripped the steering wheel, whether from nearly being arrested or my close encounter with the God of Acts, I wasn't completely sure. One thing I was sure of was that I wasn't in Kansas anymore.

Upon reflection, I probably would not have prayed *for*, but *against* the weirdo who yelled at cars with a megaphone if I'd passed him on the street. But I have since asked myself who is crazier, the man shouting on the street with a megaphone, telling people that they are going to hell, or the person who believes they are, but does nothing about it?*

IF AT FIRST YOU DON'T SUCCEED, TRY, TRY, AND TRY TO GO TO JAIL AGAIN

Shortly after the incident with the megaphone, I was almost sent to the slammer for the second time. God had been poking me, nagging me to go to the high school campus across the street and start evangelizing at lunch. After procrastinating for a few months, I finally mustered up the courage and went to the classroom used during lunch. On my first day, I met with some Christian high school students who said they would invite their friends if I turned up to preach. Reaching the campus, the dean of the school cornered me. After an interrogation,

---

* For the record . . . yelling at people on the streets with a megaphone . . . not a fan. Good open air preaching that is legit is as rare as bona fide Elvis sightings.

she threatened to have me arrested if I was ever found on campus again. She was doing her job, and the law was the law after all.

Returning to my study, ready to wash my hands, absolving myself of the responsibility, I couldn't shake the calling. God whispered, "I've got your back if you go back." I can't even describe to you the struggle that ensued over the next seven days. I saw myself cuffed and thrown into the back of a cop car. I mentally read the headlines that could be printed. "Weirdo Youth Pastor Arrested for Pestering Kids Receives Restraining Order." I know. Twenty years on, I hear how it sounds. Looking back on it now, going at all was nuts. Going back was insane. I went back anyway.

Every week.

Without incident.

For three years.

Each time, I passed by numerous security guards who greeted me by name and smiled, but I never saw that dean again. Ever. It was like Jesus's miraculous slip through the crowd in Nazareth. I was such a punk that I eventually started parking in the teachers' parking lot every week. God was demonstrating that miracles don't just happen when you're smuggling Bibles into communist countries. I was learning that miracles happen whenever we trust God, as we move onto the front line for the kingdom wherever we are. I was also learning that Paul's enterprise of stepping out was a risky business, as Tolkien warned through Bilbo, "It's a dangerous business, Frodo, going out your door. You step onto the road, and if you don't keep your feet, there's no knowing where you might be swept off to."[8] Somehow, I'd thought I could reach the unreached by playing it safe.

LEGENDARY WEAKNESS

When we pick up a biography of a man or woman of God, it's because we already know that person's great exploits. We've heard rumors of legend, and want to read the story behind the scenes to catch a glimpse of what made their greatness tick. Unfortunately, legends are the only selective tales told that allow us to see the best bits.

When Bilbo matches wits with the Dragon Smaug, it's the zenith of his journey. Since Bilbo is invisible, Smaug can smell him, but not hear him, and asks what he calls himself. Bilbo taunts:

> I come from under the hill, and under the hills and over the hills my paths led. And through the air, I am he that walks unseen.
>
> I am the clue-finder, the web-cutter, the stinging fly. I was chosen for the lucky number.
>
> I am he that buries his friends alive and drowns them and draws them alive again from the water. I came from the end of a bag, but no bag went over me.
>
> I am the friend of bears and the guest of eagles. I am Ringwinner and Luckwearer; and I am Barrel-rider.[9]

The legend that Bilbo compiles sounds impressive. But he conveniently leaves out the part about being paralyzed with fear and unwilling to start the journey, like we all do. The internal monologue sounds nothing like the dialogue with Smaug, as Bilbo constantly panics, and second guesses his every statement. Maybe this is why the gospels tell us what the Twelve were really like. They got it wrong. They gave up on people (Acts 15:38). They wanted to send people home (Matt. 14:15). They wanted to burn people with fire (Luke 9:54). They drove children away (Matt. 19:13). They got excited about the wrong things (Luke 10:20). They didn't have much faith. They were afraid of the bogeyman (Luke 24:37). They ran away (Mark 14:50). I take great comfort in the fact that Jesus picked imperfect people to reach the unreached world. Like us, their transformation happened during the journey to every village and hamlet throughout Judea when he sent out the twelve with the seventy-two (Luke 10). During that short-term mission, the apostles got a taste of adventure, venturing out of their comfort zone. Jesus hadn't allowed them to take any extra provisions so that they could experience utter reliance upon God alone. Like us, they had absolutely no clue what they were doing, but as they preached the gospel of the kingdom, they encountered situations where they were completely out of their depth doing miracles and casting out demons, but God worked powerfully through them despite their inadequacy. Gandalf tells Bilbo that he'll have some tales of his own to tell when he comes back to the shire from his adventure. Bilbo asks if the wizard can guarantee his safe return. Gandalf says no, but he can promise he'll be changed.

In God's eyes, willingness often makes up for our weaknesses. The willingness of the seventy-two was met with power that compensated for their weakness, and they returned singing a different tune than when they'd left. The thrill of adventure tinged their voices, "Lord, even the demons submit to us in your name!" (Luke 10:17). Their joy was real, despite Jesus's warning to rejoice more in the gospel itself, than the effects of it. They had been changed along the way. Every serious international traveler will tell you that once you begin a trip, the itinerary falls apart. Whatever goal you had for the journey gets eclipsed when the unexpected twists and turns happen, making your trip a story worth telling. Our plans, after all, don't always line up with God's, but he'll use them or divert them as he wills to accomplish his purposes. Dwight D. Eisenhower, Supreme Commander of Operation Overlord, also known as the D-Day landings of the Allied forces in Normandy, said, "Plans are nothing. Planning is everything."[10] Your plans will fall apart, just as they did after the D-Day launch. Nothing seemed to work right, but they won the battle because they went, and their going provided an opportunity to fall back on their training. As Mike Tyson so eloquently put it, "Everybody has a plan until they get punched in the face." But like I said, getting punched in the face can have a significant upside.

YOU DON'T HAVE TO BE READY

If you don't feel ready to spread the gospel, the good news is that you don't have to be ready. He doesn't wait for us to be ready because *he* is. With God it's always a "ready or not, here I come" affair. I'm convinced that if the twelve apostles applied to the majority of modern mission boards they wouldn't make the cut. That's not a slight against the mission agencies that must maintain standards. It's just that the disciples were unlikely candidates for mission work, and would not likely have met those standards. They would raise every red flag and activate every tripwire that any self-respecting mission board set up. Perhaps Jesus called these men because they were the opposite of what he was going to make them, thereby bringing him more glory. The beauty of Jesus's training methodology was that he didn't wait until his servants were ready, but threw them into the deep end when they were still learning to swim.

The secret of how God works is found repeatedly throughout the Scripture in this vital truth: God doesn't use the able or qualified. He qualifies the unqualified and enables the disabled. Jesus trained the twelve as if he was building an airplane while it was in the air. He looks at the eleven remaining disciples before they'd ever experienced the baptism of the Holy Spirit, and promised (or threatened) them that they would change the world forever. Within months of following him, Jesus sent the seventy-two out to cast out demons, do miracles, and heal in his name when they weren't ready, because that's the *only way* anyone truly learns dependence upon God (Luke 10:1–23). The Greek word for sent in Luke 10:3 is *ekballo*, which translates to "forcibly expel," or "fling out" as if it were against their will. Jesus, who invented birds, pushed the disciples from the confident perch of security as if he believed that the only way we actually learn to fly is after flailing our arms in the panicked sensation that we're falling.

The reality is, if you've never fallen, you've probably never tried to fly. Jesus threw his followers out into the open air so they could learn about faith, and sometimes that means we have to fail. If you never failed at trying to do something for God, it's because you didn't do anything that involved risk. Peter attempted to walk on water. He also followed Jesus to the courtyard when everyone else had fled. Yet after his failure, nobody would have ever used him in ministry again. Nobody but Jesus. The difference between a weed and a flower is a judgment call. Thankfully Jesus is the one who makes the call.

No one is truly ever ready to embark on a mission. At least I wasn't. When the anchor is pulled up, and the sails are full, it's with the wind of the Holy Spirit, not our self-supplied hot air. Remember the times when you lay in a broken heap at the feet of Jesus, crying out to him to forgive you, wash you clean, and inhabit you? In those sacred moments, where the cross stands at the intersection of God and humanity, you were brought to the end of yourself. Perhaps that's why reaching the unreached is more addicting to me than anything else in Christianity. Our great mission constantly brings us to that place of brokenness, insufficiency, and dependence all over again. We taste again that same despair of self, and utter dependence upon Christ and him alone as we did at our own salvation.

It's not an accident that the one who'd been broken in the most places, Peter, was used by Jesus the most powerfully. Following Peter's miserable failings in the upper room, the garden, and the courtyard, was a private interview with Jesus as they walked down the beach. During this second interview, Jesus restores Peter to ministry. But in 1 Corinthians 15:5, Paul mentions a secret meeting that Jesus had with Peter before that walk down the beach. It's not penned by the authors of the gospels, perhaps because it was too sacred, or Peter could never discuss it without breaking down into a crumpled, weeping mess. My guess, however, is that secret first meeting with Jesus was simply about restoring Peter's soul, not his ministry. Peter had always been a powerful mustang of a man, every ounce of him charged with power. Strong hands, a fierce grip, and powerful shoulders that hoisted a huge net of fish, and all of it failed him because he needed a different kind of power. And he didn't have it. In his brokenness, Peter finally felt how weak he truly was. And that made the crucial difference.

Peter, from that day on, was like a lost puppy, following Jesus wherever he went, knowing that he needed Jesus more than Jesus needed him.

PREPARE TO BE INVADED

Perhaps God waits until we've given up, failed a little, or completely quit before he's ready to use us. Perhaps that's because that is the moment we finally surrender. It was Peter's breaking point that was his turning point. For Jacob, it was his wrestling with the angel, and being broken at the hip. It was in utter defeat that Jacob laid his head on a stone in the desert when he was on the run, and had a dream in which he witnessed heaven invading earth. I believe God wants us to have a vision of the kingdom of God coming to earth. Snapping out of his dream, Jacob cried out, "Surely the Lord is in this place, and I was not aware of it" (Gen. 28:16). Imagine looking at the world around you with the awareness that God was working powerfully all around you. The fulfillment of that dream was Christ himself; God hasn't retracted that ladder yet. Heaven's invasion of earth is still happening but it starts with him invading your world first. He wants you to know that he's the God of Abraham, Isaac, Jacob—and *you*.

God began to invade my space, just as he'll invade yours. He didn't start answering my prayer overnight, but he seemed to throw a lever that tripped a sovereign process into motion. My guess is that God is answering your prayers today. You've probably forgotten about prayers desperately whispered in confused moments of panic, but he hasn't. He hasn't forgotten your earliest dreams and hopes to lift up his name. If they originated with him, he still wants to make good on them. Your story isn't finished being written yet. As the great philosopher, Anonymous* once quipped: "God's providences are read like Hebrew letters. They can only be understood by reading them backwards."

Who knows if having my head beat in has been the gift that keeps on giving. After the beatdown on the streets of Port Talbot, my wife and I started doing risky things. I began a metamorphosis from a

---

* Don't search for him online . . . you'll find he said a lot of things, but it's not a real person. Had to explain the joke because I threw my editors off. If you care to look, there are multiple jokes hidden in this manuscript. The biggest joke is you bought this book . . .

sedate, sedentary bookworm, to a frontline missionary with a hunger to impact the world, even if still in my pupa stage. Every weekend we hit the city streets of Wales. On weekends, the streets were dangerous after 10:00 p.m. Alcohol fueled the fighting and raping, and the streets were barricaded to keep people from being run over as they staggered through the streets by the thousands. There's nothing like it in America, except perhaps Mardi Gras or spring break, but this was a weekly event, not an annual one. Police regularly turned up in riot gear to quell the mayhem. As dangerous as it was, we began to hit the pubs and nightclubs with a video camera. Something about aiming a video camera at people who were out at night to chug beer, dive into a punch up and one-night-stands, and asking them what they believed in God, resulted in them pouring out their life stories through floods of tears. My wife, the hardcore missionary who'd spent time in Thailand rescuing kids from prostitution, began to witness something awakening deep inside my soul. I had no clue what I was doing, but doing something felt better than doing nothing.

Gangs talk about jumping an initiate in by beating them mercilessly, and I'd been initiated into the gang of the apostles. True, I'd been beaten less for Jesus, and more for being a stupid driver. My assailant threw that punch because of his juice-amped emotions, but I walked into that fist out of concern for my witness for Christ. Something about shedding my blood had affected a change in me.[11] Being able to say that I bore on my body the marks of Christ Jesus served as a rite of passage, placing me in the coolest secret club since the *Little Rascals'* He-man Women Haters Club. Sailors traditionally marked the crossing of the equator with tattoos, but I'd crossed more than a physical milestone. I'd crossed a mental, emotional, and spiritual one. Besides, when you've got scars, tattoos are for posers. Evel Knievel said, "bones heal, pain is temporary, and chicks dig scars."[12] Maybe Jesus digs them too when they are borne for his sake. Missionary to India Amy Carmichael once famously wondered about Christians who had no scars like our Master.

Hast thou no scar?
No hidden scar on foot, or side, or hand?
I hear thee sung as mighty in the land,
I hear them hail thy bright ascendant star,
Hast thou no scar?

Hast though no wound?
Yet I was wounded by the archers, spent,
Leaned Me against a tree to die; and rent
By ravening beasts that compassed Me, I swooned:
Hast thou no wound?

No wound? No scar?
Yet as the Master shall the servant be
And pierced are the feet that follow Me;
But thine are whole. Can he have followed far
Who has no wound nor scar?[13]

Now that I had a scar, I felt ready to risk. The worst had happened, and I'd survived.

Don't get me wrong—a healthy fear of danger is a sane emotion, but before my beatdown, I was more afraid than I should have been. The fear of danger, rejection, or failure was enough to stop me from risking for the kingdom. Often it's being afraid of being afraid that holds us back more than anything. Franklin Delano Roosevelt steeled the iron nerve of the American public by challenging them that their own fear was the real enemy, stalling them from taking action. "The only thing to fear is fear itself." Similarly, Paul mentions the flaming arrows of the enemy, which can be enough to keep us held back, safely behind allied lines, out of range of the archers. To advance, one must take up the shield of faith to extinguish the fiery arrows of fear. Perhaps you've felt the tension of feeling challenged and scared to advance at the same time, feeling subjectively scared, objectively unready, but desperately hungry for adventure. Humorist Will Rogers quipped, "Even if you're on the right track, you'll get run over if you just sit there." You can prepare endlessly for a trip that you never embark on. You can draw up the blueprints and obsess over a house you'll never build. You can pray unceasingly for people you'll never talk to. But at some point, you need to get a passport, swing a hammer, or open your mouth.

I have a theory that every Christian is a sleeper cell waiting to be activated. The Bible stories we read unfolded in real time, yet the central characters were unaware their actions were caught, captured, and recorded in the Scripture. One thing you can be sure of, however, is that when they stepped out with alternating steps of faith and fear, they felt confused and lost. Gideon was scared, yet barreled forth and sawed off the Asherah poles with trembling hands under cover of darkness. When the angel first appeared to Gideon, he was cowed in his favorite hiding place in the bottom of the winepress. He was a fugitive from the Philistines, but the angel hailed, "Fear not, mighty warrior!" It seemed like a joke because Gideon seemed anything but brave. He *was* brave, however, not because he wasn't scared, but because he didn't let fear hold him back from his calling. Doubt mingled with fear and an added dash of confusion has been the purchase price of nearly every square inch of kingdom ground that has ever been gained. This is why God repeated the imperative, "Do not be afraid" to Joshua not once, but five times after giving him the terrifying mission to take the land of Canaan (Joshua 1:9). Joshua was used to trailing along behind Moses, leaving the heavy lifting to the professionals, watching God's "special servant" strut his stuff on stage. There comes a time for all of us, where God asks us to audition for a supporting role and stop being an understudy. In this life, we get one shot at letting God take center stage and shining the spotlight on him for all the world around us to see. We dare not treat it like a dress rehearsal when we get our big break.

A student who had come to Christ while attending our urban

Long Beach church plant got a shock when visiting other churches. She said it was like watching a show, and although she enjoyed watching movies, she would rather be in one. She had played a part in the epic drama. But she was used to the action as a stuntman, not an actor who got all the best lines, but never messed their hair. She had become a daredevil by doing, and been scared every step of the way. Those who bungee jump, ride motorcycles over rows of trucks, and parachute out of airplanes, know the thrill of victory when fear is overcome. God seems to favor those who fear free-falling into his hands, and he picks those who are scared of doing spiritual stunts. We imagine that God uses spiritual daredevils and holy adrenaline junkies but I don't know if they even exist. I certainly wasn't one. Gideon wasn't. Paul wasn't either when Jesus called him. I think Paul was quite the transformed character. Pharisee of the Pharisees, he boasted, "I was advancing in Judaism beyond many of my own age among my people and was extremely zealous for the traditions of my fathers" (Gal. 1:14). The poster child of orthodoxy, Paul made the grade to study at the feet of one of the most famous Jewish rabbis in history, Gamaliel. Paul's great learning hadn't driven him mad, but that didn't stop his enemies from accusing him of crossing the line separating brilliance and insanity. Paul would have probably gone down in history as one of the most prolific rabbis of all time, but God wrecked his fancy plans. In his conversion, God transformed Paul so that he was no longer a man more comfortable with ideas than people. He ripped him inside out, from a Princeton archaeology lecturer to a temple raider. He'd been wrecked as a religious leader, but was molded into a loving, compassionate, soul-winning ninja. God has repeatedly wrecked people for vocational ministry and made them dangerous weapons for the kingdom. Ask Wesley, Whitefield, J. Hudson Taylor, William Booth, Mother Teresa, and others who had to venture outside of the four walls of the church to truly effectively reach the unreached. There are people who will spend their lives content with being "Dr. Jones," lecturing in the Princeton halls about what others have done in the past. But there are also those like the cast of characters above who will risk it all for God's glory and in a mix of fear and faith, take their place as Indiana swashbuckling gospel adventurers.

Luckily for us, Jesus finds us where we are, takes us as we are, but doesn't leave us as we are. He doesn't wait for us to be ready before he beckons us out to walk with him on the water . . . or into the story he's still writing.

CAREFUL WHAT YOU WISH FOR

This isn't a book for ministers. I've stopped believing that ministers will change the world anyway. Steve Addison summarized Roland Allen's point that in seminary, ministers learn the lesson of inactivity.[14] Upon graduation, they emerge no more competent to do most of what Paul did in the book of Acts. Many seminary grads who once dreamed of "tearing it up" for Jesus become pulpit pundits, protecting Christian orthodoxy from heresies over pour overs with other theologians, yet are unable to do nearly anything that might change the world, or even the neighborhood they drive through to get to church. With noses buried in texts, they are out of touch with their contemporaries, or as Spurgeon mourned, "at home among the books, but at sea when it comes to men."[15] If you are a minister, I'm calling you out, but I'm also calling you *out*.

We've got to be good at more than just talking. Unfortunately, ministry makes us pretty good talkers, but Paul was able to say that he and his fellow missionaries were men of action, not simply people full of good ideas, or "empty talkers" (Tit. 1:10 ESV). Everything I learned to do on my journey with God to make me effective at reaching the unreached didn't require me to be in ministry. It was actually a benefit for me not to be in it anymore. All that was required was for me to be willing to do something. Anything. Spurgeon urged, "Brethren, do something. Do something. Do something. While committees waste their time over resolutions, do something. While societies and unions are making constitutions, let us win souls. Too often we discuss, and discuss, and discuss, while Satan only laughs in his sleeve."[16]

If you listen closely at church, there is an emphasis on telling stories. But there is a difference between a Christian who can tell stories from a pulpit and a Christian who has stories to tell from the streets. Talking can give a mental release for an angst building up inside of us, and make us feel as if we've done the thing we're talking about. Without actually doing anything, talking is a way of letting off the steam of inactivity. But the more we talk about doing something, the more content we become with talking as the substitute for doing. I've interviewed many authors, conference speakers, and thought leaders over the past few years, and I've noticed many of them haven't done what they speak and write about. It is reprehensible when a guy on stage punches the air for impact with clever sound bites in front of a crowd of thousands, but when off the stage, never says those same things to lost people. But it is common. It's called performing. As an author and field journalist, Ernest Hemingway was disgusted when he saw this type of hypocrisy in authors. He believed he should never write about something that he hadn't personally done. He wrote about fishing, bull fighting, safari hunting, and war because they were adventures he'd lived himself. He was wounded on the field of battle, survived a plane crash, boxed as a prize fighter, and did more things by the age of thirty than most will do in a lifetime. His potent motto was taken from Benjamin Franklin, "Either write something worth reading, or do things worth the writing."[17] That quote has been written by the doorway to my office to remind me where I should be. Out there. Charles Spurgeon said, "When we hold our church-meetings we record our minutes and resolutions, but the Holy Spirit only puts down the 'acts.' Our acts should be such as to bear recording, for recorded they will be."[18]

What about you? Are you ready to start your own journey so that you're ready "not many days from now"? Are you ready to have your life invaded? Are you ready to do things worth writing about? On the other side of the adventure, I pray you'll hear something like Gandalf's evaluation of Bilbo, "My dear Bilbo! Something is the matter with you! You are not the hobbit that you were!"[19]

Discussion Questions

(For Dr. Jones, the Princeton professor in you)

1. What scares you the most about something God is asking you to do? Why?
2. How has God been rapping on your door in the last:
   - Month?
   - Year?
   - Five Years?
3. What do you intend to do about it?
4. What do you think will happen when you take action?

Adventurous Actions

(For Indiana, the Temple Raider in you)

1. Hand your answer over to somebody else in your group. Have them make an action plan for you based on your answers from the discussion.
2. Follow that action plan for one week.

CHAPTER 4

YOU WILL RECEIVE POWER

Want God's power?
Do something that requires it.

You will receive power when the Holy Spirit
comes on you; and you will be my witnesses.
JESUS (ACTS 1:8)

Lightning . . . fire . . . power of God sort of stuff.
INDIANA JONES TO G-MEN

Few from this current generation will ever understand how *cool* Evel Knievel was to millions of people during the 1970s. If you like extreme sports, you have Evel and my generation to thank for it. Every kid growing up in the 70s owned the Evel Knievel stunt cycle, and we carried on his legacy by imitating his many jumps on our BMX bikes, landing us in the emergency room, just like our hero. Knievel was the infamous motorcycle legend who jumped over buses, through rings of fire, and attempted to jump the Snake River canyon. Yes. *That really happened.* He became a household name—for no other reason than he was willing to do what nobody else thought possible—and risk multiple fractures. Over his career, he made seventy-five ramp jumps, held the world's record for the most jumped cars, and suffered 433 bone fractures. Knievel admitted that he wasn't the best motorcycle rider in the world. He'd built his entire career on risk. He once said, "Nobody wants to see me die. They just don't want to miss it when I do." Like missionaries through the ages, Knievel flung himself into the air, convinced that the glory of it was worth the broken bones.*

The difference between the missionary and the daredevil is whose glory they're flying for. When we commit to reaching the unreached, risk is inevitable. It could be the risk of rejection, being misunderstood, or losing friends. Alternatively, the risk could pay off, bringing God glory, winning souls, and seeing the kingdom come into your neighborhood. Flinging yourself out into the unknown, like a punk doing a stage dive, means you believe God will be there to catch you. We're not talking jumping off of any temples, and tempting God to act to the tune of rock and roll suicide bravado. We're talking about doing the things Jesus asked. Preaching the gospel. Making disciples. The early church was willing to embark on front-line mission work in the confidence that his acts through their acts would lead to the effects recorded in the book of Acts. The British Special Air Service commandos' slogan is "Who Dares, Wins." It's true in modern warfare and its truth echoes in the kingdom.

Risk. Adventure. Power. They are all connected. The power of God often comes after prayerfully seeking him, and then stepping out to do the impossible. Without that flair of adventure that comes with the risk of failure, there is no place for faith. God generally works his power in response to faith. The good news is that even the bestowing of God's power comes from his presence, and his presence is always guaranteed by his grace. He wants to pour his grace out on you as badly as he wants to pour it out on those who are lost.

JACKED UP

Making my way across the grounds of the "Next Hippest Thing" Christian conference to meet with a colleague, I'd already made up

---

* For what it's worth, Knievel became a hardcore follower of Christ at the end of his life. We'll see the glory boy in glory.

my mind about this conference. I couldn't stand it. Despite so much effort poured into making it seem hip, hopping, and happening, it was so lame it needed somebody to lower it down through the roof to Jesus. Although I like my music hard, fast, and furious, I craved a dose of mental Dramamine simply because what the conference lacked in musical taste, it compensated with volume.*

I was still suffering from "mission hangover," a condition commonly experienced by anybody who's returned home after a significant time on the mission field. Returning from a twelve-year overseas mission bender, my head struggled to process America's Burger King Christianity: Jesus your way. Knowing it's that way or the highway, many pastors sell out to it. After all, bags of cash are needed to keep the religion-as-big-business machine running. If the beast must be fed, then spiritual leaders feel forced to cater to the crowds and give them what they want, rather than what they need. Lest you feel too sorry for them, understand that it's a symbiotic relationship. Leaders use the people to keep paying the bills, and congregations use their leaders to put on a good show and make them feel better about doing nothing in Jesus's name. The zenith is reached when football stars and celebrities are hired to "preach," elaborate stages are built like sets, and thousand-dollar props are brought in as a draw. After all, when God isn't enough, giving people an incentive to come back is costly; especially when competing with other leaders who've got the same idea. In the absence of a genuine spiritual encounter, they've opted for the best of spiritual entertainment. Thus, the responsibility of telling *the greatest story ever told* is replaced by attempts to throw *the greatest show on earth.*

When you're running church like a circus, it's safe to say there's something you won't find in the center ring—God's presence.

---

* Apparently, time had not improved on C. S. Lewis' criticism of Christian music as "second rate lyrics set to third rate tunes." But as I tuned into Christian radio, the kicker was the commercials that aired during the breaks. Plastic surgery was marketed as a way to improve your witness because people can see you smile again after a little nip and tuck. Christian divorce lawyers prominently pervade station breaks to help you "do it God's way."

After being on the mission field with a Bible in my hands, I was too jacked up for spectator Christianity. I'd just been on the greatest adventure of my life. There would be no going back to "normal" expectations. Cutting-edge to me was no longer about being cool. It was about being on the front line. Therefore, I struggled as I stumbled through the booths, past the food trucks, Jesus-junk vendors, and hipster carnival rides catering to Christians who wanted to be entertained. The airwaves competed amid the comedian, the live band on stage, and obnoxious music blaring from the coffee house, giving the conference the unintentional vibe of a three ring circus. To my right, people were riding a miniature Ferris wheel, whooping and shouting, "Wheeeeee!" To my left, people were shooting paintball guns filled with opaque paint at a ginormous picture of Jesus. People ran around with croquet mallets, paintball guns, and all kinds of entertainment props. Others slept on hammocks placed all throughout the green, apparently too pooped to party. This place had nothing on the temple in Jerusalem when Jesus upturned tables, cracked the whip, and screamed at them to leave (John 2:13–22). It's fair to say that if Jesus had been at the conference, he might be reaching for the croquet mallets for a different reason. The worst thing of all was that the intentional sensory overload was cranked way up to produce an illusion that everybody was having a good time.

Except they weren't.

A lingering glance at the attendees told me they were bored with fun. What they really craved was an adventure. The conference was just another force-feeding in an endless stream at the buffet table of entertainment, except this time, it was stamped with religion. People have settled for entertainment-based Christianity aimed at enticing people in, and keeping them there by pumping the volume up to harder, faster music, and by offering a plethora of cheap thrills. I walked away from that conference convinced of one thing. The church has substituted fun instead of adventure.

CHRISTIANS ARE BORED

The result of circus Christianity is rooms packed with Christians who are bored of sitting in rows and staring at the back of each other's heads. People are tired of being treated like an audience even if they don't realize it. Deep down, they know they're bored, they just don't why.

In 1986, U2 front man, Bono, visited African shanty towns, and something in his soul was awakened as a result of the experience. He penned the song "I Still Haven't Found What I'm Looking For," but perhaps no song in Bono's career has been so misunderstood. Bono wrote, "I believe in the Kingdom Come. Then all the colors will bleed into one."

Wait for it. The chorus comes back around.

"But I still haven't found what I'm looking for." Christians shook their heads, calling Bono an apostate. Bono calls it a gospel song with a restless spirit. That restlessness was Bono's confession that in embracing God, it raised even more questions than he'd had before he'd fallen at the feet of the cross. For Bono, believing was just the beginning of the journey. Bono knew that there was something *more*.

Something bigger than the mind-numbing "fun."

He was called on an adventure. To go "Where The Streets Have No Name." To make an impact in the world. When Bono penned the words to that song after spending time in villages and humanitarian relief stations in Africa, and it had created a hunger for something more. He had gotten a taste of his real purpose, and it was so much better than being a rock star.

If we're honest with ourselves (and we so rarely are), would we say we experience all that God has for us? We all are made to crave the wild, the freedom, the element of danger—great things sought and risked and accomplished. We need to venture into the deep. *Moby Dick*, the ultimate classic adventure tale about the mysterious pursuit of God in the form of a legendary white whale, expresses this longing:

Whenever I find myself growing grim about the mouth; whenever it is a damp, drizzly November in my soul; whenever I find myself involuntarily pausing before coffin warehouses, and bringing up the rear of every funeral I meet; and especially whenever my hypos get such an upper hand of me, that it requires a strong moral principle to prevent me from deliberately stepping into the street, and methodically knocking people's hats off—then, I account it high time to get to sea as soon as I can. This is my substitute for pistol and ball. With a philosophical flourish Cato throws himself upon his sword; I quietly take to the ship. There is nothing surprising in this. If they but knew it, almost all men in their degree, sometime or other, cherish very nearly the same feelings towards the ocean with me.[1]

There you have it. The confession of the damp, drizzly November soul that it was made for something more. Paul expressed it when he said, "I press on to take hold of that for which Christ Jesus took hold of me" (Phil. 3:12). Paul desired to know his purpose, to achieve it, and to leave a lasting impact.

So ask yourself, what is your desire?

I believe when we are saved, our desires are at their strongest. Our sense of adventure is intact. The Spirit of God comes to live inside of us, and we are thrilled with his presence, believing that anything is possible. But soon, somebody tamps us down, douses the fire within us, or steps on our dreams, telling us that's not how it works. So we settle. Our problem isn't that our desires after fleshly things are too strong. It's that our spiritual desires aren't stronger. According to C. S. Lewis, it's that our desires aren't strong enough.

In the absence of our soul's truest desires, we settle for an illicit affair, a bottle, vengeful fantasies, even though none of these things ever lead to fulfillment. There's a raging ocean of living water inside each of us that only Jesus can still, redirecting the powerful flow of our existence. The soul can become a submissive entity that conforms to a container, or water can flow wildly out of control, spilling everywhere. Sometimes water is at peace, and at other times it is a tempest of destructive force. When a Christian isn't doing what he or she is made for, they become restless, just sitting in rows, staring at the back of each other's heads.

New Christians have pent up energy intended for mission. As Paul says, the Spirit of him who raised Jesus from the dead dwells in you (Rom. 8:11). That's a power greater than the neutron bomb. It was deposited in us because we were meant to be fighting alongside the armies of the host of heaven, taking enemy territory, taking captives, and taking names. If we don't use that energy to impact, it can become a destructive force.

Our souls were hardwired for the adventure which requires the presence of the Holy Spirit. In the absence of experiencing that power, we crave spiritual stimulation and go looking for it in other areas. These usually get us into trouble: an extramarital affair, shady deals, or violent encounters like those pictured in *Fight Club*. Bored with a life of mundanity, we vainly attempt to satiate the restlessness by substituting our adventurous calling with entertainment and stimulation. Gorging nightly on a multi-media frenzy, we live vicariously through viewing the titillating lives of fictional characters like Jack Bauer or the exploits of "real-life" sports superstars. Like taste buds that crave sugar, while the body craves nutrients, the deeper cry of our soul is silenced by the deafening sound of society's soul-numbing idolatries. C. S. Lewis remarked, "When the modern world says to us aloud, 'You may be religious when you are alone,' it adds under its breath, 'and I will see to it that you never are alone.'"[2] We never are. We are constantly bombarded by virtual images of others who are living the adventure we should be living. As a result, we find ourselves unable to sit in stillness. We lose the capacity to reflect on our disease of dis-ease. Media is incessantly crammed at us through the buzz of messages and "push notifications." We are never at peace, even as we sit on the toilet, drive in our cars, and wait in the checkout line. Although Friedrich Nietzsche claimed that religion was the opiate of the masses, somewhere along the way entertainment became our drug of choice. Rather than supplying an alternative, the mainstream evangelical church has become all too happy to supply the injection. It all amounts to the same thing—a substitution for living the ultimate adventure that Jesus set before us in Matthew 28 when he said, "Go and make disciples of all nations."

I'm firmly convinced that Christians were made for the conquest of mission. Jesus said, "You will be my witnesses" (Acts 1:8). Our function in the world gives us purpose. Like UK garage hip hop band The Streets rapped, "Geezers need excitement. If their lives don't provide them, they seek it out in violence." Christians need to kick out the jams on mission, or they become Christians-gone-wild.

I can tell you one thing. Nobody wakes up in the morning and thinks, *You know, I'd like to ruin my life and create a scandal that will break my wife's heart, rip my family to shreds, and destroy my name, haunting me to the grave.* In fact, they don't think about it at all. But somewhere, lurking under the surface, there's an underlying restlessness in a person before they get into trouble. King David got into trouble when he was bored. "In the spring, at the time when kings go off to war . . . David remained in Jerusalem" (2 Sam. 11:1). David decided to take it easy, and he got bored. He was designed as a war machine to whoop up on Philistines and kick Amalekite butt. But when he wasn't out doing what he was made for, he ended up doing someone's wife. That wasn't the type of conquest that God had mapped out for him. Think about it from this angle. Every believing Christian has been invaded by the Holy Spirit, who's chomping at the bit to lead them on the adventure of their lives. If they're not living the adventure, and chasing the Holy Spirit's dream for their life, they can still feel the inner conflict caused by the spiritual inertia. Paul spoke of the Spirit's power for mission when he said, "To this end I strenuously contend with all the energy Christ so powerfully works in me" (Col. 1:29), and Paul found an outlet for that power through mission. Make no mistake. There is a resulting restlessness inside of every Spirit-inhabited believer aching to unleash the Spirit's power as they fall blunderingly forward on a mission bigger than themselves.

And our churches have done little to help us release the tension.

The part of us that's made for eternal glory kicks up, kicks off, and kicks out. Christians want to live the glory of the kingdom and see it unleashed in the lives of others around them. They don't want to be catered to. They don't want to be entertained. They don't want to be pampered with programs. Much of what we do in church is designed to put a finger to the mouth, and gently shush them back to sleep. What if Sundays were about awakening something that lay dormant within us? What if Sunday mornings were about hitting the streets? What if our times together were about making an impact?

THE SECRET SAUCE

I want to let you in on a secret. When the church prayed its guts out in Acts chapter one, they had an ulterior motive. Jesus had unfolded the Father's plan, telling them that they were the divine secret weapon to reach the ends of the earth with the gospel. There was no plan B. The plan A team knew they couldn't pull off their mission without power, so they fell on their faces in desperation to seek it. When confronted with a naturally impossible mission, the apostles realized they needed the power of the presence of the living God (Acts 1:8). Every great story involving God on the move is summed up by a "Holy Spirit or bust" mentality. This is why the apostles saw radical conversions and whole towns (like Ephesus) caught up in a spiritual revival.

We need to reawaken the awareness of God's promised power in our midst. It starts with re-engaging with our radical mission from Jesus. Greater empowerment by the Holy Spirit starts with the helplessness we feel in "facing a task unfinished / that brings us to our knees."[3] Being overwhelmed is the first step to getting back where we belong. Even Paul said, "Who is sufficient for these things?" (2 Cor. 2:16 ESV). The front line of mission is where the church has always belonged, and waxed strongest. The world's deep need for salvation won't just go away, but the power and authority will if we ignore the mission for too long. When pastors trade in their role of front line gospel workers and instead become spiritual, behind-the-counter cubicle clerks, locked away from the people they're called to reach, they lose their gospel edge. Our church structures encourage us to take our best leaders out of the world, pull them back from the front lines, and employ them as pencil pushers for Jesus. Look, some desk time is fine, but shouldn't we be walking the beat as well? The result is that the average believer comes into contact with more people who need Jesus by noon on Monday than their pastor will in an entire week.

The front lines are where Jesus promised that the Holy Spirit would be with us in power. Without the risk inherent in the mission of Jesus, we would have no great need for his power. He guarantees he will go with us into "no man's land," kicking butt, and taking names. The power of the Holy Spirit is promised *only* in in the context of mission. Jesus promised his *presence* as we gather, but his *power* when we spread out.

Note the link in the following passages between Jesus sending us out, and the promise of the Holy Spirit's power to accompany us as we go: "All authority in heaven and on earth has been given to me. Therefore *go* and make disciples of all nations . . . And surely I am with you always, to the very end of the age" (Matt. 28:18–20, emphasis mine). So first, Jesus tells them he's got all the authority they need to reach the unreached to the ends of the earth, and the promise is that he'll be with them as they go. The going and the empowering are inextricably linked together like peas and carrots, Forest and Jenny, Beavis and his unmentionable friend. Again the link between power and mobilization is inherent in the verses that are the theme of this book "But you shall receive power when the Holy Spirit has come upon you; and you shall be witnesses to Me" (Acts 1:8 NKJV). Power is always given for witness, not for running a show.

Note how Luke and Paul link mission and power together:

- "With great power the apostles continued to testify to the resurrection of the Lord Jesus. And God's grace was so powerfully at work in them all" (Acts 4:33).
- "My message and preaching were not with wise and persuasive words, but with a demonstration of the Spirit's power" (1 Cor. 2:4).
- "Our gospel came to you not simply with words, but also with power, with the Holy Spirit and deep conviction" (1 Thess. 1:5).

The Holy Spirit is always with his people (Matt. 18:20), but he seems to show up with special power when his people are out of their depth. That's because the secret ingredient for the secret sauce of power is *risk*. After all, why would the Comforter comfort people who are already comfortable? He comforts those who have ventured out of their comfort zones. The Helper is especially present when we actually need help because we're doing things that take us out of our depth. During a prayer meeting, one of our leaders addressed the church, "We pray for more power from the Holy Spirit, but why would he pour himself on us when we continue to do nothing?"

We may long to experience more of God's presence, but maybe *we aren't doing anything we actually need him for.* If our goal is to cram a room full of people, we don't really need the Holy Spirit to accomplish it. Tozer said, "If the Holy Spirit was withdrawn from the church today, 95 percent of what we do would go on and no one would know the difference. If the Holy Spirit had been withdrawn from the New Testament church, 95 percent of what they did would stop, and everybody would know the difference."[4] I've been to seminars where church growth barriers are discussed without even a *mention* of the Holy Spirit. Because of the waste of time, I usually got up and left the room halfway through, convinced that the apostle Paul would have done the same. Trying to fill seats with butts, instead of engaging in the radical front line mission we read about in the book of Acts, is something like straddling a Harley Davidson, gripping the throttle and saying, "Vroom! Vroom!", but without ever turning the ignition. It's cute, but there's no *power*. In the twenty-first century, most of what we call "mission" doesn't actually require God's power, it just takes a building. If most of our churches lost their buildings overnight, they'd be forced out onto the streets first-century style.

Out there.

Where we belong anyways.

MISSION: THE MISSING INGREDIENT

If the goal of church is to cram record numbers of people into a building, what is the goal once they get there? I've been in ministry for twenty-two years now. The greatest favor I ever did myself (or anybody else) was when I stopped pastoring like I was babysitting Christians from the pulpit, and started unleashing missionaries from the pews. Besides, "You will receive power" doesn't make much sense if the main activity we engage in when we come together on Sundays at 11:00 a.m. is sitting on our collective duffs.

When I was a youth pastor a few decades back, I vainly attempted to transform bored, pew-sitting Christian kids into missionaries engaged in their culture. Like most Christians, they sucked at reading their Bibles, praying, attending church, sharing their faith, and giving their money.

Nothing I did was working. Then, a dramatic change came after our first short-term mission trip. I loaded all the students on an airplane and turned them loose on mission in Eastern Europe. During that trip, I began to witness a transformation taking place within those kids as they sensed God's presence. The only difference between home and abroad was their intentionality. Like the apostles, they faced an impossible mission, felt out of their depth, and were willing to risk stepping out nonetheless.

On a train whistling through Hungary, I walked through successive cars to check on the high school students spread throughout its carriages. Passing through the compartments, I witnessed sixteen-year-old girls weeping together with Hungarian families as they got on their knees and came to Christ. A young man in another carriage had his Bible open on his lap, talking to a businessman through a Hungarian interpreter. That train became a moving Holy of Holies.

God was in the house. You could feel him.

From that trip forward, God's presence and the thrill of the adventure catapulted those youths from spectators into active disciples of Jesus. No leader ever had to tell them again to read their Bibles, pray, serve, or give. Prior to this experience, nobody had ever told them *why they should.* Now they *knew* why, and it had to do with fulfilling bigger purposes in their lives than just themselves. It had to do with mission, and these things were tools necessary to accomplish it. But beyond that, they hungered to do these things now, because they understood how desperately they needed to walk in the presence of God, and because they were enjoying him, they were no longer bored. The spiritual disciplines of reading, praying, giving, and serving were never meant to be the ends themselves, but the means to an end. They are what a drum kit, power amp, microphone, and bass guitar are to a band. The goal was to play a song, not to play instruments. God being glorified was the song, and it's a tune best played on mission. Without the tuning fork of mission, the instrument of Christianity sounds off key. These kids who had multiple Bibles, preachers who preached exemplary sermons, and devotional guides aplenty, needed the outlet of mission to tie it all together.

And our church services hadn't provided it.

THE POWER VACUUM

The Holy Spirit was like the wind. As his first order of business after Jesus's ascension, he tore through the upper room and lit fires in his followers that turned the world upside down.

He's powerful.

Untamable.

Unpredictable.

But what if I told you I could predict where the Holy Spirit was guaranteed to turn up in a profound, unmistakable way? What if I told you I could spread out a map, and stab pushpins into areas I knew the Spirit was raging in a spiritual tempest? Those who build wind tunnels have to know where to harness the wind. Wherever Christians are venturing out of their comfort zones, battling on the front lines, you will find him being faithful to his promise to give us power. He is found at work when they go to places, or do things where they *need* him to be the God of the book of Acts. A return to first-century risk and mission will guarantee a return to first-century power.

Whenever a Christian embarks on mission, they enter the slipstream of the Holy Spirit. Have you ever sensed God speaking through you as you're talking to somebody about their soul? "We are therefore Christ's ambassadors, *as though God were making his appeal through us.* We implore you on Christ's behalf: Be reconciled to God" (2 Cor. 5:20, emphasis mine). There is a power in evangelism that any Christian, at any time, can experience. God just waits for us to enter into how he's already working in the world. The Spirit works powerfully, and as believers, we experience a jolt—because we're doing what we were made for. The ignition key to the old Harley Davidson turns, and as it does, we experience a rev of power from the Holy Spirit. He courses through us like fuel flooding into a carburetor. It becomes as addictive as hitting the open road, and the appeal of adventure eventually replaces every other cheap thrill. Like grizzled old bikers, missionaries ride to live and live to ride. Although pitied by Christians sitting at home doing nothing, the missionaries are privileged to live the adventure and tell all the best stories. But it doesn't have to be that way.

Have you noticed the scandal? The missionary stories recounted by bored Christians are only told in hushed whispers over our coffee like rumors from a strange land. Sure, most missionaries may dress like nerds, but they live like spiritual Jedi. As foreign missionaries unfold the tales of their adventures, such as smuggling Bibles into

China, or into Russia before the fall of communism, those in the pew wonder why they've never experienced these wonders, but deep down they already know. Many Christians have never left the garage and taken the hog out for a spin where they could fully open up the carburetor. Maybe they've never embraced the Force like young Luke Skywalker and run off half-cocked to save the world from the dark side. Their biggest thrill is rushing into Toshi Station to pick up more power converters. Deep inside, their souls yearn for something more.

I have a theory. Missionaries witness God on the move because being on mission is like having a front row seat to what God is already doing. The more frontline you go, the more of his activity you'll experience. Let me be clear here. The front lines are any time you engage somebody who doesn't know Jesus. Any Christian can do that at any time, and God will have gotten there before you. After returning from the mission field overseas after twelve years, I was determined to *stay* a missionary, in America. This is why I targeted urban areas, the trenches of dangerous, sleazy neighborhoods, where the mainstream Christian church rarely ventures.

When young moms start playgroups in parks intending to let the children play, but also lead other moms to Jesus, that's front line. I've witnessed churches running kids' karate, ballet, or dance lessons for underprivileged families and single parents who couldn't afford it. They brought in unbelieving instructors from dojos and dance studios and witnessed loads of people being saved. Your front lines could be talking with a friend, or inviting your neighbor to dinner. It could be your office or community gardening group. What makes the difference is your intentionality. The disciples received power because they were about to *do* something. And you have the same power if reaching those Christ died for is your aim. Christians who are dejected and destitute, but desperate enough to break out of their frustrated boredom, find themselves meeting with God himself. After all, that's where Jesus concentrated his ministry during his three years—not in the church buildings, but in public spaces.

In the 1980s my mentor, pastor Peter Jeffery, came back from a Reformed evangelical minister's conference convicted that he wasn't doing enough to reach the lost. Personally discipled by Martyn Lloyd-Jones, he'd been a minister in Rugby, England for years, but seeing little fruit. He returned from that conference determined to step out in faith and evangelize. Nobody can fully explain it, but the result was that the Holy Spirit started ripping through that town so powerfully, that somebody was converted every week *for two years straight*. The clincher? Nobody was saved by any of the outreaches that they put on after that conference, but something had changed. God turned up and started working in them, around them, and in spite of them.

Jesus promised that his authority, presence, and power would *continue* with them as long as they *continued* on mission. "Surely I am with you always, to the very end of the age" (Matt. 28:20). Conversely, when the church has lost its mission, you can guarantee it has also lost the power of the Holy Spirit. He may be there, but not with the depth or the roar that he could be. Why? Because we're not even taking the first steps toward reaching the unreached. We may cry out with Gideon, "God, why don't you go out with our armies anymore?"[5]

The answer is, *we* don't go out.

RUSH THE STAGE AND DIVE

I know that most of you won't plant churches, and that's cool, but nowhere else have I witnessed people change from pew sitters to urban missionaries. A team of ordinary people was transformed into pioneer missionary church planting daredevil commandos. After being in Europe as a front line missionary, I promised the core team of this church plant that they'd see things they'd only read about in books. I told them that crack addicts would get clean. Gang members would miraculously come to faith. Experience from twelve years in Europe had taught me that anyone can go full frontal missionary without having to buy an overseas plane ticket. As soon as your foot hits enemy occupied soil, the Holy Spirit answers the call with an air strike. It takes faith to abandon security. When a believer jettisons their security, a temporary vacuum is created. That vacuum sucks in faith like a carburetor and gives mission its power. Isn't that the story of every biography of a man or woman powerfully used by God? Their stepping out in faith was a direct invitation to the Holy Spirit to team up on a date with adventure. As men and women of faith, they finally went radical enough to rush the stage and dive. J. Hudson Taylor is said to have remarked, "Unless there is the element of extreme risk in our exploits for God, there is no need for faith."

Embarking on scary mission endeavors that take us out of our depths, out of our comfort zones, are activities that the Holy Spirit promised to help with. The things that most people run from are the very things he runs to. Keep that in mind if you ever want to have a crash collision with him. In other words, run toward what the church seems to be running from—the place where the unreached are waiting—and you will crash into God himself. It's not the only way, but it's one of the fastest. That is what every hero or heroine of the faith has done throughout church history. Bold faith that takes prayerful risks* makes the crucial difference in living a power-filled, adventurous life.

NOW OR NEVER

When the Spirit moves through his people and reaches the unreached, adventure is in abundance. Don't be fooled by all the talk of urban mission floating around these days by middle-class hipster church planters. The truth is, they're not going into the wound with the salve, but are going around the edges. We still aren't reaching the urban people. We're reaching the suburbia as they move into urban areas through gentrification. Where's the adventure in that? I'll use a typical Sunday in Long Beach as an example of the wild ride mission

---

* I owe this phrase to Mac Lake, one of my mentors and a phenomenal leader.

can be. A prostitute stood up and announced she wanted to leave the sex trade. A guy tried to make change from the offering. One of our Sunday school teachers was bitten by a pit bull. A once-hopeless heroin addict stood up and shared how God took away his suicidal thoughts and was helping him keep clean. A recently converted ex-con asked to train for ministry.

I've lost count of how many people at our church have confessed to committing murder. Our record for prison time is held by Tommy, a former FBI Most Wanted poster child and a thirty-eight-year inmate. His record is hard to beat, but some come close. Some tell stories of running drugs for the Mexican Mafia and some tell of their partners being murdered. One of my leaders remarked last Sunday, "Either this grace thing is real, or we're in trouble, because these are some really dangerous people." One night early on in our church plant, while doing an open mic discussion in a coffee shop, I spoke with a young man who recently moved to Long Beach, "What takes getting used to the most?" I asked. He was from the South, so I expected to hear complaints about the pace of life. He told me the hardest thing to adjust to in Long Beach was being awoken by gunshots most nights.

At our church, we baptized the ex-gangster brother of one of our leaders. He was shot dead by police before the year was out for being in the wrong place at the wrong time. I knew planting a church in a dangerous park in the heart of the urban Long Beach would be tough, and we'd need the Holy Spirit, badly. On our first day, somebody tried to steal our sound system out of the truck before we'd even unpacked it. But the Spirit turned up, I preached in the open air, and a woman got saved on the spot. We decided to keep meeting outside, and crowds of people would line up around the perimeter and listen. We saw people miraculously delivered from years of crack addiction, prostitutes leave the sex trade, exorcisms, and some radical conversions in the first eighteen months of ministry.

It didn't start off like that, but I remember the day that everything changed.

At first, my core team had been along for the ride, but they hadn't yet hopped into the driver's seat. Two thousand years ago, the disciples of Jesus turned up one day to hear him teach like he had been doing each day. As they took their places around him, he waved them good-bye, "Go into all the villages in Judea," and sent out the seventy-two (Luke 10:1–23). They weren't ready, but Jesus forced them on an adventure. Like me, they stumbled into it as they reluctantly dispersed on mission.

Church planters get to experiment on churches a lot. I decided to "pull a Jesus" on my team and send them, unprepared, to reach the pimps, prostitutes, homeless, dealers, families, and everyone else who met in various areas in the sixteen-acre park. I preached for ten minutes, then told them to take the food and feed the homeless, and we'd see them back in forty-five minutes. They stood and looked at me blankly. That only got me more excited, "There! That's the exact look that Jesus got from the seventy-two!" As the realization dawned on them that I was actually serious, the blank looks on their faces morphed into wide-eyed disbelief, eventually settling into looks of undisguised fear. I laughed to myself as it became clear why Jesus did this to his disciples. They had no idea what God was about to do, but he did. And so did I.

Forty-five minutes was a joke. Two and a half hours later the last of them circled back to our meeting point. Without exception, all who returned had joy on their faces like the disciples who marveled that "the sick were healed, and even the demons listened to us." Until that day, they had never led people to Jesus before. They were hooked.

Addicted.

Ready.

These days, I've come to believe that being ready looks a lot like simply being willing.

PITCHING A TENT IN A BEAN FIELD

During an interview for my first book, *Church Zero: Raising 1st Century Churches Out of the Ashes of the 21st Century Church*, a radio host introduced me as a church reformer. Although I'd never thought of myself as one, as a missionary in Europe, I suppose I had to be. Nothing we did in American churches seemed to work there. In Europe you can't just rent a building, announce a series, drop leaflets, hire a band, and expect Europeans to fill a room. You've got to go get them. You need to compel them to come in.

I'd come from the Calvary Chapel movement, where a forty-five-year-old pastor named Chuck Smith was used by God to ignite a counter-cultural, generation-changing movement by hitting the beaches with the gospel in the daytime. And at night, bringing people into a tent set up in a nearby bean field. Not content to hide within the four walls of a church, Smith and his hippie preachers hit the sand and actively went after a lost generation.

The tent was a bold, radical move. Smith risked losing the fifty existing congregants who were used to literal pews, fancy Sunday-go-to-meetin' clothes, and "pew sitter" church. The story about Chuck telling his church he'd rip out the carpet and upholstered pews and replace them with concrete benches he'd hose down every week is legendary. He was a man on a rescue mission to seek and save the lost generation in front of him, and the further he stepped outside his comfort zone, the more the Spirit fell upon the people.

According to Ed Stetzer, nearly every contemporary church owes its style to the Calvary Chapel movement. The stylistic changes that Chuck's hippie church instituted to remove roadblocks from the lost youth culture have somehow become about us again. We play our music, preach to amuse ourselves, and tailor services to cater to Christian crowds.

I watched the memorial service for Chuck Smith a few years back. The leaders of the movement recounted the stories of how God used to move, and questions surfaced in my mind. *Shouldn't we be out there today, still doing radical and risky things? Shouldn't we be motivating our people to launch out away from our comfy megachurches and get back onto the beach? The urban areas? The parks? The halfway houses? Shouldn't we be out reaching the marginalized, unchurched, and out of touch in today's society, instead of recounting stories about how we did it four decades ago?*

The lost world around us won't wait for us to figure it out. They'll continue to go to hell while we gather around our campfire telling stories about when giants once walked the earth, men beat their chests, and women swooned. Radical is as radical does. Radical is stepping out. Radical is trusting. Radical is the leap. It's not where you're leaping, but who you're leaping towards—the unreached.

Reaching the "hippies" or whoever is unreached in our community, is costly. Mission is uncomfortable. It takes sacrifice. It takes the kind of radical Christianity that pitches a tent in a bean field and calls it church. And until the Spirit of God moves upon his people again, I'm afraid that will continue to be a rare thing in these days. But if the church won't head to the front lines, it won't see the God that our spiritual forefathers saw. As long as she stays huddled in the bunker, sheltered from the action of the battlefield, she'll never know the power of the air support that the Holy Spirit can bring in. We'll be depressed and fearful like Gideon, thrashing wheat in a winepress, asking, "Where are all his wonders that our ancestors told us about?" (Judg. 6:13), when we should be a city upon a hill. Gideon felt that God had abandoned his generation, but wanted to see power in his generation, not just hear about what God used to do. Jesus is beckoning his church to walk out on the water again. However, like the old saying goes, if we want to walk on water, we're going to have to get out of the boat! According to the promise of Jesus, in Acts 1:8, where there is little risk, there is little power. And in the words of daredevil Evel Knievel, "Where there is little risk, there is little reward."

Discussion Questions

(For Dr. Jones, the Princeton Professor in you)

1. What things are you running from right now?
2. What's the riskiest thing you've ever done for the gospel?
3. How have you seen the Holy Spirit work in an unbelievable way in your own life?
4. What crazy, risky thing could you do to really make a difference in the world?
5. What would it take to get you to take the next step towards making it happen?

Adventurous Actions

(For Indiana, the Temple Raider in you)

1. Contact a missionary this week asking them what's the riskiest experience they've had as a missionary.
2. Ask them what experience they've had that seemed like it was from the pages of Acts.
3. Attend a church plant in a needy area for two weeks.
4. Make plans to visit a missionary within the next year.

CHAPTER 5

WHEN THE HOLY SPIRIT HAS COME UPON YOU

When we dedicate even our weakness to God, his power consumes us.

*They that cling to worthless idols turn
away from God's love for them.*
JONAH 2:8

Throw me the idol, I'll throw you the whip!
SATIPO TO INDY AT A CRITICAL MOMENT

A red laser scope pinpointed the forehead of an innocent, random Sarah Connor in a midwestern town who ill-fatedly shared the same name as the future mother of the world-savior, John Connor. In the eighties flick, *The Terminator*, the real Sarah escapes the T-800 robot assassin. In the sequel, *Terminator 2: Judgment Day*, the story flashes forward to a future where she's a pumped, ripped, lean, mean, terminator-fighting machine. In the years that follow her narrow escape, Sarah Connor devoted her life to prepare for the coming rise-of-the-machines apocalypse. Sarah's transformation happened when she mentally shifted from hapless victim to determined victor.

The mission before us shares many similarities to the *Terminator* storyline. Sarah Connor may be able to tell us the secret to success-fully reaching the unreached of the future. The ironic opening of *Terminator 2* shows Connor in a psych ward, even though she's the only sane one on the planet. Sarah Connor suffers a recurring vision of an incinerated playground, and she bears the burden of knowledge that Skynet will detonate an atomic bomb, destroying civilization.

Being an American returning from Europe was like being John Connor disembarking a time machine into the past to save the world from the coming future. Ministering in Europe is like traveling to the future and back, knowing where America is heading. If we compare Britain's slide into darkness following the Victorian age to America's current state, they also experienced a few punctuated surges until the 1950s. But then the 60s hit Britain like a Mac truck and everything changed. Just like it has for us following the 80s and 90s.

Consider the following figures about church attendance in America today from Alan Roxburgh:

- If you were born between 1925 and 1945 there's a 60% chance you're in a church today.
- If you were born between 1946 and 1964 there's a 40% chance you're in a church today.
- If you were born between 1965 and 1983 there's a 20% chance you're in a church today.
- If you're born after 1984 there is less than a 10% chance you're in a church today.[1]

Add those numbers together and it equals the yawn of an irrevers-ible generation gap.

Sarah's repeated attempts to wake up and prepare them for Skynet falls on deaf ears, so she prepares herself. She alone knows what's coming tomorrow, and her vision drives her to prepare, while everybody else is carried about by blissful ignorance, living mundane lives. Paul told the Ephesian church it was not time for sleeping, but to be alert, because the night was fast approaching, "Be very careful, then, how you live—not as unwise but as wise, making the most of every opportunity, because the days are evil" (Ephesians 5:15–16). Our lives, wisdom, and use of time must be used to strategically prepare ourselves to aid in the salvation of the world in the darkest of days. Like Sarah, we prepare ourselves by anticipating the future, equipping for tomorrow, today. Noah, like Sarah, had a vision of the coming apocalypse, he prepared, and the world survived. In the same way that years of training chiseled Sarah Connor into a hardened fighting machine, those ten days the apostles set themselves apart for the Spirit's coming in the upper room provided the necessary cutting edge to save the world against impossible odds.

CHEMISTRY THAT DOESN'T SUCK

Jesus told them the Holy Spirit would come upon them, but how can we ensure this for ourselves?

It is not enough to tell me Jesus promised it to the apostles if it can't happen to me. Why does he come upon me? When and what conditions need to be met? It's not rocket science, but it might appear that I'm drawing a formula on the blackboard. For the record, I hate chemistry, math, and anything involving numbers, so in my book, formulas suck. There are, however, New Testament principles from Scripture that stake a lightning rod in the turf when the storm is approaching. We cannot manipulate God with formulas. The Spirit is as wild as the wind and blows where he pleases. Nevertheless, Jesus predicted where he would be—like a weatherman, and we can at least trace some wind patterns. Understand that God wants to come upon you more than you want him to. Perhaps he's been waiting for you to want him to.

Aware of their insufficiencies, the disciples spent ten days praying and fasting for power to come on them, so they could go out and share the good news. In regards to the Spirit, Jesus said that we only needed to ask, but the Greek verb tense is continuous, "keep asking." Have you ever wanted something so bad it has consumed every fiber of your being? Or that you would sell all you had to possess it? If you're really hungry, God will not leave your belly empty. The men and women we read about in church history were desperate for the power of God and can recall a time of wandering like vagabonds from hovel to hole, searching for something missing in their ministries. Like A. W. Torrey, they could trace all of their successes back to the Holy Spirit's presence arriving in their lives:

> What did the world do during these ten days while the early disciples were waiting? They knew the saving truth, they alone knew it; yet in obedience to the Lord's command they were silent. The world was no loser. Beyond a doubt, when the power came, they accomplished more in one day than they would have accomplished in years if they had gone on in self-confident defiance and disobedience to Christ's command. We too after that we have received the baptism with the Spirit will accomplish more of real work for our Lord in one day than we ever would in years without this power.[2]

The book of Acts ends with, "He proclaimed the kingdom of God and taught about the Lord Jesus Christ—with all boldness and *without hindrance*" (Acts 28:31, emphasis mine). Acts leaves us with a cliffhanger—the gospel *unhindered*, advancing rapidly in power. Written on the tombstone of famed Scottish Presbyterian missionary John Geddie was, "When he landed in 1848 there were no Christians here; when he left in 1872 there were no heathen." Homeboy needed the power of God for that! Especially since people held him back for so long, believing that he was an unsuitable candidate, due to lack of ministerial experience.

There would be times things would slow down, but the apostles would repeatedly return in desperation and beg for God to give them a bolus injection of faith and power. The result: "After they prayed, the place where they were meeting was shaken. And they were all filled with the Holy Spirit and spoke the word of God boldly" (Acts 4:31). They would keep asking for fresh bursts of anointing, power, and authority after Pentecost until the world was flipped upside down.

Earlier, John the Baptist had confessed that his baptism of water was for repentance only, but that there would be another baptism that would be even more powerful. "I baptize you with water for repentance. But after me comes one who is *more powerful* than I, whose sandals I am not worthy to carry. He will baptize you with the Holy Spirit and fire" (Matt. 3:11, emphasis mine). The people must have wondered what that meant.

The answer came in the form of fire and wind coming upon them in the upper room at Pentecost. The only thing firefighters dread as much as fire is a gale wind stoking power upon the flames, spreading them like, well, like wildfire. I've been in forest fires that traveled so quickly over a ridge, we escaped with our lives only by jumping onto a moving fire truck, trailing uncoiled fire hoses behind us. On Pentecost, the apostles became the fuel, and the Spirit was the wind and oxygen igniting them to a contagious blaze that burned across the map. That fire that sparked in Jerusalem on Pentecost was the combusting of living sacrifices. They had offered themselves to prayer, consecrating themselves completely to the mission before them. After ten days, fire came from heaven to fill them and consume everything in their path.

The key to being consumed with the fire of God is surrender. Paul wrote, "I urge you, brothers and sisters, in view of God's mercy, to offer your bodies as a living sacrifice, holy and pleasing to God—this is your true and proper worship" (Rom. 12:1–2). Because of the finished work of Christ on our behalf at the cross, anything we offer to him is made holy and acceptable. The *desire* to be offered to God actually comes from being overwhelmed with the grace that grips our souls. Having our eyes opened to the wide scope of his grace, "in full view of God's mercy," offering ourselves becomes a reflexive response.

God first works in a soul before he works through it. He goes deep with grace in our heart before asking us to go wide with it in the world. This is why reformation historically precedes revival. A rediscovery of God's grace happened in the lives of Luther, Whitefield, Count Zinzendorf, Chuck Smith, and others. They returned the church to God-glorifying, Soli-Deo-Gloria-style exaltation of the finished work of the cross. Jesus said, "When I am lifted up, I will draw all people to myself"[3] and when the Spirit comes, "He will glorify me."[4] Nothing glorifies Christ like the cross, the focal point of his grace. That's why the apostles experienced the cross and resurrection personally before experiencing Pentecost. Each soul must make the same journey.

Attempting to reach the world effectively without the preparation of offering ourselves completely to God as living sacrifices is like a king going to battle against an army he can't defeat. Jesus concludes that you must sacrifice everything to him in consecration before the battle (Luke 14:31–33). As a veteran of the battle, Paul said we should offer our bodies as *weapons* (literal translation) of righteousness. Any believer offering themselves as sacrifices in response to Christ's sacrifice becomes an embodiment of the cross and resurrection. "We always carry in our body the death of Jesus, so that the life of Jesus may also be revealed in our body" (2 Cor. 4:10). Satan fears nothing more than a walking, talking example of the finished work of Christ and the power of the resurrection that ultimately defeated him. Describing us as weapons, Paul invites us to change our stance so that we're not solely defensive, but also on the offensive. At the dawn of the Great Awakening, George Whitefield wrote in his diary, "I offered my life up as a blank checque to God, telling him that he might write whatever he wanted on it." The resulting power in Whitefield's life should not surprise us. When the Spirit finds somebody completely surrendered in prayer to his purposes to lift up the name of Jesus, and is ready to be poured out for others, they are ready to be filled with God. A person like that is like a lightning rod staked in the ground to attract his power because they are aligned to his purposes.

THE HOLY COMBUSTION TRIANGLE

Paul's picture of surrendering ourselves as a living sacrifice refers to the whole burnt offering from the Old Testament. In order for the whole burnt offering* to be considered "holy and acceptable" in Leviticus, there were two conditions and one result.

1. It had to be set apart (separation).
2. It had to be dedicated to God (consecration).
3. The result: it would be fully consumed by the flames (combustion).

Separation. Consecration. Combustion. Put these three together, and you have the biblical concept of holiness. The word holy literally means to be set apart. Two aspects of holiness are revealed when looked at under a microscope. There is what you're set apart from (separated from sin), and what you're set apart for (God). Therefore holiness has a negative and positive aspect to it. Romans six emphasizes the positive and negative aspects of offering yourself to God, "Count yourselves dead [negative] to sin but alive to God [positive]" (Rom. 6:11, insertion mine). Paul continues, "Do not offer any part of yourself to sin as an instrument of wickedness, but rather offer yourselves to God" (Rom. 6:13). To become a whole burnt offering means to be wholly separated for that task, wholly consecrated to God, and wholly consumed by him.

The result of Levitical separation and consecration was combustion. Whenever a burnt offering was made at the temple, the priest would allow it to be wholly consumed by flame to remind them of the fire that fell from heaven that licked up the sacrifice in Moses's day, and visibly demonstrated that God had accepted the sacrifice as holy and acceptable. The fire in the upper room and Pentecost's power

---

* Leviticus is my favorite book of the Bible. I know, I'm a freak, right? You can catch my eight-minute chapter expositions of it on the Through the Word app.

outside of it was a visible sign that God had received their offering of themselves to the mission of going to the ends of the earth with the gospel. The answer was power. Fire from heaven.

Separation.

Consecration.

Combustion.

Those same Old Testament principles are the application of offering yourself as a living sacrifice in the New Testament era and will lead to New Testament power. But to be powerfully set apart *in* your generation (combustion), you need to be set apart *from* your generation (separation), and more importantly, to be set apart to God *for* your generation (consecration). Combustion means you are holy in the biblical sense, a living sacrifice ablaze with the fire of the Holy Spirit upon you. Separation means to be free from the bondage holding your generation down. Finally, consecration means an all-out, no-holds-barred passion for seeing them saved at any cost, even if, like Paul, it meant you were willing to be cut off for them (Rom. 9:3). Paul's dedication to the Jewish people emulated Jesus, who had been cut off from his Father for our sake.

Lloyd-Jones said it this way:

> You only have to read Christian biographies and the story of revivals, to see exactly what I mean. There is always this stripping. Men and women are aware that they have been doing things that they should not do. Not very harmful things, perhaps, in and of themselves, but they stand between them and God, so they must go . . . They strip themselves. And they give themselves to God, in a new consecration, and in a new dedication. This, I say again, is of the very essence of repentance. But we realize that we must act. We have got to take some steps. It is not for me to tell you what they are, because if I do, I shall be speaking to some and not to others. But every one of us has got to be stripped of something. Every single one of us, without exception.[5]

Maybe you're like me; chemistry is not your friend. The back label of my deodorant understands this and tells me, "Contains odor-fighting 'atomic robots' that 'shoot lasers' at your 'stench monsters' and replaces them with fresh, clean, masculine 'scent elves.'"* In the spirit of my deodorant, and in fear of chemistry, let me sum it up by saying holy people catch fire more easily! They should come with a warning label: Spontaneous spiritual combustion imminent.

COMBUSTION

Let's talk about combustion first. It's the effect of the two causes, separation and consecration. When those conditions are met, like the whole burnt offering, the power of God consumes a believer with a contagious fire that effectively spreads his message. It doesn't matter if you're thoroughly waterlogged wood and fear you'll only smoke and stink in the fire. The good news is that the consuming fire will consume whatever is offered upon that altar of separation and consecration. I once watched a documentary about an amateurish eccentric man who kept lions on his ranch. He'd lost a foot to a lion once because his boot went slightly into the cage during feeding time. "A lion is a territorial animal," he said, "and he'll own whatever crosses that line. If it's a tire, a hunk of meat, or a boot, once it's in there it's his." Remember, Aslan is a lion. Whatever smacks against the slab of that altar as a living sacrifice will be consumed. He'll own it. But it has to be freely offered to him for service. That's how it works. Everything gets sacrificed to the fire that will consume it all, burning it up until we burn brightly for him.

Tozer said, "We do not need to worry about getting more of the Holy Spirit, but see to it that he gets more of us. We can have all of him if he can get all of us."[6] In order for the fire to spread through you to others, you first have to be caught alight yourself. In order for that to happen, you have to be under the rule and reign of the Holy

---

* Old Spice—ask for it by name!

Spirit. He must possess you, own you, control you. It's less about us harnessing him, and more about him harnessing us—finally. And when he consumes us like fire, his power begins to unleash itself through us. Like a fire consuming all that's in its path, there are no hindrances to his helping, no roadblocks to his moving, no thwarting of his purposes.

Founder of the Salvation Army, William Booth, was once summoned to appear before Queen Victoria and receive a commendation for the countless souls he'd rescued from alcohol and ruin. The queen asked him why he'd had such widespread success whereas many others had failed. As tears began to well in his eyes and run down his cheeks, he looked up and said humbly, "I suppose your Majesty, that it is because he has all of me."[7] Whitefield said something very similar about his time spent in prayer, which is really a time of submitting yourself upon the altar.

> Early in the morning, at noonday, evening and midnight, nay, all day long, did the blessed Jesus visit and refresh my heart. Could the trees of a certain wood near stone house speak, they would tell what sweet communion I and some others enjoyed with the ever blessed God there. Sometimes, as I was walking, my soul would make such sallies as though it would go out of my body. At other times I would be so overpowered with a sense of God's infinite majesty that I would be constrained to throw myself on the ground and offer my soul as a blank in his hands, to write on it what he pleased.[8]

Normally we do the opposite, filling in the check for the amount we want, we ask God to sign approvingly on the dotted line. But Whitefield handed God a blank check with his own signature at the bottom, inviting God to fill in whatever he wanted. When that happens in people, history changes.

Does he have all of you? In *The Enduement of Power*, Oswald J. Smith writes about a horse dealer who agreed to break in a horse purchased by a city-slicker. "That'll be fifty dollars," he says to the dude. After a week or so, the city-slicker comes back to pick up his horse. The horse dealer tells him, "Okay, you can have him, but you can't ride him; not like this." "Why not?" says the slicker. The dealer responds, "He's only half-broken right now. I broke his left side, if you want his right side broken, that'll be another fifty bucks." Many of us, he concludes, are like half-broken horses; broken only on one side. Until what Jesus has done breaks us completely, we won't offer all of ourself upon that altar of combustion. Having bought us once with his blood, we still ask him for another fifty bucks to make it all worthwhile. But Paul urges us, "In full view of God's mercy, to offer your bodies" (Rom. 12:1). Was what Jesus did for us on Calvary enough? Isaac Watts thought so when he penned, "Love so amazing, so divine, demands my life my soul, my all."

When Jesus told his followers to wait until the Holy Spirit came upon them, they were not entirely unfamiliar with the work of the person of the Holy Spirit. In Old Testament times, the Spirit came upon David before battle, or upon a prophet as he prophesied. The Spirit came upon Samson before he laid hold of a jawbone, *Left 4 Dead* style, and gave 1,000 Philistines the epic beatdown of all beatdowns. And before Jesus exhorted his followers to wait in Jerusalem, he previously blew on them in John 20, saying, "Receive the Holy Spirit," imitating Yahweh breathing into Adam's nostrils. Jesus used the Old Testament terminology when he told the apostles that the Spirit would *come upon* them. But when Luke recorded the events at Pentecost he introduced a new term unique to the New Testament. The apostles were *filled* with the Holy Spirit. When somebody has the Spirit within them he saturates every ounce of their being, and they become filled. This filling was secondary to their salvation but necessary for empowerment.

This experience of power was not foreign to them. They knew there were times when they didn't have what it took to accomplish the mission. When Jesus was on the Mount of Transfiguration, the disciples were wrestling all day with a demoniac. They'd cast out demons before, but this one wouldn't budge. Jesus cast it out with just a word. The disciples asked, "Lord, why couldn't we do it?" Jesus's answer, "This kind can come out only by prayer" (Mark 9:29). Because they were not set apart and consecrated with prayer,* they were not powerful enough weapons in his hands.

Lest you imagine being filled with the Spirit to be an optional extra, like an app for your iPhone, perhaps it's better if you think of it as the operational system like a Mac OS X, or Windows 10. Without it, your Christian life is stuck on DOS programming. Talk about boring. Being filled with the Holy Spirit opens up new windows of contagious efficiency. The pilgrims in Jerusalem thought Peter was drunk because the power and persuasion that manifested in him demanded an explanation. In Ephesians, Paul exhorts the believers, "Do not be drunk with wine, but be filled with the Holy Spirit" (5:21). Being filled is not an option, but an imperative. The phrase to "be filled" with the Holy Spirit is literally, *keep being* filled. This is something that *you* are responsible for. It's no good to say, "Holy Spirit, come and fill me," when you're drunk off your butt. Being filled with something else, or under the influence of something else, you can't be filled with the Holy Spirit. Sin acts like alcohol, influencing your thoughts, affecting your actions so that you do and say stupid things. It is addictive, has consequences that hurt like a hangover when the party is over, and eventually ruins your life.

We must be careful to avoid the pitfall of confusing justification with sanctification. Your justification was entirely the work of Christ. He earned your holy standing before God, but the process of sanctification is a joint effort. "As obedient children, do not conform to the evil desires you had when you lived in ignorance. But just as he who called you is holy, so be holy in all you do" (1 Pet. 1:14–15). The Holy Spirit strives to make us holy, but it's our responsibility to work in partnership with him, to make his job easy. Therefore Paul says if we

* Some manuscripts include fasting, which is an even greater discipline of consecration.

want to be weapons of righteousness, we must yield ourselves entirely, piece by piece; body part, by body part (Rom. 6:13).

Therefore, to be filled with the Spirit, you have to stop being filled with sin. In preparation for our first date, I cleaned out my Plymouth Duster. I cleaned that hunk of junk like Joseph cleaning out the saliva-strewn manger that would hold the baby Jesus. Know why? Because I was going to have a real, live pretty girl in that car, and I didn't want her to find any boogers under the seat. Yes sir, my wife's a lucky girl. In the same way, it's probably a good idea to scrub your life clean of disgusting things before you ask the Holy Spirit to fill you. I can't be filled with the Holy Spirit with a brain packed with porn. Ready for some tough talk? Jesus talked tough when it came to sin. This is something that *you* can do. No, scratch that. It's something that you are *commanded* to do. And for the sake of the lost, it's something you *must* do if you want to reach them effectively.

"Jesus returned to Galilee in the power of the Spirit, and news about him spread through the whole countryside" (Luke 4:14). He had been in the wilderness, learning to rely on his Father. He was tempted, but he separated himself from sin and consecrated himself to do the will of God alone. My hope is that the church will return from her long sojourn in the wilderness, and the name and fame of Christ would combust and spread like wildfire in our cities.

This was the heart of missionary to India, Amy Carmichael, "Give me the love that leads the way, the faith that nothing can dismay, the hope no disappointments tire, the passion that will burn like fire. Let me not sink to be a clod: make me Thy fuel, flame of God."[9]

SEPARATION

If holy people are set ablaze, then most of us probably feel like Jack London's doomed character in London's short story *To Start a Fire*—hopelessly ignorant in the vast Alaskan wilderness, unable to catch anything aflame. As I wrote this chapter, I wasn't too far from the famed Lewis and Clarke Trail, where hardened mountain men braved impossible odds and rough terrain, fueled only by guts and whiskey, in an embodiment of the true American spirit. Today, the American spirit is the emotional equivalent of an overly hormonal junior high school girl, weeping and crying if somebody looks at us the wrong way. Any talk of holiness and separation from sin, and we cry "legalist" because talking about sin might make us feel guilty, judged, or "yucky." Hudson Taylor said, "An easy-going non-self-denying life will never be one of power."[10]

That said, I can't stand legalism in any shape or form, but according to Scripture, holiness isn't an option. Even Jesus stated that you need to metaphorically cut off sin wherever you find it. Even if it's something you're pretty attached to, like an eyeball or right hand. John the Baptist was accused of being a legalist, and the people said he had a demon. And by the Pharisees' standards, Jesus was a Sabbath-breaking, prostitute-loving, wild-party attending, wine bibbing, gluttonous man-versus-food champion.[11] Yet Jesus was the embodiment of holiness. With that, I'll leave you to work out your feelings with your inner child. Alternatively, you could wrestle with the angel until you receive the blessing. And of course, Jesus is always ready to spar a little bit more with us.

Does the word "holy" scare you? Holiness is so important that Peter warns, "Without holiness no one will see the Lord" (Heb. 12:14). If the Holy Spirit is in you to begin with, it's his job to make you holy. You should have been clued into that by the fact that we call him the "Holy" Spirit. But don't be afraid of the word holy, as if some big swarthy-toothed madman will suddenly spring out of the bushes with a Bible big enough to choke a mule, spouting frothy specks of spit. Being holy doesn't mean that "you don't drink, smoke, chew or go with girls who do." When the rubber meets the road, holiness means to be like Jesus. After all, he was the only truly holy human being to speak of. But when we live under the influence of his Holy Spirit, walk in the Spirit, and are filled with the Holy Spirit, we can't help but have a greater effect on the people we are around.

Separating ourselves from sin is the negative aspect of holiness, and although not popular today, it was understood in ages past to be a key to effectiveness. Charles Spurgeon, while lecturing ministers-in-training on the connection between their lives, quoted Ecclesiastes 10:10, "If the axe is dull and its edge unsharpened, more strength is needed, but skill will bring success." He likened the Holy Spirit to a workman who can work faster with a sharpened tool. That tool is a holy life. Spurgeon's lecture was titled "The Minister's Self-Watch," and was an appeal to holiness so that we are "anointed with the sacred consecrating oil, or that which makes us most fragrant to God and man will be wanting . . . Sanctity in ministers is a loud call to sinners to repent."[12] Without holiness, we lose our cutting edge for mission.

Paul exhorted Timothy, "Therefore, if anyone cleanses himself from what is dishonorable, he will be a vessel for honorable use, set apart as holy, *useful* to the master of the house, *ready for every good work*" (2 Tim. 2:21 ESV, emphasis mine). This doesn't just apply to ministers, but like Paul said, "if anyone" cleanses themselves from what is dishonorable, they will become useful, and ready for every good work. Becoming useful and equipped for mission is a choice, but comes with a hefty price tag. For some, the cost of becoming effective is too steep a price to pay. But those who are willing to lay themselves at the feet of Jesus become an effective tool, ready to do God's work. Salvation Army founder William Booth asked, "Will you go to His feet and place yourself entirely at His disposal?"

Holiness is not an optional extra if you want to see people around you get saved. Because this generation is addicted to everything, you can't afford to be addicted to anything. People today are tangled up in addiction to drugs, alcohol, gambling, rage, debt, video games, social networking, and pornography, like a cat tangled up in Christmas lights. Lest you think that addiction is unique to twenty-first-century living, the New Testament calls it the bondage of sin, and after being set free from it, Paul calls us not to "be burdened again by a yoke of slavery" (Gal. 5:1).* Gospel passages aren't always popular at gospel-centered conferences. The gospel is good news, but it's less than great news if it can only set me free from sin's guilt, but not sin's power and dominance over my life. The good news of the gospel has been undersold for years. The gospel is not merely, come to Jesus and he will forgive you your sins. It is that and so much more. The gospel is that Jesus will set you free from the sin's penalty and set you free from the bondage of sin.

How will we minister to addicts if we're still addicted? In that condition, we wouldn't even make it as a sponsor in Alcoholics Anonymous, not to mention as a minister of the gospel. Lives are on the line, and if we're going to rescue them from the undertow of sin, we need to be in shape to swim against the current. Fat lifeguards don't save lives.

I've laid my hands, Mr. Miyagi-style, on a crack addict held in bondage for twenty-five years and seen him liberated instantly. I graduated from college as a registered nurse and worked as a psych nurse in drug rehab. I know that God doesn't always set people free immediately. It angers me when people insist he must. Sometimes people need to work the twelve steps. Although our justification was immediate, our sanctification is an ongoing battle, as the nature of the flesh constantly drags downward like dead weight, like the law of gravity. But now the much stronger supernatural power works within us like the law of aerodynamics, which can supernaturally overcome the natural laws of sinful gravity and get us airborne. Paul found a "new law" at work within him that helped him rise above. Jesus does not expect me to be sinless, but he does expect me to sin less. The stakes are high. Souls hang in the balance. "Wake up from your drunken stupor, as is right, and do not go on sinning. For some have no knowledge of God. I say this to your shame" (1 Cor. 15:34 ESV). Mission was a powerful motivator for holiness in Paul's life, and in his mind, the two were connected.

If we're not walking in the power that frees us from sin's bondage,

---

* Paul may have been talking about legalism or sin, or both, depending upon the interpretation.

and not just its guilt, then trying to reach this trapped generation that has succumbed to their passions is going to be difficult. Personally, we don't have much to offer them except a half-baked gospel, as fake as the gospel of works. We don't get to choose between the cross and the resurrection. They are both part of the gospel. The cross represents grace, but the resurrection represents power. To reject the power is to leave Christ in the ground, dead and buried as if he died for your guilt two thousand years ago, but can't really do much for us today.

Separating yourself from sin is going to hurt. I don't know about you, but a part of me likes sin. In *The Great Divorce*, C. S. Lewis envisions Jesus separating a man from his sin, with the sin personified as a seditious red lizard whispering warnings in his ear about Jesus. After the man gives permission for Jesus to kill the lizard, Jesus's touch on the lizard starts to burn the agonized man. The man cries out for Jesus to stop, fearing it will kill him. Jesus replies, "I never said I wouldn't hurt you. I said I wouldn't kill you."

Suddenly the lizard begins chattering loudly, "Be careful. He can do what he says. He can kill me. One fatal word from you and he will! Then you'll be without me forever and ever. I'll be so good. I admit I've sometimes gone too far in the past, but I promise I won't do it again."[13]

Putting to death the sinful desires of our bodies is a painful process of tug of war. Beating the crap out of something hurts your fists as well as the object you hit. Starve it. Hurt it. Beat it until it dies and your flesh cries "uncle" under the dominance of the Spirit, instead of the other way around.

Perhaps you're reading this tough talk thinking God got the wrong guy. The right guys always think that. Despite all this talk about distancing yourself from sin, you will still fail. But through your failure, and refusal to quit, lies victory. Every time you resist, there is greater power, like Jesus returning from the wilderness. Every time you fail, Jesus proves to you the validity of the gospel and demonstrates a love that will not let you go. After repeatedly drinking deeply from the bottomless well of his unfathomable love for you, sin becomes a broken cistern that fails to satisfy. When the well of the heart has been deeply excavated by grace, having sin scooped out of it, it longs to be filled with holiness. Stripping grace from holiness is a formula for the making of a perfect Pharisee. They were experts at separating themselves, and having the form of godliness, but there was no power in it (2 Tim. 3:5).

Therefore, sinless perfectionism is garbage. Jesus handpicked you like he did the apostles. He died for your sin so that he could send his Spirit to inhabit the mess of a state you are, mistakes, flaws, and all. He was aware of how condemned the building was before he bought it, and he's got a restoration blueprint that nobody, maybe not even you, can see. Peter tried telling Jesus he got the wrong guy once. But as soon as Peter netted an impossible haul of fish, he knew he'd been caught. "Go away from me, Lord; I am a sinful man!" (Luke 5:8). Through deep shame and frustration with himself, Peter failed to grasp the lesson that the fish were there to teach. Jesus was essentially saying, "Peter, you keep hauling, and I'll keep doing the impossible." It's more what Jesus can do in each of us than what we ourselves can do. Peter couldn't catch a single fish after toiling all night, nor could he do anything else of any spiritual significance, but Jesus was looking for partners in his business of fishing for people. They needed to be keenly aware that God used flawed but surrendered people, and nobody knew that better than Peter as he stood broken, but filled with the Holy Spirit's power on Pentecost. Holiness doesn't mean being perfect. It means being sacrificed to the one who was sacrificed for us. J. Hudson Taylor said, "God uses men who are weak and feeble enough to lean on him."[14] Peter valued holiness because he valued grace. God had broken him before he used him.

One man said, "I'm not what I should be. I'm not even what I could be. But by the grace of God, I'm not what I used to be." With the work of God in your life, the same can be true for you.

CONSECRATION

Consecration is the flip side of the record, and like most B sides, this one is rarely played. If you thought side A was tough, this one's even harder to listen to. I promise not to ask you to dance to it. Speaking of music, Francis Havergal summed up what it means to be consecrated, with the hymn "Take My Life and Let it Be:"

Take my life and let it be
consecrated, Lord, to Thee.
Take my moments and my days;
let them flow in endless praise.

Take my hands and let them move
at the impulse of Thy love.
Take my feet and let them be
swift and beautiful for Thee.

Take my voice and let me sing
always, only, for my King.
Take my lips and let them be
filled with messages from Thee.

Take my silver and my gold;
not a mite would I withhold.
Take my intellect and use
every power as Thou shalt choose.

Take my will and make it Thine;
it shall be no longer mine.
Take my heart it is Thine own;
it shall be Thy royal throne.

Take my love; my Lord, I pour
at Thy feet its treasure store.
Take myself, and I will be
ever, only, all for Thee.

This time we're not talking about what you're separated *from*, but what you're separated *to*. Now that we've refused to allow sin to control us, it's a matter of not taking the control ourselves. It's the constant struggle to keep handing over the reins of our lives to Jesus, as our King and rightful ruler. In Romans 6:13, it reminds us to yield yourself to the Holy Spirit to become a weapon of righteousness. Like my buddy Adam Stadtmiller said, "Holiness unlocks doors of purpose in your life a lot faster than any to-do list or seminars and books on purpose filled living can. If you commit to holiness, your purpose will hunt you down and lie at your feet."[15]

When I'm filled with either wine or the Holy Spirit, I come under its control and influence. If I fill myself up with wine, I'll be under its influence. Likewise, if I fill myself up with the Spirit, I'll come under his influence. Let me illustrate. Years ago, I was playing a massive multi-player online game called *The World of Warcraft*. Even now, I slightly drool when I think of it. As dumb as it sounds, it was consuming me. Killing boars, looting snobolds, and fastening epic armor to my toon avatar was all consuming. But you can't be consumed by Wow and wowed by the Spirit at the same time. Believe me, I've tried. While a committed warrior of Azeroth, I could not be a warrior in the kingdom of God with the same efficiency. Playing video games took huge bites out of my prayer life, time preparing to preach the word, and even my marriage.

In the first year of our church plant, our leadership went away for the weekend to seek God for direction in a place that literally looked like Hobbiton. There is a book written about that place called *The Grace Outpouring* that hadn't been written yet, but the Hound of Heaven was hot on my trail during our time there. The Spirit hounded me about the cat-and-mouse I was playing with him. On my knees in prayer, I begged God to rip the addiction out of my heart because I was unwilling to let it go. After about four hours of struggling silently, one of the other leaders had a word for me. It was something like this, "Peyton, God wants to use you, really use you. But there is something in your life that is blocking the influence and activity of the Holy Spirit. God is calling you to sacrifice that to him, but he won't take it from you. It has to be given. And when you do, he'll be able to fill you with his Spirit."

Busted.

Yet being busted never felt so good. It was the taste of freedom for a guy who was languishing in prison. I didn't know how to stop wanting what I wanted so badly and because I was unwilling to let it go, I prayed the only thing that I knew how to pray, "God, make me willing to be willing." If you're not willing to offer it because you love the kingdom of Azeroth or the state of Pornizona more than the kingdom of God, then you need to ask God to make you willing to be willing. It's the starting place, and God welcomes prayers that echo, "I do believe; help me overcome my unbelief!" (Mark 9:24).

I have to warn you, prayers like that are dangerous. They're prayers inviting God to come into your inmost desires and shake them up. It will wreck what you have now. I mean, heck, we're supposed to be praying this way daily, "Lead us not into temptation." That prayer is a way of saying, "Help me to *not* want what I want when I shouldn't want it." I always misunderstood that prayer as meaning God would steer the external temptations from my path. What it actually means is that while I walk down temptation way, my internal GPS doesn't malfunction, but safely navigates me out the other side. The entire Lord's Prayer is a prayer of consecration, asking God to change our hearts so we're not diverted from his glory, his will, our dependency, our repentance, or our mission.

Coming under the influence of the Spirit means to want what he wants! Consecration is all about the submission of wills, saying as Jesus did, "Not my will, but yours be done" (Luke 22:42). The key word here is surrender. I come under his influence by yielding to him; offering myself to him as a living sacrifice; offering my desires, my will, my dreams. That's why Romans uses the language of offering sacrifices with the word yield, or surrender, "Therefore do not let sin reign in your mortal body so that you obey its evil desires. Do not offer any part of yourself to sin as an instrument of wickedness, but rather offer yourselves to God as those who have been brought from death to life; and offer every part of yourself to him as an instrument of righteousness" (6:12–13). When you separate yourself from sin in order to consecrate yourself to God as a weapon of righteousness, you put your toe to a spiritual line, and enlist as a commando. Trust me when I say wimps need not apply. There's going to be a bit of a fight ahead of you before you get to settle down into eating the fat and drinking the sweet. Like Joshua, you're going to have to fight for every inch of ground, because to be frank with you, the enemy you're fighting on this front is primarily yourself. When Indy is in the cave at the end of the Last Crusade, he also realizes the true enemy that needs to be fought is himself. His father tells us the same thing ours does, "Let it go."

FIRE!

To sum up, power in witness is the result of meeting these two conditions: repentance and surrender. It would have saved time if I'd just said that at the beginning, but it'll save you time in life if you repent and surrender. Life is like a mafia thug sometimes, offering us the choice between doing this thing the easy way or the hard way. Surrender seems hard at first, until you've done things the hard way. D. L. Moody said, "I do not know anything America needs more today than men and women on fire with the fire of heaven. Not great men, but true, honest persons God can use."

When Blaise Pascal, the famous mathematician died, they found a piece of paper detailing an encounter he had with God sewn into the liner of his coat. This encounter has become known as Pascal's "Night of Fire." On that scrap of paper was written the words that would set almost any heart ablaze.

It reads:

> The year of grace 1654 . . .
>
> From about half past ten in the evening until half past midnight.

FIRE

"God of Abraham, God of Isaac, God of Jacob," not of philosophers and scholars.

Certainty, certainty, heartfelt, joy, peace.

God of Jesus Christ.

God of Jesus Christ.

My God and your God.

"Thy God shall be my God."

The world forgotten, and everything except God.

He can only be found by the ways taught in the Gospels.

Greatness of the human soul.

"O righteous Father, the world had not known thee, but I have known thee."

Joy, joy, joy, tears of joy.

I have cut myself off from him.

They have forsaken me, the fountain of living waters.

"My God wilt thou forsake me?"

Let me not be cut off from him for ever!

"And this is life eternal, that they might know thee, the only true God, and Jesus Christ whom thou hast sent."

Jesus Christ.

Jesus Christ.

I have cut myself off from him, shunned him, denied him, crucified him.

Let me never be cut off from him!

He can only be kept by the ways taught in the Gospel.

Sweet and total renunciation.

Total submission to Jesus Christ and my director.

Everlasting joy in return for one day's effort on earth.

I will not forget thy word. Amen.

I can hardly ever read that without being moved by Pascal's demonstration of incredible intellect, suddenly overcome by emotion during a head-on collision with God. It's obvious that words fail to express the enormity of his experience. Whatever his experience, he uses the words "total submission," "renunciation," and "surrender all" in connection with fire. At that moment, he was a man consumed.

George Whitefield was consumed when he flung himself on his bed in desperation and cried out, "I thirst!" The Spirit flooded in that day and Whitefield surrendered and was consumed by a holy fire. At the moment that the Holy Spirit rushed in, he laughed that it had all been so simple and cried out, "Joy, joy, unspeakable! So full and big with glory!" At that moment, Whitefield became a spiritual millionaire. When he spoke, it was out of an experience of a satisfied soul, nourished from a well that sprung up within him into everlasting life. Not only that, it spilled out over the rim of the well of his heart and created streams of living water others used to quench their thirst. That well of the Holy Spirit wants to well up within us so deeply that you never thirst again, and out of that abundance, offer others freely to drink from the streams of living water. And Whitefield knew power. Eyewitness accounts attest to the powerful undertow of the gospel that pulled at their souls when he preached.

Whitefield's counterpart John Wesley said:

Never doubt either God's presence, God's word, God's pity, or God's power . . . but whatever else you do, deal much with God. People say, 'this man has talent,' and 'that man has talent,' depend upon it, the great secret of usefulness is close dealing with God . . . walk humbly with God. Acts of self-condemnation are, next to acts of faith in Christ, the most profitable of devotional exercises. I have grown best and done best when most frequent in them.

The reason people get nervous about this stuff is that it can make people raging, jerkhole Pharisees. This is because they can be tempted to feel self-justified that they've set themselves apart to receive power in their lives. But remember, we don't become holy in our souls by any other means than the blood of Jesus, so that as Paul said, boasting is excluded (Rom. 3:27). The problem is, we'd rather have a lack of power, and stifle these verses, than have raging jerkholes. But the current hour calls for humble, broken people, consumed with Jesus, and unimpressed with themselves.

That's what it's about, by the way. There was a time when I was obsessed with seeking power for witness at the expense of seeking Jesus. Feeling no better than Simon the Sorcerer who tried to buy power from Jesus without walking with him, I repented. Make no mistake, the disciples were seeking the Father, Son, and Holy Spirit, not his power. Power is always a result of something else. It's never something to be sought directly. I've begun to get to know Vance Pitman, who has been used powerfully in the city of Las Vegas to reach the unreached and plant many churches. He has repeatedly said that his life changed when he realized ministry was what God did. Therefore, ministry was not his first calling. His first calling was intimacy. If he pursued that, God would work all around him in power.

THE POWER OF ONE

Back to Sarah Connor. In the Terminator franchise, only one lone warrior could be sent back in time to save the world. Sarah Connor shifted from a hapless victim to a determined victor. She focused with the intensity of the laser that drew a bead on her forehead. Those who labor, sweat, fast, and pray during the "silent years" have been the ones that get to see God turn the tide of the war through a revival. They are those, who like Elijah, pray for rain during the years of drought. They are categorically out of place, like prophets born out of due time. They pray when they see nothing on the horizon, in anticipation of seeing a cloud the size of a man's fist. Anna and Simeon kept lamps trimmed and burning in the temple and held the infant Hope of Israel in their ancient arms. They stayed focused. They were tired, but remained awake, watching and waiting. As Paul said, "Let us not be like others, who are asleep, but let us be awake and sober" (1 Thess. 5:6). E. M. Bounds said, "Men look for methods. God is looking for men."[16] He's looking for people that will focus on him, looking only to him as the answer to the mess we're in.

This kind of talk is not popular. It's not going to make it into most pulpits, Christian magazines, or popular conversation. It's seen as extremist and strange. It'll get you locked up in padded rooms of solitary confinement and make people want to shove a needle in your glutes. That's okay, I'm in good company. Didn't you know that everyone thought the prophets were crazy? You wouldn't have believed their message either. They were specifically sent into times that needed, but didn't want, their message.

In the psych ward, Sarah is pounding pushups and pull-ups in her cell to keep herself in shape for the coming war. She stayed tough and ensured she could wield a machine gun and use her fists. She trained in martial arts, explosives, and schematics. She trained her mind, spirit, and body in preparation for a future she knew would follow.

She is like those apostles on the eve of Pentecost, focused, determined, and all in. They knew what it would take to save the world. Like Joseph in prison, Moses in the wilderness, Daniel in Babylon, and David on the run from Saul, they knew their time was coming. Soon. They prepped. They sought God. He ignited them.

Discussion Questions

(For Dr. Jones, the Princeton Professor in you)

1. What areas do you think you need to surrender to God?
2. How would your life be different if you submitted those areas to him?
3. How do you continually live a holy life without becoming a Pharisee?

Adventurous Actions

(For Indiana, the Temple Raider in you)

1. Spend a week focusing your prayer life on surrender to God.
2. If there are areas of your life in bondage to sin, ask somebody to pray you through whatever struggle you're having. Talk with them on a weekly basis. If it's a serious issue, consider getting counseling from a pastor or licensed and Spirit-filled professional.
3. Spend a day praying and fasting and asking the Holy Spirit to fill you.

CHAPTER 6

YOU WILL BE MY WITNESSES

Your gifts are designed to reach the world for Jesus. So what's holding you back?

You will be my witnesses.
JESUS (ACTS 1:8)

Yes, you're a man of many talents.
MUSGROVE TO INDIANA JONES

When I was converted to Christianity, I waited as the phone rang. My best friend picked up on the other end.

"What's up, man?"

"Nothing. Just playing a video game."

"Cool. I gotta tell you about something cool, but don't laugh."

"I can't promise."

"Well, you're not going to expect this, and you're probably going to think I'm joking, but I'm being dead serious."

"Shoot."

"I'm a Christian."

(silence)

"You want to hear about it?"

"Um . . . yeah."

"Okay, check it out. Jesus loves us, man. He died for us. He wants to forgive us for all the crap we've done. Man, he watches us while we sleep, he's got the hairs on our heads numbered. He loves us so much that he'd do anything to have us get to know him. If we don't accept his friendship, we stay his enemies, and when he comes back to judge the earth, we're screwed, man. I became a Christian the other day and there's nothing like it, man. You need to let me come over right now, and I'll tell you more."

"Okay."

"Well, what do you think? Think you wanna become a Christian too?"

"Okay."

"Cool, man, I'll be right over to show you how to pray it right."

My first and easiest convert ever! Over the phone even! I can remember thinking, *Man, this Christianity stuff is going to be easy.*

Little did I know. In fact, I pretty much knew nothing about anything.

But there was one thing I did know.

God used me.

And that was all I needed. I was hooked.

Looking back now, I realize the Holy Spirit used me when I knew next to nada, had zero skill in sharing the gospel, and didn't even know the definition of the word "ministry." God was real to me, and because the Holy Spirit was real in me, he was busting loose through my fumbling attempts to do the simplest of things for him. Without knowing I had "gifts," I was using them. I'd subconsciously become his witness despite myself. When people are released in their gifts, Jesus becomes unleashed on the world.

As the Spirit channeled through the disciples, he expressed himself through spiritual gifts. Ephesians chapter four says that when Jesus left the world, there was a Jesus-shaped-hole in it. That might seem like Jesus took a few steps backward in kingdom expansion, but his plan to "fill all things" was by distributing spiritual gifts to mankind (Eph. 4:7–13). As the body grows and matures, it expands, in turn filling that Jesus-shaped hole. The body grows as "each part does its work" (Eph. 4:16). Jesus replaces his life on earth through our lives, as the gifts flourish. Jesus's work on the cross may be finished, but his ministry in the world is not. He continues his ministry through the powerful outworking of the gifts of the Holy Spirit, in a way that's unique to you. Peter preached, but you may never speak a sermon. And that's okay if that's not your calling. Nobody can crack that whip like Indiana Jones, and nobody can use your gifts just like you. Indy's fedora was shaped to his head, and nobody will be the Indiana Jones that Harrison Ford is. Your gifts are as uniquely tailored to you as that fedora. Indy was kitted out with a leather jacket, revolver, map, and a bag of sand, but you've got your own necessary tools to accomplish your mission.

TIME TO GET WET

We've been expecting our church services to be the witnesses when we were told that we *ourselves* would be his witnesses. For decades the church bombarded the enemy with powerful mortars, like a massive battleship, while we safely stood on the deck behind the armored plating, swabbing the decks, and doing other church chores. That worked great in the eighties, but in case you haven't heard, the eighties were over a quarter of a century ago. Those days are done. That's why those battle tactics won't work anymore, and it's time to regroup.

Reaching the unreached in the years to come will require people to infiltrate communities like Navy SEAL teams. Our military brass entrusts some of our most critical missions to SEAL teams because they can perform extractions where naval battleships fail. In the case of reaching the unreached the splinter cell approach is the right tool for the job. The average believer can infiltrate enemy territory throughout the week with the stealth of an airborne ranger, duck-dive over the railings, and plunge into the deep. If immersion into hostile waters is an occupational requirement of being a Navy SEAL, we've been unable to accomplish the mission because we've been afraid to get our feet wet. Just being you, filled with Christ, will bring you many more conversations and experiences to proclaim Christ than seeking out a "mission."

Stories have piled up about communities changed by small unassuming everyday believers discovering new and innovative ways of connecting with individuals as they blunder into mission. Big doors turn on small hinges. Tugboats turn tankers. Splinter cells can win wars. We're in a different kind of battle, where individual guerilla tactics make you a fast moving, light-footed, low to the ground reconnaissance weapon of witness. You won't be effective in big numbers in the future. You won't need the heavy artillery. You're perfect for the job in a way that your church never will be. No matter what we do, no matter how many programs we launch, stadiums we fill, or outreaches we put on, statistics from Lifeway Research tell us that sixty percent of the unchurched American populace will *never* come to church. Period. It's up to you. There is no cavalry riding over the hill, no big guns, no backup ground support, no rescue team coming.

Just you.

Don't underestimate your size, or undervalue yourself because you can't operate with the sound and fury of a big church. It's a myth to think that megachurches are God's big guns. God has always operated in small numbers, scored with the underdog, and favored the dark horse. "Judge me by my size do you?" Yoda asked Luke Skywalker. And when push came to shove against Count Dooku, Yoda proved more dangerous than a midget on fire. That works for my short man syndrome, on both a physical and spiritual level. You probably didn't even realize that to join the Special Forces of the American military you only have to be four foot ten.* Without drifting into the Napoleonic monologue from *Time Bandits*, about how all the world

---

* Technically, four foot ten is classified as a little person. They used to say midgets, but that insults circus performers. You can't say dwarf anymore either since *Lord of the Rings*. Dwarves carry axes now.

conquerors were "tiny guys," I'll just say big things come in small packages. Mother Theresa was a tiny woman who made a huge impact in her world. Armed with the gift of compassion, she was willing to strike out on her own, leave the walls of the convent in Calcutta, and care for the poor and dying in the streets of India, and became more inspirational to the world than the entire Roman Catholic Machine in Rome. Similarly, when Abraham Lincoln met Harriet Beecher Stowe, the author of Uncle Tom's cabin, he exclaimed, "So this is the little woman who started the big war." Your life could be a small meteor that leaves a huge impact crater because it has the force of heaven behind it. C. S. Lewis was hinting at the uniqueness of every human being and their capacity for eternal significance when he said, "There are no ordinary people. You have never talked to a mere mortal."[1]

The powerhouse potential of each believer is squandered when our churches value one person's gift on the big stage, while an entire room of unused gifts come to listen. In the system of "one large gift to rule them all," believers are seen as small cogs in the big wheel, doing church chores, giving time, money, and energy to keep the machine going. Instead of being quick, punchy, risky, and powerful, we become tame, housebound safety officers. The systematization of religion fosters the illusion that "you need us to do mission work for you. Bring people here. We'll save them." In the beginning of the church, it was not so. Jesus didn't set the church up this way according to Ephesians 4:11. The speaking gifts of apostle, prophet, evangelist, shepherd, and teacher have their place, but their role is to equip the body for the work of the ministry.

The gifts of the Holy Spirit were given to the church, but like an old tie or wool knit sweater from grandma, they can remain folded and unused in the bottom of the drawer. When your gifts aren't needed in church, they lay there dormant, or you begin to find other outlets for them outside of church, using them unawares. God still moves through you, but because you're not in touch with them, you may not recognize that it's him. But others do. They're going away wondering why you're so different. Business experts talk about the unconscious competent, but you're the unconscious witness to Jesus.

Perhaps the largest travesty among church goers is that many are unaware they even *have* spiritual gifts. One of the most powerful evangelists of the nineteenth century, Dwight L. Moody said, "For years, I really believed that I could not work for God. No one had ever asked me to do anything."

Read the open invitation to allow the Holy Spirit to make you his witness: "But grace was given to *each one of us* according to the measure of Christ's gift" (Eph. 4:7, emphasis mine). You won't easily identify your gifts by asking what you've been allowed to do up until now. You find your gifts by noting what thrills you every time a particular gift is mentioned. This is because a person's gifts aren't too far removed from their passions. The gifts of helps, compassion, and giving are often unwittingly acted out when a believer is constantly helping people who can't help themselves. People with these gifts find themselves giving money, time, or services (like fixing a car) without fully understanding that Christ is expressing his heart through them. The unchurched recipients scratch their heads and wonder why you've spent so much time helping them, as you become a living epistle, preaching God's undeserved grace and favor to them in tangible, practical ways. In silent moments, when their guard is down, for a brief moment they catch a glimpse of Jesus, as you do the things that Jesus does. You've just unwittingly become his witness by being who God made you to be: Jesus wearing a "you" costume. Never underestimate the spiritual connection that a simple act can make to a person's soul. Men have married women for simply baking them cookies, for the proverb is true that the way to a man's heart is through his stomach. The way to a person's soul may be through fixing their car. And although this can happen through you while you're completely unaware of it, it does not make it any less real. When a believer becomes aware of it, they simply become more strategic in how they implement and deploy their gifts to God's glory.

IF YOU MISSED THE CONCERT,
YOU CAN STILL WEAR THE T-SHIRT

Despite what you may have been led to believe, the church services you attend are *not* the key to reaching the unreached. You are. God desperately wants to reveal to you what he can accomplish in the world through *you*. We rob ourselves when we hand the adventure map and temple raiding over to the pastor, church, or program. We assume the gifts belong in the church service, but at Pentecost, we see the gifts effectively utilized outside the four walls of that room. I interviewed an underground missionary so cool, he has a secret identity like Superman. Knowing that he was on the front lines of mission, I asked him what gifts were operating from the book of Acts. He shifted uncomfortably, leaned in, and asked, "Is this on the record or off?" I assured him it was off the record. Unsure that I'd believe him, in a hushed whisper he said, "Bro, we're seeing the dead raised." He was a Baptist, and they aren't allowed to talk crazy talk.

When the Spirit fell at Pentecost, the apostles became witnesses by taking their gifts to the street. As a one-time request only, the apostles played an international set list of "tongues" so unique it was never repeated. It was a one-time concert, like the time U2 played the impromptu concert on the roof of the downtown Los Angeles liquor store in 1987, immortalized in the video for "Where the Streets Have No Name." You were either there and got to see it, or you heard stories about it later. It still kills me that I lived down the road when it happened, and didn't know it was going on. You may not have been in downtown Los Angeles when the cops shut down Bono and the band on the rooftop on that historic day, but the T-shirt is still available online. You may have missed the show two thousand years ago when Peter rocked the mic at the one time epic international Pentecost show, but you can still wear your own T-shirt and be a witness to the world of what Jesus has done. Incidentally, T-shirts are one of the best ways of advertising things because it transforms you into a walking, talking billboard. You may not have been present at Pentecost, but you can still be an indirect witness to the epic nature of the concert today by utilizing your spiritual gifts.

The beauty of Acts 1:8 is that it's about what would happen once the crowds dispersed. Jesus promised we would be his witnesses, rocking to the end of the earth, to the end of the age. That means the offer still stands today, and he's still got a T-shirt in your size. He's still got gifts tailored to your personal calling. When you use your gifts, it's like putting on a U2 concert shirt that makes people wish they could be there and hear the music. You've just glorified God without even trying.

When the Holy Spirit fell, the crowd was reacting to the gift of international tongues, a one-time stadium filler, but Peter told the people that being witnesses isn't just for rock star apostles. He said,

> In the last days, God says,
> I will pour out my Spirit on all people.
> Your sons and daughters will prophesy,
> your young men will see visions,
> your old men will dream dreams.
> Even on my servants, both men and women,
> I will pour out my Spirit in those days,
> and they will prophesy.
>
> ACTS 2:17–18

Peter was quoting the prophet Joel, who prophesied that the Lord would pour his Spirit out on "all flesh," including sons and daughters, wrinkly old men, and prune-skinned women. They'd dream dreams, prophecy, and experience visions. Everyone was a participant. Pentecost was an all-inclusive, crowd-swelling revolution that opened ministry up to everyone. Nobody was excluded according to Joel's prophecy. You weren't too old, too young, too male or too female, too poor, or too enslaved. Anyone could be God's witnesses. Zoom in close, and you can see yourself waving in the satellite picture of that verse because Peter is explaining that Joel's prophecy is also talking about you, "And you will receive the gift of the Holy Spirit. The promise is for you and your children and for all who are far off—for all whom the Lord our God will call" (Acts 2:38–39).

Paul Pastor wrote, "'I will pour out my Spirit on all flesh,' God said. He was addressing a culture that understood the work of God among humanity as mediated work—to the people through a prophet, a priest, a king. Poured out on *all*? This was a new thing."[2] Let this bullet sink into your brain a bit and it will end your life as you knew it. In order to accomplish the mission, God gave you a unique set of gifts that are strategically meant to fill a you-shaped hole, as the body of Christ collectively fills the Jesus-shaped hole left in the world after his ascension!

I AM EVERYDAY PEOPLE

At Pentecost, Jesus was going global and everybody was supposed to be in on the ground level. The most rapid kingdom expansion movements around the globe are happening through ordinary people empowered in their gifts. Throughout church history, epochs of reformation and revival have resulted in God energizing the men and women, old and young, whether cause or effect, no one knows. Nonetheless, they go together like Forest and Jenny, peas and carrots. From the releasing of Scripture into the hands of the commoner during the Reformation to the ordaining lay preachers and setting up home-based experience meetings during the Great Awakening, God has been pouring his Spirit out on everyday people.

William Booth gathered misfits, rejects, ex-cons, and alcoholics and God dredged the gutters of Victorian Britain. Count Zinzendorf opened his estate to pauper gypsies, and the Moravians became the largest missionary movement the world had ever seen up to that point.

During the Evangelical Awakening, Wesley ordained lay preachers, launched circuit riders, and trained them to recruit people who could disciple small groups known as "experience meetings" or "societies." The societies were strategically placed to empower, equip, and release everyday believers after the field preachers blew out of town. That groundswell was the strength of the movement, and without them, there'd have been no Great Awakening. The civil rights movement found a voice in leaders like Martin Luther King, Jr. and Rosa Parks, but it was the Freedom Riders who made it a movement.

Throughout church history, pew sitters have turned gospel jockeys and the trajectory of kingdom growth has skyrocketed as a result. Following suit, the solution for the church's plight will come from an activation of the pew sitters, not a mandate from the pulpit. When the gifts in the people are activated and unleashed, the church becomes God's witnesses in power.

Jesus handpicked a small band of twelve that nobody else had time for, and used them to turn the world upside down. He empowered the woman at the well to preach the gospel, resulting in an entire village taking a second look at Jesus. Few would have placed value in that woman's life. Not a single person Jesus chose was clergy material. Unless we value the individual believer as more potent than a program, we're not going to be effective.

Tozer said:

> We would do well to seek a new appreciation of the inarticulate many who make up the body of the church. They do a large share of the praying and pay most of the bills. Without them not a preacher could carry on, not a Bible school function. They are the flesh and sinews of the missionary program. They are the private soldiers of the Lord who do most of the fighting and get fewest decorations. The big stars of the Church get a lot of their glory now; the plain Christians must wait until the Lord returns. There will be some surprises then.[3]

FIRST-CENTURY STYLE LEADERSHIP

The apostles had to learn to encourage and disciple ordinary, everyday believers in their gifts because as church planters, the apostles didn't stick around too long. Some think the apostles merely evangelized, and then got the heck outta Dodge. But Paul laid a foundation by reproducing himself so others could build on it, continuing forward momentum once he'd blown the popsicle stand. Paul told Timothy how to develop and empower everyday disciples, "Entrust to reliable people who will also be qualified to teach others" (2 Tim. 2:2). Look at that verse a little closer. Do you realize that there is discipleship development going four levels deep packed into that small verse? Everyday believers are a part of it, and if you look closely, you'll see yourself hiding in that verse, no matter what you do in church.

Here are the four levels of discipleship in that verse:

- Paul—penning the instruction to the guy he's discipled, Timothy
- Timothy—being taught to pass the gospel down to reliable people he can disciple or "entrust" it to
- Reliable people—who are able to train and disciple others
- Others—everyday ordinary believers living out their calling

The "others" would eventually become disciplers as they were discipled. How do I know this? Because after launching a number of churches out of our urban Long Beach church plant, we could do nothing else. We trained up our first string candidates, the "Timothys," and sent them out to plant. Our second stringers, or "reliable people," needed more time practicing, or incubating. I poured into them and tied them off like a water balloon and launched them. Finally, I looked around at my third stringers, "the others," and sent them out too. By the fourth church plant, I'd run out of candidates for ministry and just started looking for warm bodies. That's what happens when the coach looks into the bleachers for replacements. Our spectator stands were full of fence salesmen, financial planners, and DJs. When you run out of traditional leaders, you're forced to disciple people who would never go into "vocational ministry" and leave their day jobs. I quickly discovered, however, that anybody I discipled became leadership material. Rather than waiting for people to emerge as leaders, I started producing my own. This radically changed my theory and paradigm of leadership development. Whereas I used to look for the young people who seemed eager to preach or take the conventional ministry path, I now disciple whoever is immediately in front of me. I learned that everybody has gifts and that discipleship pulls those gifts out of people faster than anything else. It dawned on me recently that the main reason I may have been in leadership younger than most people is because, from day one, I had people discipling me nonstop. D. L. Moody said, "If this world is going to be reached, I am convinced that it must be done by men and women of average talent."[4] I've been witnessing it in action.

The fact that God uses ordinary people shouldn't come as a surprise as we look at the model of the early church. The model of the New Testament is not to leave it to the professionals, but to get the professionals to leave. The early church sent out their best: Paul, Peter, and John. Only James stays behind in Jerusalem. Take Paul himself. Paul had nearly reached the pinnacle of organized pharisaical ministry prior to his conversion. After losing it all, he called it a butt-load of crap saying it had cost him more than it was worth (Phil. 3:8). He became the most effective tool for the gospel after he'd "left the ministry" and gone back to the family business of making tents. I sometimes wonder if Jesus called Paul simply to show he could use ministers to do something useful after all, because his first choice was ordinary people like fishermen, government employees, and anti-establishment punk rock zealots, like the rest of us. Jesus himself was a carpenter fully surrendered to God. Spirit-empowered construction workers for the win! The most powerful ministry I've ever done was after I'd left the ministry and worked as a firefighter, factory worker, or barista. I've learned that there aren't any magic powers that are given to ordained people. Far from it. If I really want to be effective at reaching the unreached, you'll see me working a day job somewhere in Everywhere, USA. At the time of writing this, I'm currently working for a large mission board, training church planting trainers. My team leader is a great friend named Mac Lake who checks up on me to see if I'm okay because he knows I yearn to be surrounded by lost people again. Although I have the most amazing job on the planet, training the next generation of church planting trainers, I confessed that I'd recently put out an application for a senior writer at a major video game company, simply because of my apostolic bent. A combat soldier in the Asian Theater during World War II radioed in his position, "We've got the enemy to the North of our position, to the South, East, and the West . . . and I'm pretty sure they're not getting away from us this time, sir." Similarly, my gifts become fully activated when I'm fully surrounded by the unchurched. Park me in a room full of people who don't know Jesus and my gifts are activated and unleashed. I'm not bad, I'm just drawn that way.

PRODIGALS, NOMADS, AND EXILES

Like-minded millennials are the future of North American mission. A few years ago, I spoke with my brother-in-law who leads the mission program at a Christian university. He told me the kids coming through gunning for ministry are no longer studying theology, but business or global economics. They are going to give their lives to serving God with everything they have. They just aren't going to be doing it in a church building. And it's not just the ministry that they've left. Often it's the church itself.

David Kinnaman, in his book *You Lost Me*, tells us that there are currently three categories of people who've left the church: prodigals, nomads, and exiles.

- Prodigals don't believe anymore, so church doesn't make sense.
- Nomads still believe, but left church because it still doesn't make sense.
- Exiles believe so strongly, that they've given their lives to mission and can no longer find an outlet in churches because they don't make sense to the leadership.

Put simply, the exiles found their way into mission without us, and believe too strongly in it to just attend a show on a Sunday morning. They've left the established church as outward-bound missionaries because they were too dedicated to the mission of Jesus to be held back by our insular ways. In the public sector, they're running missions, and they feel alive as God is moving through them. They're functioning as a missionary station in Nepal or a small medical clinic in Africa, but on home soil in cubicles, collaborative spaces, and through relationships. A small band, low to the ground, and effective. They've followed the currents of traffic in the marketplace, and constantly share Jesus with people through their lives and conversation. They are tomorrow's gospel activists who just couldn't sit in church anymore and think *that* was the big event of their spiritual week.

What I'm saying is not popular, but necessary. Having been a firefighter, I'm no stranger to doing unpopular things to save people's lives. I've debrided MRSA wounds that exposed skin layers, fat, muscle, and bone. I've inserted nasal gastric tubes into paralyzed people while their eyes confessed the agony it was causing, begging me to stop. I've held family members back from rushing into a burning house where the kids were confirmed deceased; rushing in meant certain and unnecessary death. I've had to do and say a lot of things over the past few years that weren't pleasant, but I believed they were right and necessary. I realize this isn't easy to hear, but what if the exiles are right?

They didn't want to be like the sportscasters commenting on the game, viewed as experts, talking about plays. They wanted to get back into the game, feel the crunch of the shoulder pads and crack of a helmet making contact. They wanted to sweat, and risk, and win. So they're outside the church walls doing what those inside are talking about doing.

CHECKED AT THE DOOR

Our lack of action within the walls of the church is due to how we've set church up to run like a spectator sport instead of a contact sport. We invite people to a Sunday set up, treat those in attendance like an audience, then spend the entire sermon pleading with them to be active participants when they leave. They sit there and listen, but we don't provide them with any model or means of carrying out the mission. We assume they'll make it up when they leave us. It's about as successful as the dentist asking people to floss every day once they leave the dentist's office. Um . . . yeah.

My approach as a church leader changed after I accidentally planted a church in Europe. My wife and I stumbled into running a book club in the local Starbucks, intending to discuss *The Da Vinci Code* for a "one night only" event, but then it became a church after unchurched people asked us to do it every week. We set up chairs in a horseshoe pattern around coffee tables that allowed everybody to interact with each other. This was how Paul "reasoned" with people (Acts 17:2, 17; 18:4) in an interactive style of discussion called synagogue-style evangelism. It was powerful. Everybody sitting in that small group inadvertently became an evangelist, and every visiting unbeliever could ask questions, answer, or just listen. Ezra employed an interactive method when he read the law to the gathered multitude in Jerusalem. His scribes moved throughout the crowd and met with clumps of people, fielding questions and entering into discussions "giving the meaning" of what was read (Neh. 8:8). We found that people's gifts were best activated in circles, not in rows. Suddenly, people were evangelizing, encouraging each other, prophesying without realizing it, serving, and praying with one another. We provided people with an opportunity to interact. We gave the gifts a chance. That environment was like giving birth underwater, and the new believers born to us there naturally knew how to swim and hold their breath. All I had to do was get out of the way, as their gifts naturally emerged in the right atmosphere. Once you've tasted interactive spiritual outreach gatherings, you can't go back to church as you knew it.

In most churches, the worship "sets" run like well-oiled machines leaving no margin to use the gifts of the people. Watertight services are so perfectly choreographed that there's hardly a crack for the gifts to slip in. Spiritual gifts get checked at the door. Could the Holy Spirit be as much a spectator as the people sitting in the pews, watching the leaders do everything? Or if the gifts are the channel for the Holy Spirit to glorify Jesus, has he been checked at the door along with the gifts? "I stand at the door and knock. If anyone hears my voice and opens the door . . ." (Rev. 3:20). When you refuse to allow the people to participate, you block one of the ports of entry where the Holy Spirit often breaks in. Whereas when you let people participate, the Spirit begins to flow through the gifts and ushers in a sense of the presence of Christ. When the gifts are exercised, an opening is created, as if by a linebacker, so that the Holy Spirit runs the football through to make a touchdown, and scores the winning connection with his people. If people are the running backs, their spiritual gifts are the power plays.

Because spiritual gifts are expressions of God's presence among his people, they change the atmosphere of the entire room. Paul said when the nonbeliever came into the gatherings of the Corinthian church, it was possible for them to experience a Jacob-style awareness that God was in their midst. The use of the gift of prophecy would allow God to speak in a way that "the secrets of his heart are disclosed, and so, falling on his face, he will worship God and declare that *God is really among you*" (1 Cor. 14:25 ESV, emphasis mine). In other words, the unbeliever experiences what he doesn't believe in: the presence of God, through the gifts of the Holy Spirit. Of course, if that happened in one of our Sunday services, we'd probably apologize for making him uncomfortable and give him a coupon for coffee in the foyer to ensure he returns the following week.

Paul places the gifts in the category of a witness to the gospel, rather than entertainment for Christians. Thankfully Paul laid down ground rules that hedged decency and order, and he told the Corinthians to stop driving lost people away with all kinds of crazy. Their false beliefs about the gifts and their tendency to hype them up were actually obscuring God's true presence as much as somebody who quenched the Spirit by not allowing him in at all. Paul told them they were sacrificing the most powerful opportunity believers have to experience God's presence. The gifts amplify his presence, especially for witness to the unchurched. When believers exercise their gifts, it changes the atmosphere, making everyone aware of the supernatural aspect of Christianity, but therein lies the rub. Somehow we've reduced Jesus's mandate to spread the Greatest Story Ever Told, to running the Greatest Show on Earth.

YA FEEL ME?

The presence of God is the one thing that can't be successfully duplicated or manufactured. It can, however, be substituted with something else. A Pentecostal church leader once confided to me, "The weakness of our movement is that we aren't comfortable when God isn't moving so we tend to whip it up, rather than falling on our knees, patiently waiting on him, and asking the right questions." When the king of Egypt raided the treasures of Rehoboam's palace and plundered the gold shields Solomon had made, Rehoboam tried to keep up appearances by replacing them with shields of bronze to mask the shame of defeat. E. M. Bounds observed, "All around us we see a tendency to substitute human gifts and worldly attainments for that supernatural, inward power which comes from on high in answer to prayer."[5]

On the front lines of mission, bereft of church trappings, I've had "take your shoes off" moments as I stood on holy ground and felt the overwhelming presence of God. Have you ever been in a room where the felt presence of God was so overwhelming that everyone sensed him? I've been in prayer meetings where it seemed a mere forty-five minutes had elapsed, but when we all glanced at our watches, we were shocked it had been five hours! That only happened once, but happened it did. Blown away, we were. Talking like Yoda unnecessarily, I am.

I can remember a baptism in an old Welsh chapel where the presence of God was so thick in the room you could cut it with a knife. As I stood wading in the water of the baptistry, God seemed to fill the room in a way that was tangible. I can count on one hand the number of times I've been afraid of the manifestation of God's presence and my hands began to tremble. That night we baptized a notorious heroin addict who, before coming to Christ, had previously slit his throat in the entrance of a supermarket. Another woman was baptized and her two construction worker brothers felt God's presence and were saved on the spot and set free from addiction. We baptized a college student who had invited his friends and a couple of them also came to faith that night. I glanced into the eyes of the nonbelievers from the water, wondering if they could sense his presence. Yep. Their eyes were wide with fear. The litmus test of whether God is moving isn't how many Christians you've crammed into a room, but the effect upon the lost. The "Big G" was in the house, and it was evident to all.

Drew Dyck writes, "God is always present, I believe. But he doesn't always manifest his presence in the same way. The remarkable thing about these experiences is that they seem to take me by surprise. In those services in which I have sensed his presence, it wasn't because the music was particularly good or the prayers particularly profound. It was because there was a collective sense of God's power and glory, of his holiness. I recall standing in a room with three hundred people singing 'How Great Is Our God' and it felt like we were blending into heaven."

When the Organized Atheist Church in the UK can replicate an average Christian service, and without any noticeable difference, it's time for the Church of Christ to take a pulse. If all it takes is songs and inspirational talks to mimic us, then we've lost the vital felt presence and demonstrable power of God in our midst. Yet Paul boasted, "Our gospel came to you not simply with words but also with power, with the Holy Spirit" (1 Thess. 1:5). Can our churches boast the same?

How would you know that God was in your midst?

Conversely, how would you know that God was *not* in your midst?

You would have to know what the presence of God felt like to know how to answer both questions, but our churches don't seem to put stock in the "felt presence" of Christ.

When I was serving as the evangelist in Martyn Lloyd-Jones's legendary church, Sandfields, where the Spirit had powerfully moved in the 1930s, the elders would huddle in prayer before the service kicked off. Assured that Jesus had promised to be present when two or more gathered, they still yearned for more. They consistently prayed that his "felt presence" would be among them. The waves of revival that Wales had experienced had left an indelible mark on how they prayed. They expected God to turn up, and if he didn't, they begged for him to do so the following Sunday. As I reflected on what they meant in praying this way, my mind went back to all the times that God promised to be in the midst of his people.

God has a habit of crashing the party. Isaiah ministered faithfully in a business-as-usual manner as priest and prophet, but one day, God tore through the rafters of the temple and the hem of God's garment wrecked Isaiah's world. Moses was hidden in the cleft of the rock and could barely absorb the after burn of God's glory. A frustrated, obedient "Holy Club" devotee George Whitefield threw himself on his bed at Christ's College in Oxford and cried out, "I thirst!" and as the Spirit fell upon him, the evangelical world irreversibly shifted. God interrupted. God broke in. What if God wanted to break in on us?

We haven't left him any room.

In the same way that God's presence can't be manufactured or duplicated, it can't be purchased or bought. It has to be sought. We have plenty of money, but a lack of power. But in order to experience

New Testament power, you need New Testament prayer. Jesus found that making church a house of prayer, rather than a circus of religious entertainment or a money-making scheme, upset the status quo too much and interfered too much with what the people were trying to accomplish. The local church won't return to prayer anytime soon, for the same reason we're not praying in the first place—we don't think it will draw, hook, or keep a crowd. When a church is concerned with numbers, it's usually doing things that eventually lead to decline, which is what the nineties taught us about the eighties. Unfortunately, many didn't learn.

Maybe leaders are right. Maybe it would drive people away.

Praying might . . .

Get people involved, which might . . .

Cause them to interact with God, which might . . .

Expose their lack of spirituality, which might . . .

Make them feel uncomfortable, which might . . .

Make them leave . . .

And we can't bear that.

Or it might truly transform the church.

It might even bring revival if you believe in that sort of thing.

The fact that many don't, is telling in and of itself.

A pastor once confided to me that he felt most of what he did was smoke and mirrors, giving the crowd what they wanted so they would keep coming back. Anything to keep the crowds coming, even if it means God isn't—at least not in a way that he can be experienced.

Thank God that prayer was all the early church had. It's why they also had power.

OUTREACH SHOULD BE GIFT-DRIVEN

That power the early church had, like all energy, needed an outlet. Gifts were never really intended for internal use, but external. That's why the power Jesus spoke of in Acts 1:8 is connected with mission.

It's why the apostles immediately went outside when they began to speak in missional tongues as a witness.* It's also why Paul spoke of the gifts in 1 Corinthians in the context of unbelievers experiencing God through them. When the gifts get stuck within the church's walls, they lack the outlet that they were intended for. The gifts were intended for what happens *outside* of the four walls of the church. The beauty of Acts 1:8 was that Pentecost was the catalytic event, but the process was intended to repeat in the epoch of every age until we've hit the ends of the earth. The ripple effects continued beyond the big meeting, and into the rest of the week, month, year, decade, century, down through the millennia, until today. We denude that power of being his witnesses when we imagine spiritual gifts are intended for Sundays. The gifts aren't something we do for an hour every Sunday, they're an integral part of who we are. Os Guinness said, "The truth is not that God is finding us a place for our gifts but that God has created us and our gifts for a place of his choosing—and we will only be ourselves when we are finally there."[6] The gifts flow out of us on Sundays and the six days in between. If the gifts authentically operate inside the church walls, they will be outside as well because they were never intended to entertain believers. They were designed to serve as witnesses to Jesus's glory.

The world's needs are greater than any one congregation can meet. Nevertheless, the anonymous maxim applies here, "I can't do everything, but I can do something, and I will not let everything I cannot do, keep me from doing the something that I'm called to do." You can do something, or rather, God can do something through you, to reach the community around you.

When that happens, we call it *gift-driven ministry*. Business models operate with the idea that you can draw lines across a whiteboard, predicting what you're going to be doing, and how you're going to branch out in the next couple of years. That's nifty when you're flipping widgets, but not so good when you're dealing with Holy-Spirit-filled

---

* This does appear to be unique from the other types of tongues mentioned in the Scripture.

believers. We plan outreach using concentric rings instead of lines. The first inner ring represents our church. The second represents the unreached in our community. Inside the first ring is our team symbolized by a bunch of dots. Each dot represents a person with unique gifts, and their gifts are represented by arrows going out from them, beyond the circle, representing our church. As people come to faith, we draw arrows to the dots once they are reached. Here's where it gets fun. We draw a circle around the dots outside of the original circle redefining the "inner circle" representing the church to encompass them too. Now we have more dots. More dots means more arrows. More arrows equals more gifts. More gifts means more ways to be a witness in that community. Our chief concern becomes finding out what the arrows are, or the gifts that God has placed in our midst. Therefore, the question that anyone who wants to be effective in outreach has to ask is, "How has the Holy Spirit equipped the people in front of me, on my team, to reach this town?" It's not what I want to do to reach my community that counts, it's what the Holy Spirit has gifted the people in front of me to do.

If we've just reached three creatives, then we explore whether the Holy Spirit wants us to engage in creative outreach next. If we reach three bikers, then maybe we create space for people to do stuff tough guys like. If he brings us three single mothers, then we may start a mother's support group. It could be three addicts coming to faith that triggers a recovery group. We never know who we're going to reach ahead of time, but we have a pretty good clue where to start by following our gifts. All of these are relational and involve these people getting involved in their own communities with things they are already familiar with. They're not following us into battle; it's us accompanying them. They perceive us to be leading, but our leading looks a lot like following, as we empower them to reach their community in the unique way God has hotwired them to release their powerful witness. Then we release them to do things through the power of the Holy Spirit that they never dreamed possible and empower, equip, and support them in whatever way we can.

Last year, our Christmas outreach started with a toy drive to support a local women's and children's shelter through which we forged relationships. Through that process, we discovered more than physical needs, and although we hadn't really seen a need for a women's Bible study at our church, a women's discipleship group began to take shape out of necessity. Our women were already being used for evangelizing, exhorting, and admonishing one another regularly, but witnessing the brokenness of the women from the shelter, we had a *reason* to start a discipleship group. The gifts of the disciplers and the gifts of the disciple were simultaneously awakened in the process.

A DOOR KEEPER IN THE HOUSE OF MY GOD

When I started my first church plant in Europe, I'd been in ministry for fourteen years, and a missionary for five. I was burned out. I'd actually quit ministry and was simply acting as "a doorkeeper in the house of my God," holding the door for the Spirit to come out, and for the lost to come in. I told God that I quit. I was done working for him and if he wanted anything to come of the book club at Starbucks, he needed to do all the heavy lifting. I told the church-planting team I had a broad canvas, and a few brush strokes, but they needed to fill in the details. They didn't know what I meant, so I told them I didn't want to be in ministry anymore. I just wanted to be a normal guy. I was fed up trying to climb over grumpy Christians to reach the lost. I told this motley crew in my living room that I didn't have a red Batphone to heaven that was ringing off the hook with calls from the commissioner. Plus, I didn't want to be Batman. (Did I really just say that?) So we looked around the group and asked, "What gifts do we have here?" We couldn't use a business model or five-year plan, but decided to use an organic model with no clue what we were doing. All we knew was that if the Holy Spirit was real, he'd lead us, move us, and reach the people through us that he was gunning for. Being a doorkeeper meant I got out of his way, but inadvertently, it also meant I'd stepped out of everybody else's way, and given them room to do the work of the ministry.

We had people who liked films, so they started a film critic's club. We used films like *I Am Legend*. That movie scared the pants off me, yet it was laced with signposts of redemption. The movie opens with a shot of an old poster on a brick wall, reading, "God has not abandoned us," and ends with a guy sacrificing himself for humanity after screaming, "I can save you with the blood!" Weaving that conversation back around to Jesus in a film club discussion is easier than beating a one-legged man in a butt-kicking contest. The only thing that would come easier is if a chariot pulled up in the middle of the desert and an Ethiopian asked you to explain Isaiah 53 to him (Acts 8:26–40)!

We had two professional chefs, so a group kicked off that taught single teen moms how to cook healthy foods because the mayor told us that if Jamie Oliver knew what they were eating, he'd have a heart attack. We had college students who were addicted to *Halo*; we started tournaments. Don't laugh. More people got saved from that missional community than any of the others. They also got their butts kicked at *Halo*. Our guys were good. Our key to effective evangelism was allowing people to be who they really were. *Really* real. Be themselves. Once we started doing church like this, we started finding out ways that people could be used in their passions.

Jesus specifically placed the hand-picked combinations of gifts perfectly formatted to your calling. Everything about you can be harnessed and put to use for the Lord. Even your personality—for some people, that's pretty redemptive! Shy people can be just as effective at welcoming new visitors to one of our gatherings, simply because they're seen as good listeners, and not intimidating. It's a big myth that loud people make the best evangelists.

Your passions matter. Your hobbies matter. Because how you've been wired matters for mission. We've been told for too long that hobbies are just idols that get in our way. But the Bible redeems hobbies for us. The temple artisans were made into ministerial craftsmen for a living, because their creative skills were outlets for revealing God's glory. Your creativity or physical activity can also be a way of expressing who God made you to be. Eric Liddell always wanted to travel to Africa and be a missionary, but something in him beckoned him to compete athletically despite what others thought. When his sister urged him to drop it for the mission field, he replied "God made me fast. And when I run, I feel his pleasure."

Time to get running.

Discussion Questions

(For Dr. Jones, the Princeton Professor in you)

1. What do you think your gifts are? What evidences have you seen of them?
2. Ask somebody else what they observe in your life.
3. Compare the lists of the gifts in Romans 12 and 1 Corinthians 12, knowing that neither is a complete list. Consider what gifts you may have. Do you have a gift that is not listed in either?

Adventurous Actions

(For Indiana, the Temple Raider in you)

1. Grab a newspaper and circle every need you find in your city
2. Circle the top two needs that you want to do something about.
3. The chances are that you've circled something that has to do with your gifts. The reason why is that your gifts are connected to what you're passionate about.
4. Now join your community in creatively practicing that gift in mission, or start something with others in your community.

CHAPTER 7

IN JERUSALEM

Where is the front line of God's mission?
Look out the window. Yes, *that* window.

You will be my witnesses in Jerusalem.

JESUS (ACTS 1:8)

Beloq: It only takes a little nudge to make you like me.
Indy: Now you're getting nasty.

RAIDERS OF THE LOST ARK

She stormed up to me, irate, as I basked in the Californian sun during our outdoor service. "There's a transvestite in the women's room. What should I do?"

I smiled at her calmly.

"Wait for him to come out?" I said quizzically as my smile turned to a smirk. I knew what was coming. Told you I was a punk.

There was no response, just a blank look. Her eyes narrowed with apprehension of what I was suggesting we do: nothing. With a huff, she stormed off to find another leader and tell on "that bald guy over there" who didn't give her the answer she wanted. I'd planted this church a few years earlier, but when I returned occasionally, few knew who I was. Just some bald guy; and that was the way I liked it.

I knew the transvestite she was talking about. We had three prostitutes in the church at that time, but Marcel was a cross-dressing ex-construction worker who was coming to church regularly. It had taken months for us to earn his trust. In fact, the first time I asked how to get in touch, he handed me a paper that had an email including "4rent" in the address. When I read it, tears started to form, and I nearly lost my composure as I folded it up into my pocket. Marcel had been a construction worker, and once he began to open up with a few of us, we realized he'd walked a very tough road.

The other leader who she tattled to later told me that the lady wanted a confrontation with Marcel. A pound of flesh. A showdown at high noon. She wanted me to give the nod for her to storm into the women's bathroom and demand that Marcel come out immediately. After that, she was hoping one of us would chew Marcel out for the audacity to think he could use the women's bathroom. In many churches, if I'd given the nod, the coats would pile up at my feet as others eagerly picked up stones to throw. This is where, I fear, many Christians would make a stand against all they thought was indecent. This is where they might plant the flag and hold firmly, and as they did so, they would also pierce the heart of yet another person who'd come to a church named Refuge, and was hoping it would live up to its name.

Marcel had learned quickly that very few churches were indeed a refuge. After the service, we spoke with Marcel, and he let us know that he strategically chose to go into the bathroom during the sermon because he didn't want to make anybody feel uncomfortable. Further, he'd chosen the women's restroom because he usually got beat up when he used the men's room. In a conflict like this, experience had taught me that before the day was done we would lose somebody. The important thing was quickly deciding who it was going to be. I knew exactly how upsetting my response was to the woman, but I also knew that she could find a handful of churches where people would think and act exactly like her. She'd be welcome in those churches. Marcel? We were pretty much it. Because of the large number of funerals we've done in our first few years, we call Refuge the "last stop before hell." For many people, we're their last chance at redemption before they face eternity.

You can tell pretty easily when people just talk *about* reaching lost people versus talking *to* them. Sometimes it's the way they describe a drug addict or somebody with mental illness, but there's one quality that will expose that they don't actually know anyone with those struggles—a lack of compassion. Everywhere Jesus went, if he showed one thing to sinners, it was compassion. And nothing tests your compassion like a cross-dressing prostitute on a Sunday morning.

Compassion was one of the first results we observe in the apostles at Pentecost. When the Spirit came in power, they received his heart for the community and began to see Jerusalem through his eyes. Peter had passed the beggar propping himself against the Temple Gate called Beautiful countless times on his way to daily prayer, but that morning after Pentecost, Peter saw him differently. Same beggar, different Peter. "Peter directed his gaze at him" (Acts 3:4 ESV). The Greek text implies that Peter studied him, perhaps as if he'd really seen him for the first time. Or perhaps the first time seeing him in a new way. Whatever it implies, that look was momentous. When we come under the influence of the Holy Spirit on mission, our attitudes towards our own "Jerusalem" changes. Becoming a witness in Jerusalem means going on mission in the community you've probably lived in for a long time. So long, in fact, that the way you see your city, or community, or neighborhood is in need of an overhaul. Perhaps you no longer see it all. As the Spirit consumes us for mission, we *see our community as God sees it.* Being a missionary isn't so much a matter of geography as a matter of posture. The Greek philosopher Anonymous* said, "A missionary isn't someone who crosses the seas but someone who sees the cross." Once you begin to see the people you're interacting with as people for whom Christ died, it's a game changer.

By the way, that day at the temple gates? About two thousand more men believed, in addition to the three thousand at Pentecost. Why?

---

* Yes, I know. This is a joke . . .

Simple. The apostles had become the crucified Christ's witnesses in their home turf, Jerusalem. And it all began with Peter taking a second look. It's the second look that kills ya.

I HATE PEOPLE

Every town tells the tale of two cities. There are two types of people you can choose to reach; people just like you, or people who are nothing like you at all. On Paul's first missionary journey, he and Barnabas *went home* and reached people just like them. There's nothing wrong with that; it's a good starting point when God begins working in our lives. Paul targeted his fellow citizens of Tarsus, in his native Turkey, and Barnabas the inhabitants of his homeland, Cyprus. But on Paul's second missionary journey, something shifted. Paul thought he had it all mapped out, where he would go, who he would reach, but the Holy Spirit kept frustrating his attempts to go places. Finally, the Macedonian call brought him to Greece. That was the shift away from Paul's own Jerusalem, and the beginning of the call to a specific foreign people group. Sometimes God calls you to reach one specific people group at the expense of others, and believe it or not, there is nothing wrong with that. In every epistle, Paul claimed that he was the "sent one" specifically called to reach the unreached Gentiles. Rick Warren claimed he was called to the yuppies in his Jerusalem of Southern California. During his three-year ministry, Jesus said, "I have been sent only to the lost sheep of the house of Israel" (Matt. 15:24).

Wherever you think your mission field is, it always starts in Jerusalem and expands outward from there. Like the apostles, God will initially begin to use you in your immediate surroundings, even if it's the springboard to a different destination. J. Hudson Taylor felt called exclusively to the Chinese, and in embarking for China, had to leave his Jerusalem behind.

God may never call you to South-East Asia, or to the Afghanistan tribes to share Jesus, because he may have strategically called you to stay in Jerusalem and reach the home team. There is enough broken-ness in your city to keep you busy for the rest of your natural born life. Instead of a passport and an airline ticket, Charles Spurgeon said that the two necessary items to reaching people effectively are a love for God and a love for people. Monty Python missed this as the meaning of life, but the Holy Grail of truth from a biblical worldview is that we were made to love and be loved by God. It shouldn't surprise us, therefore, that being witnesses in Jerusalem flows out from loving God and loving others.

I'll let you in on a little secret. I hate people. People laugh when I say it, but it's true. When I grew up, I escaped the heartache of my upbring-ing by reaching into the furthest corners of my imagination, represented by a universe of plastic action figures with five points of articulation. Star Wars, He-Man, G.I. Joe, ThunderCats, and plastic three-and-a-half-inch people were my friends, locked away with me in my room, because being around human people meant pain, rejection, and emo-tional abuse. In the end, I felt safest when alone. Childhood was all toys and cartoons (which probably explains a lot). When I approached adolescence, however, I lost myself in reading and music, all of which provided more opportunity to isolate myself. When I was a child, I thought as a child, but when I came to Jesus, it was time to grow up.

Many Christians grow older in Christ without really growing up in him. When I came to Jesus, his Bible kept saying that I needed to tell others about him. There was a part of me that was doing that naturally, but a piece of me felt like Jonah—loathing the people I was called to reach. It had nothing to do with them. It wasn't personal; I didn't like anybody. How was a natural born Son of Thunder to become transformed into John, the Apostle of Love? John's evangelis-tic methodology worked for me, "Call fire down upon those people, Lord." With the Vikings "Convert or Die" program in full swing, I grabbed the first scoffer that ever mocked me for being a Christian by the neck and slammed him against the wall. Fist cocked back I growled, "Think Jesus is funny now, wuss?" Tears moistened his eyes in humiliation and fear, and his quivering lip eked out "No, I'm sorry . . . just let me go."

I realized pretty early on that I had a dilemma. Jesus was trying to love people through me, but I naturally feared, disliked, and hated the people he died for. If I was going to love people, his supernatural love was going to need to trump my natural hatred, I just couldn't see how. We waste time pretending that we love people when we don't. So in desperation, I broke down and did a crazy thing. I told God the truth!

I confessed my hatred of people.

Acknowledging the truth to yourself and God is the first step in yielding your place of brokenness and helplessness and inviting him to fill you and fix your inadequacies. When we come to the end of what our natural self can do, the supernatural Holy Spirit begins to kick in. At least that's how it worked in our justification. Why not our sanctification too? In our justification, we had to come to a place of utter helplessness in our ability to save ourselves before we cried out to Jesus to save us. In our struggles with sanctification, we can't tell God, "Thanks for saving me, God. I pretty much got it from here." The Spirit rushes into that vacuum created by a spiritual bankruptcy where we've reached deep into the pockets of our own resources and come up with pocket lint and a paperclip, but no dice. At that moment heaven kisses earth, and the Spirit fills that vacuum of inadequacy and supernaturally fills us with a love for people we'd naturally hate. I've stood weeping, overwhelmed with love for the people I shared the gospel with, aware that left to my own devices, I wouldn't give a rip about them. It's inexplicable. It's what Paul naturally felt when he asserted that it was as if Christ himself were pleading through us to "be reconciled to God" (2 Cor. 5:20) and that "Christ's love compels us" (2 Cor. 5:14). You don't have to have the same love he has, you just have to let him love people through you. And with that, you win the T-shirt "Instant People Person—Just Add Holy Spirit."

Why am I telling you all of this? To reach the unreached at the ends of the earth, our Jerusalem changes only when we change first.

The revolutionary spiritual awakening known as the Jesus movement started in the 1960s with a forty-five-year-old Foursquare preacher named Chuck Smith. Problem was, he hated hippies. As they sat on the wall in front of his house on the coastal boardwalk in Newport Beach, Chuck would peer out the window at the unwashed, stinky, emaciated bodies invading his space, and grumble about what losers they were. Until his wife, Kay, stopped him dead in his tracks one day with a challenge, "Chuck, why don't we start praying for them?" You can't get any more "Jerusalem" than the front wall outside of your house. As Chuck and Kay prayed for the hippies, God started to open Chuck's eyes to the mission field of his own personal "Jerusalem." Without it, the Jesus Movement may never have had happened, and you might have been dressed in a suit next Sunday singing hymns. Remember, if you enjoy cruising church in shorts and sandals, you have the hippies to thank for it. The harvest was indeed plentiful, but the workers were few. A prayer to see hippies differently made all the difference and changed outreach as we know it.

MAKE THEM GO HOME, JESUS

The masses had been following Jesus late into the evening. The disciples were hungry, exhausted, and ready to turn them away, but Jesus, being Jesus, would hear nothing of it. He pictured them being like sheep released into the darkness—vulnerable, helpless, and harassed. His shepherd's heart was moved with compassion for the shepherdless sheep. Personally, I'd have been with the disciples all the way.

But that dusky evening was more pivotal for the apostles than for the hungry, heaving masses. Having our eyes opened is the first step to becoming a worker in the field.

"Ask the Lord of the harvest, therefore, to send out workers into his harvest field," Jesus said (Matt. 9:38). It was a sneaky little prayer of self-transformation Jesus pulled, because praying that prayer isn't about changing the lost, it's about changing us. David Wilkerson had his heart broken by a youth on trial for murder, who was pictured in a newspaper, resulting in Wilkerson's head-on collision with the Great Commission. It can happen at an intersection on a dusty road outside an African village on a short-term mission, or holding an infant in an orphanage in Haiti. It could be outside of a brothel in Bangkok, witnessing the sale of children. Each of us has a moment where our hearts are broken, and in that moment a piece of us surrenders into the hands of God.

Thy kingdom come . . . through me.

Thy will be done . . . through me.

No matter where you are in the world when it happens, it will change the world you already inhabit. My job of assessing church planters can be a bit like the old seventies *Gong* show. After the planters pitch their elaborate visions for where they want to go (Las Vegas, Los Angeles, London) and change the world, we ask them what they've been doing locally. Sometimes we get silence and blank stares. When they don't pass the test, we tell them, "Jerusalem first." You need new eyes before you can move to a new place. That's what Paul said, "So from now on we regard no one from a worldly point of view. Though we once regarded Christ in this way, we do so no longer. Therefore, if anyone is in Christ, the new creation has come: The old has gone, the new is here!" (2 Cor. 5:16–17). We often misquote and misapply that verse; it's not about you being changed, but changing the world as you see it.

Paul was the poster-child for this; transformed from a murderous, xenophobic, sinner-hating monster, into a broken man who loved people until it killed him. Just like his Master.

How can that happen to us?

IGNORANCE IS BLISS

Opening your eyes starts with the people you've already been passing by in your personal Jerusalem. But opening your eyes so you notice what's really going on in your own private Idaho can be dangerous.

Once you've seen it, you can't unsee it. Once you pay attention, the need of your neighborhood forces you to feel, and you feel forced to take action. It's like peeling back the plaster in a remodel and discovering asbestos. Perhaps you would have felt better if you'd left well enough alone, but now that you've exposed it, you've got a job on your hands. Now that you've picked at the scab, you're going to have to deal with the bleeding. Ignorance is bliss, but God doesn't want us to be ignorant. Brace yourselves and put on your spiritual beer goggles, because compassion makes the lost look a whole lot more attractive when we see them as God does.

Contrast the comfort you have as a believer with the hopelessness that an unbeliever feels daily, as they soldier on alone, and struggle to make sense of their world or find purpose in it. Maybe you've forgotten what that feels like. To flesh out what people feel like when they're without hope and without God in the world, we should ponder what it's like to have God as a compassionate, care-taking, watchful shepherd, and invert it like a negative exposure snapshot of Psalm 23. After each line in Psalm 23, I'll contrast it with what people normally feel when they don't know God as their shepherd.

The Lord is my shepherd . . .

I'm on my own. Nobody cares for me, and nobody is looking out for me. When I fall, I have nobody to pick me up.

I lack nothing . . .

I can't keep up with the competing voices clamoring for my attention, demanding to be satisfied. Nothing satisfies no matter how much I spend or buy. I still feel empty.

He makes me lie down in green pastures . . .

It's never enough. I fear about tomorrow, like there won't be enough for me or my kids. Eventually, everything and everyone fails me. I've never known the feeling of abundance and contentment.

Beside quiet waters . . .

I'm restless. I would lie down if I felt safe. The times and society keep rushing by me and I have no peace.

He refreshes my soul . . .

I don't believe in a soul. I'm a highly evolved animal. My animal instincts wear me out, and I feel like a slave to my passions as I indulge their every whim. I can never satisfy my animal appetites.

He guides me along the right paths for his name's sake

I do whatever feels right to me at the time, but why then do I always end up eventually feeling bad? Nobody else can tell me what's right to do—it's my life—but sometimes, I wish they would, and I'd follow if I knew they were right. Nobody seems to have the secret, though; we're all blindly groping along.

Though I walk through the darkest valley, I will fear no evil . . .

In life, crap happens. I just hope it doesn't happen to me. If it does, I'll probably have a nervous breakdown or need to get on stronger antidepressants, but I can't think about that right now. I could use a drink right now.

For you are with me . . .

I'd like to think that when the dark times come, my friends will stick by me, but they never have. I wouldn't stick by them either; it reminds me of my own mortality. Where's that drink?

Your rod and staff, they comfort me . . .

The only comfort I have is that I have tried my best, but mostly, I'm pissed off. Life is unfair. Why did this happen to me? If there is a God, he must hate me. I hate him for doing this to me.

You prepare a table before me in the presence of my enemies . . .

I'd like to tell my enemies how I feel before my time comes. Give them a piece of my mind, or at least get them back. But I've never been able to tell my enemies off. I've always been paralyzed by fear. Even with nothing to lose, I'm still a coward.

You anoint my head with oil . . .

How's my hair? Better to look good even if I don't feel good. I need to go to the gym and get one of those hot mom bods. At least people can still think I'm hot. At least there's that.

My cup overflows . . .

My cup is empty. My whole life has been a waste. Eat up and drink it down because tomorrow we'll all be food for worms.

Surely your goodness and love will follow me all the days of my life . . .

My life has been a goat rodeo of pain and regret. Maybe checking out early will save me more of the same. I'd just always hoped it might get better so I kept going.

And I will dwell in the house of the Lord forever.

If God is there when I get to heaven, I'm gonna flip him off and cuss him out for everything that's so jacked up with this world, and tell him that's why I don't believe in him. If he were real, he wouldn't have to play like a make-believe Santa Claus that nobody ever sees because he's up in his North Pole Heaven, checking to see who's naughty or nice. Like most children who grow up, I stopped believing in Santa long ago. It's his problem, not mine . . . but . . . I want it to be real. It's a nice thought. I just wouldn't have let people suffer if I were God. If God were ever willing to get off his high horse and come down here for a few minutes, he'd know how hard we have it. If he were willing to suffer through what we do, he might act differently. That would be a God I could believe in.

In response to that last bit, there is only one word, in the form of a name, that answers every objection in that reverse Psalm.

Jesus.

And we may not have all of the answers, but we do have the only one.

HELLA CORPORATE

When God poured his heart into the disciples, they immediately poured themselves out for their community. They distributed food to widows, sold their stuff, shared with the poor, and fed the hungry. Being Christ's witnesses in Jerusalem became a hallmark of the church's DNA that was replicated into Paul's ministry among the gentiles. When Paul recounts his first sit down with the twelve after his conversion, he tells us that they told him to "remember the poor" (Galatians 2:10). People mattered, not programs.

What does the unchurched person see when they look at the church? The average young person from this generation looks at the church with suspicion because they see our Sunday gatherings and they appear . . . expensive. They quickly calculate how much the air conditioning, lighting, and pyrotechnics cost. Then they look around the room, and according to externals, the church appears a very wealthy, religious country club. Internally, they're working out whether we are for them, for God, or for ourselves. They add up the costs of running the machine, subtracting from that the number of times Jesus said to look after the poor while noting the lack of evidence of social awareness, social accountability, or social action. It doesn't take them long to do the math.

Perhaps this is another reason why the church has lost the Nones, Dones, Mosaics, Prodigals, Nomads, and Exiles or whatever else you call them. By way of review, the Nones claim no religious affiliation.

The Dones are done with the church. The Mosaics are made up of a little bit of every belief system. The reasons they've left are more accurately described by the following terms: Prodigals are those who no longer believe; Nomads still believe but just don't come to church; Exiles believe that their gifts are best used outside of the church. We've lost the younger generation mainly because they didn't want programs to do the work of missions for them. They grew up in the age of social media interaction that got them mobilized to engage in people's struggles and championing causes. Millennials know the power of the digital groundswell communities, Kickstarter campaigns, and online charitable causes, and they've been wondering why there's a cognitive dissonance. They've been exposed both to people on the one hand who talk about Jesus, but don't take action emulating what he did, and people on the other hand who do what he said, yet don't believe in him. So they left. If they do come back to church, I guarantee you it will be to churches that pick a fight with something in their city: sex trafficking, poverty, orphans, battered women, or homeless vets. This is because the gospel can really only be understood in the context it was created for—out there. This generation needs to see the gospel doing what it was made for—changing things. Complain about the millennials if you must, but this generation gets it more than you think. They're just not waiting around for the church to get it. Many of them are already out there impacting the world around them. I've seen prodigals running food banks, exiles starting companies that promote fair trade in people's lives, building relationships, and serving the gospel to their souls. I've seen people running Habitat for Humanity campaigns from their offices, and leading their unconverted missionary coworkers to Christ as they build houses together over Christmas break in Haiti. The gospel makes more sense in action. I'm a gospel man until the day I die, and I will go to my grave believing in the importance of preaching, but who convinced us that we had to choose between action and sermons?

The CEO of Chick-fil-A told his senior leadership that he was tired of them always focusing on getting *bigger*. He changed the conversation to getting *better*. Once they got better, he created the need for the company to get bigger because people were buying what they were selling. If only reaching our generation and turning this situation around were as easy as making better chicken sandwiches. Some would like to argue that it is, and that if we just make church better, it will become bigger. Statistics show, however, that forty to fifty percent of youth who are active in church today will walk away from church.[1] Truth is, the next generation couldn't give a rip about what we're doing inside our four walls. It's what we're *not* doing *outside* of them that concerns them. They're not waiting for us to get better so that they can demand more campus franchises and floor space. They're waiting for us to get on the road and do what we talk about on Sundays. They're waiting for us to be witnesses in Jerusalem, and when that happens in our communities, they might start to give a rip about what goes on inside our churches. Ironically, the yuppie generation running the show hasn't realized the millennials see the church through the same eyes that they themselves did when they were young, anti-establishment hippies. Except now, the tables have turned; the hippies have become the establishment, forsaking their counter-cultural ideals. The Nones and Dones have left the ninety-nine to go after the one because we haven't. They know what Carl F. Henry said was true, "The gospel is only good news if it gets there in time." Perhaps the conversation is less about them coming back to us. Maybe it's about us going out to them.

ALL'S NOT GOOD IN THE HOOD

It's time for a little old schooling with Mister Rogers. He was burdened for underprivileged children growing up in neglected neighborhoods in America. Fred knew it wasn't all good in the hood. Say what you will, but Fred Rogers is one of my heroes. Not only was he an apostle of love to generations of lost kids, but beyond *Mister Rogers'*

Neighborhood, Fred was known as an activist for children's rights. I've watched footage of him in congressional hearings, advocating for children. He held his own, championing the rights of children in urban areas. He was a man full of conviction, full of faith, and full of the Holy Spirit. And he oozed Jesus. The presence and love of God rolled off of him as he sat before children, but it was in front of adults that Fred bore the authority and power of Jesus. Although he's been ridiculed often, if you read the YouTube comments to any of his videos, the laughter stops. People confess in their comments to crying, missing him, and wondering out loud why we don't have people like him anymore. Discussions about grace, love, and God surface in reverent tones from the keyboards of non-religious people, centering on his presence and persona. Why? He impacted a generation by showing them what God was like.

Rogers appeared on Joan Rivers' talk show, and during his brief but amazing interview, Fred dripped with the love of God. The clip is just under two minutes, but Joan Rivers melted in his presence and became like a little child under the power of love. Only onions and Pa Ingalls can turn on my waterworks like Fred Freakin' Rogers. Sadly, he's gotten a lot of flak over the years by Christians who are too insecure about who they are to acknowledge that Fred embodied Christ in his own way. He's been compared to Ned Flanders, and used as the straw man for how Christians are perceived as milksops, but here's a little known factoid about Fred. He went to seminary with R. C. Sproul. You heard me right! R.C. Stinkin' Sproul! Fred Rogers as a Lutheran minister was a theological animal, and could have had an amazing career as a pulpiteer had he chosen to. He studied psychology and sociology enough to know that most urban kids grew up in hellholes, shells of houses that would never be homes. Places where they were abused, neglected, and often thrown into the foster care system. Fred knew that millions of children lived in environments where nobody *ever* told them that they were loved. Fred knew that God loved them and that Jesus had a special place in his heart for children. Like the undercover radical he was, he threw everything he had into launching a public television show that had every inclination of failure. He locked his sights onto those lost kids in America and modeled Jesus to them through love, vulnerability, and service. At the peak of *Mister Rogers' Neighborhood,* eight percent of the American population was tuned in to him every single morning. You can say what you want about him, but those who push for a brawling, macho, swaggering, tough-guy Jesus have nothing on the impact that Fred Rogers made. Not a lick.

Let's step away from *Mister Rogers' Neighborhood* for a moment and talk about your neighborhood. What if you were as burdened for your neighborhood as Fred Rogers was? Solomon moaned that with much knowledge comes much sorrow (Eccl. 1:18). The more you see of the brokenness around you, the more it breaks your heart. And you can't just do nothing anymore. Bono's trip to Ethiopia in the 1980s changed his life forever. Ask Angelina Jolie about her trips to Cambodia, Sierra Leone, and Tanzania, which resulted in her giving twenty-five percent of her annual income on a yearly basis toward helping children globally. Even the most privileged people on the planet are not immune to having their hearts ripped inside out, and their lives turned upside down until they are utterly unmade, and repackaged into activists who see the world through God's eyes once they open their own.

When Michael Cheshire was in the church planting game, he founded The Journey Church, just outside of Denver, Colorado. His core team cleaned out abandoned apartments to scrape enough cash together to pay the bills. They called it doing "trashouts." Trashouts are needed when people have suddenly cleared out of a property because of dire circumstances. As Mike and his team cleaned out the remains, it was like sorting through the personal wreckage and piecing together how lives had fallen apart. They found pictures of families that had been split, letters of unrequited love written to estranged spouses, copies of divorce papers, and containers of antidepressant pills stacked up on bedside tables. The trashouts were emotionally devastating. The team felt like detectives investigating a homicide at a crime scene, piecing everything together when it was too late to avert the destruction. The damage was already done. A virtual-reality demographic study unfolded before their eyes, and Cheshire and his team were determined that their church plant was needed in that community to ensure that people in dire circumstances had hope, so that these situations played out less frequently. G. K. Chesterton said that those who would be used of God would need to hate the world "enough to change it, and yet love it enough to think it worth changing."[2]

Bordering Long Beach is a dockside community called San Pedro. You know it from *The Usual Suspects*. We're planting in Keyser Soze's neighborhood. My planter who is there grew up in a barrio, got converted in the back of a cop car, and was discipled in prison. While I teach most of my planters to pick the brains of the local authorities about the community they're planting in, my planter there had to get permission from the local homies to come onto their turf.

After driving home through the ghetto community, he wrote:

> God forbid I ever look at a person as too far gone. I got a chance to take a drive through San Pedro tonight after meeting with some brothers and sisters out there for fellowship, I cruised up Gaffey Street then drove through the projects. I have to say it breaks my heart seeing the nightlife because it's so much like the places I grew up in, and I know some of the hopelessness that resides there, that feeling of having no other way. It's a tough fight to reach the lost in a place. It's not about starting a "church" that you can minister from but going out on the streets and meeting people and being real as you share the gospel with them. If you're going to help someone stuck in the muck you better be willing to get dirty; if you're going to help the broken you'd better be ready to get hurt because the jagged edges of a broken life are sharp. I pray I'm bold enough by God's grace.

ALL YOUR BASE ARE BELONG TO US

Years ago, a video game came out depicting an alien invasion during which it repeated the phrase, "All your base are belong to us." It was classic stuff. Somebody made a video mocking it, it went viral, and the rest is history (that you probably missed). The point is, had a little more research been done, the audience might have been intimidated when the alien horde invaded, bellowing their verbal threat. Many of our efforts to reach people are equally as laughable because we simply haven't done our homework. This is where researching the people you're trying to reach is valuable.

A major help to seeing your community *how God sees it* is to know a little more of *what God knows about it*. I want to introduce you to a tool called Google. I found it on the world-wide-interweb, and it's really amazing. You can search things with it. Sarcasm aside, it has a bigger kingdom purpose than finding unicorn rainbow fairy kittens. Ever Googled your neighborhood? How many single parents, divorcees, meth users, or sex offenders are in your neighborhood? It'll change the way you look at everything. Better yet, it will give you a sense of mission. A calling. You might even start building puppets, wearing cardigans, and talking to trolleys.

The country of Wales contains a fair share of severely economically depressed areas. Valley communities exploded with people during the coal mining days, as evidenced by the row houses that snake through the valleys, packing people in like sardines. When the coal industry died, the communities were left high and dry without any industry. We started a youth outreach in the HUDs in post-industrial South Wales, where unemployment in certain communities was the chief occupation of its inhabitants. In the projects, we built relationships and saw lives changed. We had been doing outreach among working class youth. One Christmas the mayor identified the neediest families in our town so we could deliver Christmas dinners to families who couldn't afford them. While we were making the rounds, I walked into one of the homes and saw the evidence of alcohol-fueled rage and violence. There were holes punched in almost every square inch of the hallway, running from the front entry to the kitchen. As we passed the living room, I noticed the dad passed out with a bottle next to him. The mom was clearly drunk, and the ten-year-old girl stumbled up to us, smiling, with a glazed-over look from whatever she was high on.

Then Nathan came down the stairs. Nathan was a young kid who'd been coming to some of our gatherings. He had some behavioral problems at first, but had learned to trust us when he realized that we really cared. As he came down the stairs to see who was at the door, his face changed into a look of horror, as if he'd seen a ghost. That's when I saw the shame cover his expression, his eyes averted, as his mind retreated into a mantra that repeated, *Please don't be here. Please don't be here.* He didn't want me to see his home; that this was how he lived. Nathan wanted out of that room. I left as quickly as I could so as not to pour salt into an open wound, but I resolved to do what I could for kids like Nathan. I'd continue to go where the need is, not where the money is. Unfortunately, the opposite is the current trend. The church follows the trajectory of starting congregations in middle-class neighborhoods because that's what can sustain the church's existence and pay a minister's salary. Somehow I think I missed the part in Bible class where that was the point of it all.

Being a witness in Jerusalem means meeting needs.

Prison Fellowship founder, Chuck Colson, wrote during the nineties that "an estimated 36,000 homeless men and women have been wandering New York's streets at night. The city's maximum shelter capacity is just more than 3,500 and the budget is already overloaded, so Mayor Koch appealed to the city's religious leaders for help. If each of New York's 3,500 places of worship would care for just ten homeless people, a desperate human problem would be quickly solved, without huge government expense."[3]

At Refuge Long Beach, where we are a small congregation and we don't have a huge budget, we've seen a handful of people come off the streets, get jobs, move into homes, and start over. But it's come with a price tag. We've seen people take in schizophrenic young girls because they can't bear the thought of them being raped on the streets another night. We've had people looking under cars for addicts at the wee hours of the morning and saved their lives. We've literally talked people off the ledge and kept them from committing suicide. Although we're small, God is powerful.

With God, we're more powerful than we realize if we'd sit down and do the math. I hate math. Math is hard, so we just get out there and help people because we've stopped making excuses. Helping people is easier than doing math. That's our excuse.

In his book *In Deepest England*, frontline street missionary William Booth wrote "While women weep, as they do now, I'll fight; while children go hungry, as they do now, I'll fight; while men go to prison, in and out, in and out, as they do now, I'll fight; while there is a drunkard left, while there is a poor lost girl upon the streets, while there remains one dark soul without the light of God, I'll fight—I'll fight to the very end!"[4] With a heart like that, how do you not change the world around you?

WHERE TO START

As it was for the apostles in the upper room before Pentecost, reaching the unreached starts with prayer. "Ask the Lord of the harvest, therefore, to send out workers into his harvest field" (Matt. 9:38). When you do, your eyes slowly begin to open, and with it, your heart yawns open too. When I pray for the harvest, I change, despite whether the world around me does or not. Because I'm the worker that's going to be sent if I keep up all that praying stuff. How should we pray? In answer to that question, Jesus suggested the Lord's Prayer. The Lord's Prayer itself is a daily reordering of priorities, laying my life out as a sacrifice to glorify his name, begging for kingdom expansion, and submitting to his will.

- Hallowed be your name = Let your name and fame be known, revered, and loved.
- Thy Kingdom come = Let your agenda and priorities be mine as well.
- Thy will be done = Let the parts I don't like be my act of worship and surrender.

By the "Amen" part, I've begun to care about what he does. However, praying for the Lord of the Harvest to do his work should come with a warning label because it can seriously jack you up. Darren Edwards, a church planter in the council estates (think HUDs) of England, prayed for God's compassion for people. He wrote about the consequences:

> I asked God with every ounce of sincerity to "show me the way you feel about people, and give me a taste for the love that you have for your people." After all, if I was going to win people for Jesus, I needed to know how Jesus felt about them so that I could speak from truth and experience, rather than blind faith. The following Monday my wife and I were shopping in Morrison's (the grocery store) when, as I was walking up the aisle, a man stood in front of me looking at some groceries. A rush of emotions hit me as I began to feel God's love for this man, and I began to cry as God told me that this man may not make it into heaven and eternal life. My wife, in shock and horror, quickly reminded me that we were shopping in public and that it wasn't good for men to cry in public. The same thing happened again in the next aisle and I had to keep my head down the whole time that we were shopping.[5]

YOU HAVE TO EARN THE RIGHT

Once you're burdened for Jerusalem, what's next? Like Peter, returning from prayer in the temple, you have to stop in your tracks, and look.

But seeing the condition isn't enough. You have to be determined to *do something* about what you've seen. Once you've served somebody, you earn the right to speak to them. Whether it's an individual, family, city, or country, you earn the right to tell them about Christ's love after you've shown it to them.

In 2006, our infant church plant in Wales met with our mayor. Our particular councilwoman sent a newsletter around the neighborhood and it was obvious she was a woman with a huge heart, intent on bettering the community. After asking for a meeting to interview her about the needs of the community, she was shocked a church was contacting her. She said nobody had ever done that before. We learned that nobody knows the city like a local civic leader who wants to make an impact. Over the next several months we visited shut-ins, mowed lawns and trimmed hedges of cancer patients, and started cooking classes for teenage pregnant mothers, but it didn't get a single person through the doors of our church. But that's not why we did it anyways. It wasn't a program. It was Jesus in action. We were frontline—witnesses in our Jerusalem as we used our gifts missionally. We also promised all the men who turned up to do hard labor that there'd be copious amounts of grilled meat afterward.

Or instead of calling a civic leader, you could pick up a newspaper. Slap it down on the table in front of your church and circle all of the needs in the city. Then, with a red marker have each individual circle the top two that they'd like to do something about. Those red circles have just pinpointed their passions, and once you've pinpointed somebody's passions, their gifts are close behind them. There are far too many needs for your team to reach, but if you focus on those red circles, you'll find that not only do your people care about those areas, but they'll want to roll up their sleeves and do something about them. I've learned the key to mission in any given cultural context is to see how the Spirit has matched the gifts of the team in front of me to the needs of the culture I want to reach.

If I have a third of my people wanting to reach homeless people, then guess what we're going to do? Luckily for you, the Holy Spirit has already identified and targeted the needs for you and equipped your church.

The apostles were all about service. Luke tells us, "There was not a needy person among them, for as many as were owners of lands or houses sold them and brought the proceeds of what was sold and laid it at the apostles' feet, and it was distributed to each as any had need" (Acts 4:34–35 ESV).

The Jerusalem church grew rapidly because the believers grew rapidly in the esteem of the people (Acts 5:13). Here's why:

1. Good news created good works.
2. Good works created good will.
3. Good will created good soil.
4. Good soil created good response.

Entrepreneurial guru Gary Vaynerchuk calls this the "Thank You Economy." It's the philosophy that once you've done something for somebody else, they're more inclined to help you or give you their time and attention. That means listening to you. This was illustrated when we braved the open mic night in the LGBT coffee house in Long Beach. We learned that you start the night off right by buying a drink for everyone. Some are trying to study, and may not appreciate the interruption, but hey, you bought them a drink. After drinks, you announce the topic of discussion and then shut up. Let them talk. Once you've listened to others, it's your turn, and people are more gracious listeners when they don't feel preached at. Spurgeon said, start where you are. Start today.

My fellow Christians, you who have believed in Christ, it is time for us to bestir ourselves, for we have not preached the gospel to every creature, yet, by a very long way. Some persons have never preached it to anybody; some, I mean, of the very persons who are commanded to preach it to every creature. A quaint preacher says that, if some of God's people were paid ten dollars an hour for all they have done for their Lord, they have not earned enough, yet, to buy a gingerbread cake, and I am afraid the statement is true. So very little have some persons done for the spread of the gospel, that the world is none the better for their being in it. Do I speak too severely? If I do, you can easily pass on what I say; but if not, if it be so that any here have never yet fairly and squarely told out the gospel of Jesus Christ, begin at once! When you get home tonight speak of the Gospel to your nearest relative; and go out tomorrow to your next door neighbor, or to the friend whom you can most easily reach, and tell the good news that your Lord revealed to you and so help to preach the gospel to every creature.[6]

That's your Jerusalem.

Start where you're at, then love on it.

A witness in Jerusalem is a city on a hill—it can't be hidden for long, and neither can you.

Discussion Questions

(For Dr. Jones, the Princeton Professor in you)

1. What is your Jerusalem?
2. How are you currently reaching the people there? If you were to give yourself a letter grade of A through F, what would your grade be?
3. What are the challenges to reaching your Jerusalem?
4. What would you need to do next to bump it up one letter grade?

Adventurous Actions

(For Indiana, the Temple Raider in you)

1. Invite a neighbor, coworker, or family member to do something with you this week. It could be to get coffee, see a game, or help them with a project they're doing.
2. On your drive to work this week, spend the drive praying for people and places your eyes see. Ask the Holy Spirit to open your eyes to what has become "normal" to you. Note what you've passed and accepted as "the way it is."
3. Confess to God anything you've overlooked, and pray that he sends more workers to address that issue, people, or brokenness.
4. Write three action steps that "someone" could use to impact that area of your Jerusalem.

CHAPTER 8

IN ALL JUDEA

God will take you to the very limits of your comfort zone.

You will be my witnesses . . . in all Judea.
JESUS (ACTS 1:8)

You know what a cautious fellow I am.
INDIANA JONES, SARCASTICALLY TO MARCUS

It's not just getting accidentally beat up that I'm good at. I refuse to discriminate against any kinds of accidents, including ones that involve church planting. I like to think of myself as the accidental missionary. The public launch of Refuge Long Beach was a train wreck. The sun was just about to set the Friday evening before our launch, when the Batphone rang. It was the City of Long Beach. Apparently, our church plant's launch day in the community center was now a national holiday that government employees took off because it fell on 9/11. In short, no employee could unlock the doors to the community center. Having a crisis forty-eight hours before the launch of a church plant is bad timing for mere mortals, but God has never run his life or mine by my clock. I decided taking a long walk around the block with him was a better idea than hopping a train to Mexico. If it had been my first rodeo, it would have floored me in a panic, but as

I walked a few miles, prayed, and listened, I felt peace flood my soul. A strategy slowly formed in my mind. I called the mothership (our sending church) and asked to borrow their lawn chairs and some E-Z UPs;* I decided church in the park with a barbeque sounded swell. At least two accidents had been prevented, one on the ground, and one in my pants. Honestly, I had no idea if it would be the worst launch in history, but unbeknownst to me someone attached an American flag to one of the E-Z UPs, and passers-by assumed our little shindig was a 9/11 memorial service. Crowds of locals gathered that we could not have anticipated, a person from the LGBT community came to faith, and from that day forward we were addicted to outdoor church. Like the early believers in Jerusalem, we had been forced out of our comfortable "Jerusalem" and into our own personal "Judea," resulting in something radical, risky, and completely undesirable to most. But it resulted in reaching a cross-section of urban culture that was unparalleled to anything I'd experienced.

THE ACCIDENT DRIVEN CHURCH

If Rick Warren specializes in purpose driven churches, my specialty is probably the accident driven church. I once accidentally planted a church in a Starbucks in Europe! Most of what we discovered on the front lines were like what 1970s PBS painter Bob Ross called "happy accidents." He'd tell you that your mistakes could be deftly turned into trees with a few strokes of the brush. That never worked for me, but Bob could pull it off, and so can God. Maybe Bob's white man's 'fro could be explained as a happy accident. For the apostles, that happy accident was Judea. Let me set the scene about how the apostles got to Judea:

> [Jerusalem] had all the makings of a megachurch experience: thousands of people, money to do anything they wanted, and ministry

---

* The shelters. Not to be confused with Easy Ups diapers . . . although in this emergency it did feel a little like diapers for our church plant's little accident.

coming out of their ears. There was only one problem. The kingdom couldn't advance in a holy huddle. God had to give them a spiritual kick up the backside. Enter Saul of Tarsus. Persecution smacked down on the church like Gallagher's twenty-five-pound sledge-hammer on a watermelon, splattering the seeds of the church to the far reaches of Asia Minor. If the church wouldn't go out willingly, they'd be scattered unwillingly. That is God's time-tested method of getting His people to heed the Great Commission. In Europe today, postmodernism has been forcing churches to venture outside to reach the unreached.[1]

Jesus said, "You will be my witnesses . . . in all Judea" (Acts 1:8). So what did it mean to be his witnesses in Judea, and how was it any different from being witnesses in Jerusalem?

Being his witnesses in Judea is what happens when the church has to move everything out of the context that it has known and adapt to the new culture it finds itself in. It involves traveling outside of all that we've known before and taking the gospel into new territory. Like the old saying goes, "Ships are always safest in the harbor, but harbors aren't what ships are made for."[2] The church was venturing out of a safe harbor and making its first baby steps toward the end of the earth.

I'll let you in on a little secret. Antioch was planted organically during the "Judea" period without organized leadership, without permission, and without hindrance. Ordinary believers scattered northward because of Paul's persecution in Jerusalem, and preached Jesus to gentiles on their migration north like naughty little gospel rebels (Acts 11:19–26). Read the passage carefully. "Now those who were scattered because of the persecution that arose over Stephen traveled as far as Phoenicia and Cyprus and Antioch, speaking the word *to no one except Jews*. But there were some of them, men of Cyprus and Cyrene, who on coming to Antioch spoke to the Hellenists also, preaching the Lord Jesus. And the Lord was with them, and a great number who believed turned to the Lord" (Acts 11:19–21 ESV, emphasis mine). Once Peter had his vision that gave permission to preach to Gentiles, the apostles were intrigued and sent Barnabas as a fact-finding delegate up to Antioch. The nameless church planters were people that had moved through Judea—and hadn't stopped. Something about leaving the security of your comfort zone makes people a little more daring and willing to take risks. The church was adapting as it moved through Judea, witnessing conversions, but breaking all the rules because it happened before Peter had his vision of the unclean animals, and received permission for the "eat hot dogs with heathens" outreaches. They weren't technically "supposed to" preach to the Hellenists, but "the Lord was with them, and a great number who believed turned to the Lord" (Acts 11:21 ESV). But that's often the case. Those who seem to be wrecking the church are often those who are reaching the lost.

Because the spreading of the gospel to Judea was a forced move, they were out of their comfort zone, and out of their depth. The apostles must have felt as if they'd gone from chillaxing in a warm Jacuzzi in Jerusalem to a cold cannonball plunge into Judea's cold unheated pool. Leaving your "Jerusalem" is always a sink or swim affair. The Jerusalem Christians were forced to leave the houses and temple behind that they'd normally done ministry in, but that was because God was on the move. Since the death and resurrection of Jesus, God had busted out of the temple building so that the church could bust loose to the ends of the earth. God refused to allow his glory to be confined to the man-made temple anymore. Ladies and gentlemen, Elvis had left the building.

We've spent years trying to convince young leaders that if they listened to enough talks from big church leaders, CEOs, and people from Chick-fil-A, they'd have the church of their dreams. Shame on us. When the believers spread out to Judea and moved beyond Jerusalem, they were forced to leave corporate religion behind. Judea was like the Wild West, and their eviction from Jerusalem forced them to innovate new ways of reaching the unreached culture they found themselves in. Paul, ever the innovator, would have his passport book stamped with many visas before his mission was done, and each city would require some new type of adaptation to reach the unreached. In Jerusalem, they had a temple to bring the people to, whereas, throughout Judea, they had to learn the skill of taking church to the people. The Jerusalem years of the eighties and nineties when the unchurched came to our buildings ended in the new millennium, and now we must go to them. Because like it or not, like the Christians forced to be witnesses in Judea, we're running out of alternatives.

Many churches are still prepping themselves for the future that isn't coming. Our strategies rely upon utilizing tomorrow the buildings we've built today. But if Europe is an indication of where things are going, yesterday's ornate church buildings are going to be converted to tomorrow's nightclubs, mosques, and carpet warehouses. It is disheartening to stand in an intricately carved gothic stonework church building, where the gospel once thundered forth, but where the pulpit now serves as a DJ booth in a swanky nightclub. Like the subterranean Cold War bunkers buried in backyards across America, our church fortifications when the future we anticipate fails to materialize. Like Europe, the bastions of religion will serve as barriers to the culture around them and endure as lifeless monuments to a wasteful age of opulence and misguided priorities. Inevitably, there are leaders who feel powerless to change things, but are going through the motions, hoping, despite their dwindling megachurch attendance, that there will be enough money to see them through retirement. Many leaders are in a holding period, and they know it. They're hoping you don't.

RAIDING THE LOST ART

In Acts 1:8 Jesus told us it's not the time to hold ground, but time to take it. He's hell-bent on advancing the kingdom of heaven. And it's no accident that it advances most rapidly in Africa and Asia, where buildings aren't always an option. If all of this is true, then somebody who wants to be able to get ahead of the curve needs to master ministry in public space.

Recovering the lost art of reaching the unreached will involve ditching desk job ministry and getting out into the field. It will involve shedding our glasses and bow ties, leaving the lecture halls, and donning the fedora, grabbing the bullwhip, and venturing out into the jungle. If you've been paying attention to Indiana Jones, the jungle is where the treasure is found. That's why the apostles were masters of ministry in public spaces. In Acts 5:42, they met "in the temple courts and from house to house." Some have imagined that house churches are cutting edge, but nothing is more cutting edge than "temple courts." Many have misread "temple courts" in Acts 5 as being synonymous with church buildings, but the temple courts were a far more public community hub. The apostles visited the temple during the busiest time of the day, when people congregated for prayer (Acts 3:1). By preaching in the temple courts, the apostles were practicing the lost art of ministry in open venues. Being truly missional will mean gathering where people already gather. Despite the missional movement making some advances, we're still primarily inviting people into our space instead of invading theirs; albeit homes instead of church buildings. I speak with many missional leaders, and their struggles are not much different from established church leaders. They're still struggling to reach the unreached beyond their four walls, be it church walls or house walls. They both feel walled off from their communities.

The scattering of believers into reaching the unreached in the unfamiliar territory of Judea involved God working in completely new ways. They lacked the building, the money, the programs, and security they'd known in Jerusalem. Without those things, they were forced to step out in faith in a spirit of experimentation. There's just one problem; experimentation inherently involves the risk of failure. And we're as uncomfortable with failure as we are with forced moves.

But without risk and experimentation, innovation is impossible. We forget that all great innovators, regardless of their field, tended to be greater "failures" than they were successes. That's because innovation in any field, including mission, tends to fail forward. Of course in mission, the only failures are the ones who never try. Thomas Edison didn't think of his failures as failures. He once told a reporter that he didn't fail one thousand times to create the lightbulb, but that creating the lightbulb was a one-thousand-step process. Reading the life stories of Imagineers like Jim Henson, George Lucas, Steve Jobs, and Walt Disney demonstrate not only that they saw things that nobody else saw, but more importantly, they were willing to bank their entire lives on things that nobody else thought would work. There seemed no other option for them but to break the mold, innovate, and go boldly where no man had gone before. George Lucas himself believed that a sci-fi movie, if done correctly, could become a leading blockbuster, yet no studio would fund his crazy space movie in the Tunisian desert. The necessity of a ridiculously low budget dictated that he innovate new ways of filming, building props, and creating sound effects. Disney himself went bankrupt once, and for most of his career lived on the verge of a second one, going hand to mouth, from picture to picture. Once, his brother Roy called him, distraught at the banks collecting two million dollars they didn't have. Ever the optimist, Walt laughed and reminded Roy of the time when they couldn't get the banks to loan them twenty thousand dollars for a movie, telling him to be proud of how far they'd come. We love to read the biographies of the experimental innovators, risk-takers, gamblers, and game changers who had the guts to risk it all for their vision.

But nobody wants to *be* "that guy."

A famous cricketer and pioneer asked a similar question when he surveyed the church. "The gamblers for money are so many. Where are the gamblers for God?"[3] Mission seems to be lacking risk-takers in the ranks. A Steve-Jobs-caliber innovator may be as rare in the church as he was in the tech world. It's only so often that a John Wesley,

George Whitefield, William Booth, or Seth Morgan comes along. As society constantly shifts around us, churches are being forced to innovate ways to reach the unreached. Personally, my money is on the happy accidents more than the paid strategists. The church that weathers the future will be less dependent upon buildings, methods, and structures and more on natural missional engagements. God may be waiting to break through using something as radical as pitching a tent in a bean field or raising up young people as daring as Whitefield, who take the church out of the context it's always known. What if God was the gambler, gambling on a church that was willing to gamble on him, trusting his power to work in new ways?

I believe that being "witnesses in Judea" today means learning to innovate ways of engaging lost people in public spaces and leaving the "Jerusalem" of our buildings.

WHERE IT'S AT

Stephen was martyred for preaching against meeting in a building. Let that sink in. You could say the religious culture in Jerusalem was pretty attached to the temple. Stephen's main point in his sermon was that you couldn't really cage God up inside of a box, even if that box was the Holy of Holies. In the Old Testament, the building symbolized the focal point of God's active presence, but the New Testament equates God's activity with being encountered wherever one finds two or more. Incidentally, Jesus sent them out on mission in groups of two's. Are you beginning to see a pattern? That's why taking it to the streets, and letting God out of the box, is so imperative. The first result of the Holy Spirit being poured out in power was turn the church out on the streets. The apostles were immediately driven out of the upper room and into a public space with a capacity of thousands. Examine Acts closely. *The entire book practically takes place outside.* So do the gospels. Jesus sends them out into the villages and hamlets, largely against their will, feeling unprepared, ill-equipped, and in need of further training. Both before and after Pentecost, Jesus trained them to go to the people, instead of waiting for the people to come to them. Trace church history and you'll find every ground-breaking movement of the Holy Spirit resulted in the church crossing not only cultural barriers, but its own barriers as well. You can have the big gold temple, complete with a marketplace, smoke billowing out, and a revered priesthood, but still fail to reach the world around you. Ironically, we still strive to cram everybody into the "temple" for the "come to Jesus" meeting when our culture is more primed for the New Testament experience of small community than we are. They crave authenticity through social media and meet-up groups. The church should have led the way on community. Instead, churches have been desperate to return to the establishment of megacenters of worship that resemble the temple in Jerusalem with all of its wealth, power, and prestige. And that's the last thing this next generation needs.

We need Stephen's sermon as desperately as the first-century religious leaders did. "The Most High does not live in houses made by human hands" (Acts 7:48). Reaching the unreached is no longer dependent upon a building, even if we are.

Would we pick up rocks to stone Stephen if he preached to us today about abandoning our million dollar buildings? Moreover, would we be willing to leave our buildings if it meant more effectively reaching the unreached? When the church made its way to Judea, it became skilled at doing ministry in a new context.

God has been trying to bust out of the box, and we keep trying to stuff him back in. We've been inviting God to join us inside, but God has been inviting us to join him in his work "out there" for nearly two thousand years. Make no mistake. He's been waiting for us to join him in the work, but he hasn't waited to get to work in people's lives. He's already dwelling outside the camp, working hard, getting down to business.

Is that scandalous to you? It scandalized me when I began experiencing it firsthand as a missionary. It was surprising to Peter. Peter found God working in Cornelius before he, the mighty apostle, and veteran missionary, showed up. God had already been talking to Cornelius *without him*. Imagine the nerve . . .

I BRING THIS!

Over the years, I've had a number of "Cornelius Moments." These are when the Holy Spirit shows you he's been very busy, even when you haven't. One of my neighbors was a million miles away from attending any church, but God drew near to her as she desperately read an Alcoholics Anonymous prayer book in secret each night. In the pages of that book, she struggled to connect with a "higher power," struggled with alcoholism, and struggled with depression that incapacitated her and made her a recluse. My wife and I invited her and her husband to a barbecue at our house. They showed up drunk, stoned, and in an argument that turned into an epic shouting match, then left. As their screams echoed down the road, my wife and I looked at each other, disappointed that we'd probably never get to know them. We dropped by a week later to check on them, and the moment we stepped into her house, we walked into an atmosphere as thick as a jello mold with the presence of God. I remember feeling scandalized. *Wait! I bring this! I'm the missionary!* If it had been a public service commercial, the narrator would have freeze-framed over my face and narrated, "Bad little missionary boy, you've been playing in the whitewash. You are about to discover a roaring ocean of activity that God has been involved in, and has been inviting his church to plunge into for the past few thousand years." That was when my skies started falling. Oh what a dumb, dumb chicken little.

The biblical names Cornelius, Jethro, and Melchizedek are just a few of the "outsiders" God worked with outside the church, and rather than that being a deterrent from us going out, it should serve as a massive encouragement. Out of everything that gives me strength and courage, it's God's sovereign activity and his passionate heart for people outside of the church's walls that move me most. Without that knowledge, I'd be too afraid to move. No joke, whenever I talk to people my internal monologue is questioning how God is already moving in their lives before Johnny-on-the-Spot turned up. Even when they are hostile, I rely on the old proverb, "when you throw a rock into a pack of dogs, the one who yelps the loudest is the one who got hit." God is always moving. He's not confined to where we are. He wants to hitch you up to what he's already doing in the wide open world. That's why Jesus said, "My father is always at his work to this very day, and I too am working" (John 5:17). If you're fasting and praying, asking God to do the heavy lifting, you're not going to be the first one to arrive at the party, but turning up fashionably late, after God's already started the conversation with the ones you're trying to reach.

What Judeas can we venture out into that we're not currently going? Being witnesses in Judea means leaving our Jerusalem, the place where we've grown comfortable, and frequenting the spaces of people who are not like you. It's pushing the boat a little bit further out from the dock. It may not be to the end of the earth, just to the edge of your personal world. I'm talking about moving further out than you ever have without being forced to. It could be crossing the seas to engage a foreigner or crossing the street to your neighbor. It could be crossing to the other side of the economic, ethnic, or religious tracks in the city you live in. Being his witnesses in Judea means somehow going out of your way to boldly go where you have never gone before. Reaching the unreached begins when each believer crosses their personal boundaries, not national borders. When you reach the end of your personal boundaries, he'll be waiting for you in the No Man's Land beyond the barbed wire. It's like opening a door to go out at the same time that somebody is opening the door to come in from the opposite side. You end up face to face with God.

IT ONLY TAKES ONE

I've already told you I have the spiritual gift of accidents. On my second international church planting gig in New Zealand, I was leading an evangelistic team to the town square in Auckland, where the plan was to do some cool thing and then talk to hundreds of skaters congregating there. Except it didn't shake out that way. Instead, it turned out like a scene in Casablanca:

> **Captain Renault:** What in heaven's name brought you to Casablanca?
> **Rick:** My health. I came to Casablanca for the waters.
> **Captain Renault:** The waters? What waters? We're in the desert.
> **Rick:** I was misinformed.

We had been misinformed. The town square was a ghost town. There were no youth, no skaters. Worse still, to reach it we'd trekked a grueling hour, getting lost, and enduring the constant whine "Is it much further, Papa Smurf?"

"Not much further," I'd say with the same barely concealed aggravation Papa Smurf managed.

We arrived at the fountain in the middle of the square like Ponce De León looking for the fountain of youth, and about as equally disappointed at the site of no one there. It would be a gross understatement to say I was angry. Remember when David and his men pursued the Philistines, leaving their women and children at Ziklag? After the battle, David and his troops return only to find that a marauding band has carried their families away captive. David's troops picked up rocks to stone David, adding insult to injury (1 Sam. 30:6). It was kind of like that. Frustrated, tired, and ready to kill someone, I walked up to a random guy, like Jonah begrudgingly delivering his message to Nineveh. I muttered, "Hey, we're going to do this Jesus thing. You wanna watch?" He looked at me as he lit his cigarette flippantly and said, "Okay." We did our "cool thing" presenting the gospel like the little dwarves marching angrily around the eighteen-inch Stonehenge in *This Is Spinal Tap*. As we packed up, ready to walk off, I looked back at the guy standing there. Tears rolled down his cheeks. We invited him to pizza, where he unloaded his life story, sobbing the whole time. He had been living in a friend's garden shed for a few weeks after his life had fallen apart, and that night, he had determined to douse himself with gasoline and light a match. Not only did God intervene in what would have been a horrific suicide, he became a deacon of that church plant the very next year. We learned a lesson that night. We'd traveled far out of our way, like Jesus sojourning to Samaria, and we'd found somebody sitting at a well, just waiting for somebody to talk to him. Sometimes reaching the unreached is as simple as finding an out-of-your-way well to sit on.

Stepping out of your comfort zone to reach the unreached will force you to innovate like Paul, who left the religious culture he'd always known and stepped into a culture of innovation, adaptation, and freedom. Embarking for Turkey on his first missionary journey, Paul failed forward, and adapted in each port of call, and learned more about how Jesus still worked to reach people the further out he went on each successive missionary journey. He experimented with the dangerous combustive material of the Holy Spirit resulting in explosive kingdom expansion. Your faith is a result of it.

THE LOST ART OF MINISTRY IN OPEN SPACE

Once you know that God is already at work "out there" it's not such a daunting place to be. The more we invade public spaces, and meet in the temple courts, the more we find ourselves riding shotgun on divine appointments. Just ask Philip from the "witness in Judea" period as he hitchhiked in the middle of the desert and was picked up by the Treasurer of Ethiopia. A few years after launching in the open air, Refuge Long Beach tried to meet back inside after one of our team leaders convinced us that we would serve our families better with classrooms rather than EZ-UPs. Meeting in a public school our second year looked promising (because wrapping construction netting around EZ-UPs doesn't make the best Sunday school atmosphere—especially when the drunk people leer at the kids.) But to our urban, multi-ethnic church plant, meeting in the school auditorium felt as unnatural as David trying to wear Saul's armor. Instead, we traded in the wooden 1950s seats of an auditorium for the lunch tables outside in the public school yard. That was the poorest school in the district, and they served breakfast to the students so that they'd get at least two meals a day. As part of our outreach strategy, we welcomed people from off of the street, ate with them, and held our church service in the open air. According to Whitefield, "I now preach to ten times more people than I would if I had been confined to churches."[4]

Most churches get kicked out of their building.

Not us. We got kicked *into* our building.

One resident from a nearby apartment started writing us angry letters about the noise. The best part was the "P.S. Your music is NOT good." We apologized, lowered the volume, and prayed to love our neighbors better. A few Sundays later, that same man was taking out his trash when he was captivated by the gospel message on Romans 8 that drifted over the alley wall. He stopped and listened to the entire sermon while standing by a dumpster. When the sermon was finished, he rounded the corner, weeping, and told us he had heard God speak to him.

A few weeks after that, while I was preaching, another resident yelled over the wall, "You're too loud." Someone in our service piped up, "He's next!"

WALKING INTO THE STRIP CLUB

The witnesses in Judea tell us it's not hard to reach the unreached, as long as we're not making it harder than necessary by restricting ourselves to the confines of a building. I'm not anti-building by any means, but I'm convinced it's harder to reach people that way. When we first started meeting in the school, we would serve breakfast outside on the school benches before the service. After breakfast, we would move inside to worship, but some people would leave. So we conducted a controlled experiment. On the Sundays we continued to meet outside, the people who normally left after eating breakfast with us stayed for the service. Our takeaway was that a doorway isn't really a portal. It's a barrier.

When it comes to church, walking through the doorway feels as foreign as coming into God's living room like a stranger off the street. It's like an imaginary line around Les Wessman's cubicle space that many people just won't cross.[5] My mentor Peter Jeffery once quipped, "It's as awkward for your neighbor to walk through the doors of this church to hear about Jesus, as it is for you to walk through the doors of a strip club." The physical act of walking through a door means you're a part of "this," and the last thing people want is to commit to something when they walk through church doors. Rather than lower the standards of the gospel to make everybody feel comfortable, we pulled a Wesleyan maneuver and continued to meet outside on a regular basis. Heck, we pulled a Jesus. He preached in boats, fields, mounts, and graveyards. C. T. Studd once remarked, "Some want to live within the sound of church or chapel bell; I want to run a rescue shop within a yard of hell."[6]

GETTING YOUR FREAK ON

Are you hearing my thoughts on this, because I think I'm hearing yours. At one time I feared, like you probably are, that if our churches ventured into public spaces, we'd be labeled as weirdos, freaks. I've never been keen on making Christians look even crazier than we already do, so I shied away from taking church outside the four walls even though it thrilled me to read about it when William Booth or

John Wesley did it. But I eventually decided that rather than the church having an "outreach ministry," the church service would *be* the outreach. It's radical, it's risky, but it's effective, and it's taken me nearly twenty years to arrive here.

Blame Europe. Embarking for Europe as a church-planting missionary fifteen years ago, I got my first taste of open air ministry when I served at Martyn-Lloyd Jones's legendary church as the evangelist when the elders wanted me to preach on Saturday mornings in the town square. I found it awkward, but I couldn't shake the conviction that Wesley, Whitefield, and William Booth had discovered a way that could take church to the people, instead of expecting the people to come to the church. Feeling conflicted about open air preaching, I experimented with less invasive public discussion groups on university campuses and pubs and eventually launched that accidental church in a Starbucks. Spurgeon said, "No sort of defense is needed for preaching outdoors, but it would take a very strong argument to prove that a man who has never preached beyond the walls of his meetinghouse has done his duty. A defense is required for services within buildings rather than for worship outside of them."[7]

I wasn't the first one in Wales to conduct experiments. Wales is a rough place, borne out of centuries of backbreaking work, hauling coal, building ships and railways, and fueling the backbone of the expansion of the British Empire on the backs of hardened Welsh laborers. Into this poverty and deprivation stepped the three lads who founded a church planting mission known as the Forward Movement. When the churches were either going backwards or stalled in their tracks, they took the church out to the streets and propelled it forward. Their names were David Pugh, and his two brothers, Frank and Seth Joshua. One of them had been a prize fighter, so he erected a boxing ring, issuing the challenge that if anyone could take him, he'd go home, but if he won, they'd all have to listen to him preach. It worked. Rough, hardened, calloused men were won to Christ. Within fifteen years of those three lads hitting the streets, thirty evangelists had planted forty-eight centers of worship with twenty-two thousand attendees (1,056 of which were on probation). One morning, Pugh was passing by the walls of Cardiff Prison and noticed the crowds of paroled convicts exiting the gatehouse. Criminals awaited them in the crowds, ready to scoop them up and recruit them back into a life of crime, "I gotta job for ya, mate! Come with me." Within days, Pugh arranged a ministry to meet the prisoners outside the gates at 8:00 a.m. each day in time for their release with an invitation card to a free breakfast at a local tavern. After breakfast, the gospel was preached, and legit jobs were arranged. This was the precursor to the revival of 1904–1905, where God began to move in power.

None of this could have been done behind church walls.

I began to wonder what it might look like to have a "forward movement" in our generation; churches that invaded public spaces in a non-invasive way. The key to ministry in public spaces is to do the things people naturally do in those public spaces. This often happens in what sociologists call *third spaces*. What are third spaces? Back up the truck and let me run over the first two.

First spaces are where people live. Naturally, you eat together, let the kids play together, watch the game, or films, and help your neighbors do projects in the *first place* of your home. For this reason, hospitality is an evangelistic gift in the New Testament, and a job requirement for all elders who need to be able to open their homes to reach their neighbors.

Second places are where people work. It's not where you live, it's not where you want to be, it's where you *have to be* (if you want money). Paul owned this space like a boss. He found the market-place, the place where people trafficked, and penetrated it with the gospel. Paul was bi-vocational partly so that he could support his team on mission (Acts 20:4), but mostly so he could traffic with and be exposed to people he was called to reach. Although he could have asked for support from the churches he planted, and he defended that right (1 Tim. 5:18), going to the marketplace was more conducive to mission. In *Indiana Jones and the Kingdom of the Crystal Skull*, when Indy is asked disbelievingly, "You're a professor?" he replies, "Only part-time."

Third places are the places you want to be. You go to third places to unwind, relax, or be a part of a community. Again, the key to pulling off church in public space is to find a way to adapt the missional aspects of Acts 2:42 to what that third space *already does*. That's why a book club in the local bookstore coffee shop can naturally become a church, without seeming invasive. After the first night at Starbucks, when I threw a *Da Vinci Code* discussion night, they begged to meet again, and on the second night, even more people turned up. It became a book club, which eventually became a church. Recovery groups, support groups, a cooking class, the gym, or any place people traffic are all places to serve people. I personally wouldn't stand up and preach in the middle of my gym. That would be weird. Yet Paul preached in the Areopagus at Mars Hill because that's what people already did there. In places where people met for dialogue and interaction, Paul changed his tactics and reasoned with them, as he did in the synagogue. Today we have community crossroads at coffee houses, and breweries, and classrooms. As long as you're doing what's natural in that space, you can adapt mission to fit it.

One of the upcoming marketplaces is the local brewery. After watching the trendy white middle class discover microbreweries, I've realized it's all the rage. After living in the UK for twelve years, I've come to think it's cute that Americans are so impressed with their "craft beer." Europeans have been perfecting the art for thousands of years, and every village has a local brewery. Love booze or hate it, the Pharisees weren't too crazy about the places Jesus met with people either. Yet you'll spend far less effort approaching people in their space, the local pub, than trying to entice them away from the bar. A few years ago, a friend and I were having a beer at a local brewery. As he told me about his son's generation, he confessed, "I sit here, and I look around at these kids, just like my son, and I feel hopeless. How are we gonna reach this generation?" Without taking my eyes off of one of the brewers, I said, "Watch."

I kick-started a conversation, "Hey, me and my buddy were just talking about what it would look like to do church here. How do you think that would go?"

The guy sneered, and remarked that he didn't like religious people at all. Just then, a server was walking by and said, "Yeah, they're so self-righteous. They think they're better than everyone."

I asked, "But not with a beer in their hand, right? You can't think you're any better than anybody while holding a beer, or am I wrong?"

They stopped in their tracks, and the brewer said, "That might actually make a huge difference. If they could sit and have a beer, and talk politely about God, I might be open to that." For the next few minutes, we talked about what a conversation like that could look like. In essence, we had a mini-session right there with the bar-back. Before we left, my buddy shook his head and said, "I'm in shock. I can't believe what just happened here. My son would go to something like that."

Alex Early started a church in a bar that grew to hundreds of previously unchurched people. It all happened because as a seminary student coming out of church one Sunday morning, he noticed the pub on the opposite side of the street. He also noticed that the people who went to one building never went to the other, and Alex wasn't cool with that. So he pulled a "witness in Judea" maneuver. He got a job as a bar-back praying that God be the sovereign God he knew him to be. And Jesus started reaching people in the Judea of that bar.

That said, this works great for middle-class suburbanites, but where I've been lately, the last thing on earth you'd do was go anywhere near alcohol. The people at Refuge are kicking heroin, crack, and prescription meds. Alcohol is not the friend of recovery ministry, nor does it help people get clean. Besides, I've been on a beer fast for about a year now. This isn't an apologetic for drinking beer, but an apologetic for reaching people where they are (not where you want them to be). Some of you are called to drink beer missionally, and others of us are missional teetotalers.

GO TO HELL. WE DON'T CARE.

Recently, I had breakfast with church-planting legend Bob Logan. He said that he'd been called into a church that was failing to reach its community, yet doing nothing to improve the situation. All of their money was going back into improving the church building and keeping the lights on. Bob told them that if they were honest, they would arrange letters on the church sign out front to spell "Go to Hell. We don't care." Truth be told, million dollar church buildings silently scream that rich churches with bags of cash care more for their building than they do the neighborhood surrounding it. In response, people no longer trust anything that resembles a Walmart for their soul. For the millennials it's not about what you *say* you believe, it's about how you *show* it. That's actually a biblical sentiment. The apostle James might relate to the millennials more than we realize. Actions speak louder than words. They know that if our churches run like corporations, it's because we've ignored the words of our CEO, "Where your treasure is, there your heart will be also" (Matt. 6:21). They've figured out where our treasure is by where we put our money, and it's not where our mouth is. Can you blame them if they take Jesus at his word, even if we don't? What if we stopped investing our money in the buildings, and invested in the community instead? Might it build more of a monument and visible witness than our edifices?

START SMALL

According to John's gospel, conversations equaled conversions. All of these encounters I've mentioned provide opportunities to engage with live specimens out in the field. One of my church planting students was challenged when I asked them to lead somebody to Christ that week. Most students looked at me, eyes wide with disbelief that I'd assign them to actually do the very thing that church planting is all about. But one student was haunted by the fact that it seemed so challenging. He remembered something that I'd said about reaching the unreached: just get out there and have conversations.

Every morning he drove past a bus stop and prayed for the people standing there. On a cold autumn morning after the assignment, he picked up a Starbucks traveler carton, and armed with cups and creamer, parked his butt at the bus stop and started pouring out cups of coffee, handing them to total strangers waiting for the bus. At first, they looked at him like the anti-social psychotic person who missed his chance at hiding razor blades in apples or poisoning Halloween candy. But after one person succumbed to the pull of the magic energy juice, the others began to take the hot liquid like cautious, superstitious natives taking trinkets from a pilgrim from the new world. That's when the conversations started. An hour later he sat on the bench next to a middle-aged African-American employee on his way to work who missed his bus so he could listen to the gospel. Although the employee was late on his journey he'd started out on, he embarked on a new journey of salvation in the cold, gray dawn at a bus stop. Thanks to somebody starting small and just going out of his way a little bit.

BREAKING THE MOLD

To what other groups could you venture out and meet on their own turf? Sociologists speak of tribes. Harley Davidson riders are a tribe, as are users of Apple products. Cyclists in Portland, Oregon, belong to an undefined community in which the bonds are strong. Gamers, tech nerds, cosplay geeks, and hip hop enthusiasts can all be identified by appearance because they adopt the tribal dress, language, humor, rituals, and customs of their particular subculture. How would we adapt church to any of these tribes to become witnesses in Judea?

For example, what would a church that wanted to reach bikers in Daytona Beach look like? After the wake for a biker buried at a biker bar hidden in the heart of the San Gabriel Mountains in Los Angeles, a handful of bikers approached me, asking where my church was. If I planted a biker church, it would change locations every week and you'd go on an organized ride to get to the biker bar. You'd arrive, bond, eat, and do church outside somewhere. Now if I could rock a pulpit made out of a gas tank and complete with handlebars, that'd be bonus. Worship would be hard, fast, and furious, where men could raise a beer to Jesus and shout the words like a fight song. I would have more testimonies than Alcoholics Anonymous. I'd shoot straight, but preach grace in the hopes that the Spirit would fall like a sledgehammer with the gentle word that would break the bone (Prov. 25:15). Men like to laugh, so there'd be plenty of room for that. After you got baptized into Christ, you might get jumped into the church. Yeah, the biker church that exists inside my head is pretty cool, but it only exists in my head. Ridiculous, right? I'd think so too, except what I witnessed at the biker tavern funeral wasn't far off. They listened to the gospel, drank beer, laughed, wept, and came up to me afterwards, broken, and hungry for spiritual things. You can reach any tribe if you're willing to adopt that tribe's customs for the sake of the gospel.

Okay, swinging the pendulum to the opposite side of the spectrum, what would an outreach church for astronomy nerds look like? Start with stargazing at 2:00 a.m. under the night sky in the desert. Eggheads who could talk the cosmos, quantum physics, the speed of light, and power of God stuff would be a must. We'd bless the Creator and blow our minds with a Louie Giglio-style multi-media presentation of God of the universe, and everything with a flavor of Yancey, and a dash of C. S. Lewis in *Mere Christianity*. It'd be hard-core smart-people stuff. Most of you probably wouldn't understand it. There would be no chairs, we'd be laying on our backs on our sleeping bags, watching light travel. S'mores. Question time. Maybe a little number by Mozart, Wagner, or Vaughn Williams during a time people are told to "wonder," tripping on the fact that the God who made the universe also made our minds to compose and enjoy master-pieces. A talk on neuroethology. It would be a practical ambush of the soul, using David's Psalm 8 nighttime worship session under the stars wherein he marvels that God even thinks of him at all.

How would I reach fishermen on the end of the pier? Gamers? Artists?

Well, you get the picture. I could do this all day.

Your turn.

Discussion Questions

(For Dr. Jones, the Princeton Professor in you)

1. Describe life in the comfort zone for you? What is your typical routine?
2. How have you been challenged to shake it up or do something different?
3. Imagine your church building suddenly caught fire and burned down and your church had to meet without a building. Where would be the most strategic area to meet? What would you do?
4. How do you think that lost people in your community would react to it?

Adventurous Actions

(For Indiana, the Temple Raider in you)

1. Look online for some type of meetup group, gym, or coffee shop. Plan a one-time public event. It could be a discussion group or service to a particular part of the community.
2. Pray!

CHAPTER 9

IN SAMARIA

Guess what? Reaching the unreached
means reaching people unlike you.

You will be my witnesses in . . . Samaria.
JESUS (ACTS 1:8)

Snakes. Why did it have to be snakes?
INDIANA JONES

She interrupted the sermon I was preaching, "Excuse me. I don't mean any disrespect. I'm a lesbian. You're talking about all of this love and mercy. What does this mean for me?" My mind raced through the various responses available to me in that moment. It was the launch day of our church plant in Long Beach, California. I knew that whatever my answer, it would most likely cost me half of my church planting core team. As I faced the crowd, I was the only one who could see the tears glistening in her eyes as she fought back the emotion.

To the Jews, the problem with Samaria was that it was filled with Samaritans. To the horror of the Jewish remnant, Samaritans were bred into existence when the pagan Assyrians invaded the Northern Kingdom, slaughtered the men, and took their Jewish wives. The Jewish-pagan half-breed babies were known as Samaritans, and if you'd asked the Jews, they bred and infested like cockroaches, and were just as disgusting. When Jesus included the Samaritans in the equation of Acts 1:8, that was a little detail the apostles were happy to put on the back burner.

Who are the Samaritans today that the church is loath to touch?

The inclusive language used to describe the gay community is LGBT, broken down into lesbian, gay, bisexual, and transgender. To say that Long Beach has a large LGBT population would be an understatement, ranking second in California only to West Hollywood. The church plant launched that day was nestled in the rainbow district in a sixteen-acre park that regularly hosted homeless, pushers, prostitutes, skaters, families, and gangs. Across the street from the park was the city's premiere gay coffee house. It borders the thoroughfare that the Pride parade marches through, making it impossible for us to get to our building on Pride Day.

I braced myself to give her the only answer I could give.

REWIND THE TAPE

This chapter isn't about sexuality, but the current sexual revolution of the new millennium highlights the difficulties the church faces today. And the church isn't any more prepared to engage those beyond the outer fringes of the church than it was in the sixties. Or in the eighties. Nobody will disagree that the church has been in a difficult position for the last twenty years. In the eighties, the church was broadsided as movies like *Philadelphia* hit the box office, raising public awareness of the AIDS crisis. A new prejudice called sexism was the talk of *Tinseltown*, while gay-bashing was standard fare in the pulpit. Cruel cracks about homosexuals were made to masses of like-minded individuals within the four walls of the church. As the church chuckled, the rift widened between heterosexual followers of Jesus and the LGBT community.

As a young man I felt called to the LGBT community, but to reach them, I knew I would need to go outside the church. The church was miserably failing at representing Jesus in that arena, so I trained as a registered nurse, intending to apply for work in an AIDS hospice program. Years earlier, when I read the gospels as a new convert, Jesus struck me as a radical. I became convinced that if Jesus had come to earth in the twentieth century, he'd hang out in a gay bar because they'd been ostracized like modern day lepers. The Jesus I read about was always on the wrong side of popular religious opinion, alienating the "righteous," and being identified as the friend of sinners. When the law demanded death to the immoral, he sidestepped protocol. He was a master of subverting religious convention—breaking spiritual, racial, and social taboos. Two thousand years later, the church still comes nowhere close to being as radical as Jesus. Edward Lawlor said, "If God's love is for anybody anywhere, it's for everybody everywhere."[1]

MISSED OPPORTUNITY

If we're not good at reaching our Jerusalem where there are likely others similar to us, we're worse at reaching our Samaria due to xenophobia of those that are different from us. When dealing with people of questionable morals, Jesus elevated the person above the principle. Such was the case with the woman at the well and the woman caught in adultery. Jesus prioritized reaching their souls, and seemed to relegate their sins to the cross in advance of dying for them, in the same way that he nailed ours there two thousand years ago. I wonder why we find it so hard to do the same. The church seems to focus on sins of individuals outside the church, like the grumpy neighbor who calls the cops on the party next door. We've taken to fighting the LGBT community politically, instead of loving them compassionately. We've left the impression that they are the enemy, demonstrating we've learned so very little from the mistakes made in the eighties. I remember them well. Let me be clear that I'm convinced the message of the apostles on this issue hasn't changed, but I'm equally convinced that our approach has to change.

We keep approaching this issue as a theological argument, when the world is asking for social justice for the LGBT movement on the grounds of civil liberties. You can maintain a conservative theological stance while still approaching the issue liberally on a social level. This is what Jesus did when he sat with the woman at the well, and talked with her as if she mattered, challenging the racist attitudes and treatment that, as a Samaritan, she was used to from Jews.

Thirty years ago, as AIDS swept the nation, the church missed a crucial missiological opportunity. Religious figures were heard stating AIDS was the judgment of God, while the gospel took the back seat. Into a similar tension, Jesus told a parable to illustrate Israel's prejudice against their next-door neighbors, the Samaritans. Bono's AIDS charity, the One Campaign, is named after this parable, because Jesus commends the Samaritan man who is idealistically nothing like the Jewish man that he helped. In fact, the man being helped would have been disgusted by the man who saved him. Although the Jews and Samaritans were on opposite sides of the religious fence, if they'd both heard the story, they could agree on one thing; the man needed saving. Bono has repeatedly urged the sleeping giant of the church to wake up, calling them to action, to be those that love their "enemies." For thirty years, the church has missed the opportunity to be the Good Samaritan as the foremost AIDS activists. Had we done so, instead of fighting the traditional values battle, the world would be listening to the gospel. We'd have neutralized any accusation of bigotry because although we disagreed with the lifestyle, we still viewed people as worth saving. Such action would have been an embodiment of the gospel itself. As Spurgeon said, "Sometimes shepherds go where they themselves would never roam if they were not in pursuit of lost sheep."[2]

CAUGHT IN THE MIDDLE

The dilemma of reaching the unreached is nothing new. In Jesus's day, the Pharisees were committed to upholding the standards of the law, while the Sadducees were dedicated to throwing out anything that was difficult to believe. Respectively, they represented the conservatives and liberals of Jesus's generation. Neither camp fully represented him then, and neither do today's counterparts. Theological liberals have adopted a "theology of convenience" by interpreting away the hard passages of the Bible in their dedication to reaching the LGBT community, but dodge the responsibility of faithfully representing a God who is as holy as he is loving. Conservatives make the opposite error by viciously digging in for a protective last stand on the high hill of morality, while dodging the responsibility of reaching out. Both sides have managed to push people further away from the God of the Bible, but in different ways. One side erects an idol of their own imagination that only loves, while the other erects an effigy of a vengeful deity that no one *could* love. The end is the same; both versions of God are easy to ignore.

Jesus managed to glide deftly between these two extremes without throwing barriers in people's way and without compromising the standards of holiness. It probably takes a divine being to get that exactly right.

That was the dilemma I faced the day our church launched as the woman's question hung suspended in the air.

My answer came quickly, "It means the same for you as anybody else." For all I didn't know, I was confident about one thing.

Nobody gets a separate gospel.

ONE FOR ALL

Jesus didn't have any problem reaching people. Do you know why? He specifically targeted those that nobody else bothered going after. Regionally, he targeted dirty, redneck Galileans and Samaritans. Occupationally, Jesus had a thing for fishermen, tax collectors, prostitutes, and Roman soldiers. Jesus also went after the marginalized, those who fell through the cracks: women, demoniacs, and lost causes. Stop and think about the vast numbers of people who will never darken the doors of the churches that exist in your city. Now ask yourself why. Once you've answered that question, you're halfway to understanding who your church is called to go after, what part of the city it's called to go to, and what it's called to do. Everything from the location it meets in, to the time it meets, what people do when they get there, to the way the room is set up will all come into play. I'd say that for the most part, everybody plants a cookie cutter version of church with hipper music, sexier graphics, and skinnier jeans, thinking that will really reach people. But have you ever noticed that the "stuff Christians like" is often worlds apart from what a lost person really notices or desires when they come to a point of honestly seeking God?

Jesus may have gone after the marginalized, but more importantly, the marginalized flocked to him. Jesus saw the down and outs, outcast from society, lost, helpless, and harassed like sheep without a shepherd. Jesus was a man of sorrows because he was the man who knew too much. Solomon observed that more knowledge brought more grief. It increased Jesus's burdens, and after all, he came to bear them. He was the suffering servant who took others' burdens upon his own shoulders. He carried our sorrows, bore our afflictions, and was bruised for our iniquities. The same Jesus who crumpled in a heap in front of Lazarus's tomb was a Jesus who was wrecked by the consequences and pain that sin causes. The Jesus who sat on a donkey in the midst of a frenzied crowd chanting his name and bellowing prophesies about him, was a Jesus unmoved by their desire to make him king. Weeping as his face flooded with tears, he was emotionally moved as his heart understood the hard-bitten determination of unbelief, and the destruction in A.D. 70 that would result. He had come to suffer for them, not to rule over them.

As I gave my answer to the woman who stood up that Sunday morning, I audibly heard gasps from the crowd. They betrayed the mindset of those who didn't understand the grace of God. Similar gasps must have been heard when Jesus singled out Matthew with his index finger and said, "Follow me." People's mental objections hung heavily in the atmosphere like oppressive phantoms.

Then something beautiful happened.

An art professor called out, "Nobody here is any different from anybody else in God's eyes. You should get to know me. You think you're a hard case!" Ten heads over, another woman raised her voice, "God loves you. You know how I know? He took me. I was a homeless, alcoholic wreck. Nobody wanted me, but Jesus wanted me, and I know he wants you too." That day in the park, those who had been forgiven much, loved much. A well of grace was springing up from the core of their beings, overflowing to others.

The church has always struggled to understand God's grace. Many Christians still think it enables people to get away with murder, rather than catalyzing a person from the inside out. They fear that grace means the lowering of standards. Although God has never indicated that his definition of sin has changed, our lives may not be completely stitched up this side of heaven. Like everybody else, members of the LGBT community come in with a lot of baggage and their transformation isn't instantaneous.

Jesus modeled reaching out to the Samaritans by sitting with the woman at the well. John tells us, "He *had to* go through Samaria" (John 4:4, emphasis mine). Had to? It was miles out of his way, but if Jesus had to, we do to. The disciples were scandalized by the fact that he was having anything to do with the woman because (a) she was a Samaritan, and (b) because she was a she. They were further scandalized that he was holding a conversation with her. How are we going to reach the unreached if, honestly, we don't even want to be seen with them? Think of the unspoken rules your own church might have about who does or doesn't belong. Going with the example at hand, when someone from the LGBT community walks through the doors of the church our approach is crucial. If our first question is, "Are you going to stop your homosexual behavior?" we become spiritual TSA agents, erecting metal detectors and demanding that they empty their pockets of everything sinful before we let them through. It's one of the times we make sin a barrier at the gateway. To everyone else we clearly explain that God will receive, forgive, and cleanse. We emphasize that they've been given the righteousness of Christ, and that sanctification will follow along their journey. Not so here. We want a pound of flesh. We want to ensure they don't try to sneak something lethal on board that might explode the airplane. Like Jesus told the Pharisees, we shut the door of the kingdom in people's faces and prevent them from entering.

In contrast, Jesus invited scandalous sinners to follow him. Although it seemed a simple, unrestricted invitation, there was an implicit recognition of Jesus's complete mastery over every area of life. Like leaven, it would infiltrate every area of the follower's life; but it would happen along the way. Remember, as was the case with the disciples, and ourselves, it is more the journey with Jesus that facilitates our transformation than our initial introduction to him. Who can pinpoint the moment at which the twelve were truly converted on their journey with Jesus? After walking with individuals from the LGBT community, I'm convinced that transformed lives result from going on a journey with Jesus, not from making an instantaneous decision— just as it is with heterosexuals.

We want purity in the church, but at what price? We have our clean, orderly, sterile churches, and as a result, the world is kept out. If God himself made his grand entry into a slurry-soaked stable that reeked of crap, then I'm pretty sure we can handle lesbians holding hands in church as they hear the gospel. Bonhoeffer, in his classic work *Life Together,* quotes Luther, "Jesus Christ lived in the midst of his enemies. So the Christian, too, belongs not in the seclusion of a cloistered life but in the thick of foes. ... And he who will not suffer this does not want to be of the Kingdom of Christ; he wants to be among friends, to sit among roses and lilies, not with the bad people but the devout people. O you blasphemers and betrayers of Christ! If Christ had done what you are doing who would ever have been spared."

CHURCH STINKS

In my experience, the churches that are the most effective at reaching the community smell like alcohol on Sunday mornings. Lesbians have sat in our midst holding hands. Some are visibly withdrawing from substances. In order to reach people, you've got to be willing to be patient. Bonhoeffer observed, "The pious fellowship permits no one to be a sinner. So everybody must conceal his sin from himself and from the fellowship."[3]

That launch day, the woman wanted to know what Jesus thought of the homosexual lifestyle, and we shot straight with her. We were careful to emphasize that her sexual orientation may never change, but that to be tempted is not a sin. We don't choose the object of our attraction. Those with same-sex attraction don't care how you think they got that way, be it from abusive fathers, or being born that way. The reality is that the LGBT community tells each other, "It's how you are. We accept you." The church should be no different when it comes to welcoming people from every walk of life. Welcoming people as they are does not imply that God will leave them as they are. Within our rows every Sunday morning, people sit confused, silent, and suffering with conflicted desires warring within their flesh. Like Jesus, a leader needs to exemplify the courage to break away from the chatter of the Pharisees debating, "Who sinned, this man or his parents, that he was born blind?" (John 9:2) and dismiss the question altogether. Like the man born blind, the argument is irrelevant. It's not how he got there, it's that he's there now. They need the reassurance that nobody is blaming them.

COMMUNITY BEFORE CONVERSION

Although it's trendy to talk about discipleship in community within leadership circles, the LGBT community needs the church community as part of the process of transformation. When working properly, the church community actually becomes a tool of conversion. The difficulty with forcing them to check their baggage at the door is that the LGBT community is so supportive. They've come from a lifetime of rejection because of their sexual orientation and lifestyle into a community that has embraced and accepted them. In order for an individual to fully leave the LGBT community lifestyle, the church community has to be as strong as the community that they've left. This will never happen if we're in our defensive stance at the metal detector, TSA badges flashing, guns fully loaded. The community of Christ must therefore become the support system that functions like a trapeze to grab hold of before the other one can be let go.

Evangelicals have always placed conversion before discipleship, equating the unconverted as outsiders, but we've found that discipleship starts from the moment we come into contact with someone. Conversion happens somewhere along the way. This shift in approach has been the key strategy to fulfilling the Great Commission, and consequently preaching peace to those that may seem distant from the faith.

In the past, the order of belonging to a community was: Belief, Behavior, Belonging. In order to be a part of the community (or church), you had to believe (or be converted). After that, you could attend a church, but your behavior had to conform to everybody else's. Once that happened, you were no longer viewed with suspicion, and were welcomed into the community as "one of us."

In church planting, you need to reorder the equation to look like this: Belonging, Belief, Behavior. In other words, people are made to feel accepted, no matter what they're going through or doing. It's the way that Jesus operated, and it's the very thing the Pharisees criticized him for. You'll get your fair share of it too if you operate like he did. The belonging allows people to track with us long enough to hear and believe. Baptism becomes the formal transition into the community, but until that time, they've already been welcomed and feel if you could accept them, then maybe God could too. Allowing your church to function like this will also turn community into an evangelistic tool in and of itself. A number of people in our Long Beach plant have left alternative lifestyles, but we had to be patient with them. People who don't eventually repent don't last long with us, but we've had to last long with those who do eventually repent. Baptism has served as a natural unspoken barrier for people ready to change. Churches are uncomfortable with this approach, however. But who better to reach those in alternative lifestyles with the love of Christ than those from alternative lifestyles? What would it look like to become all things to all people in regards to this cross-section of Samaritan culture?

A CHURCH JESUS WOULD GO TO

When I was planting in Los Angeles County, I had moved to San Diego County in hopes of handing the church off to another planter. My neighbors would see me drive off to Long Beach and ask me what my church was like in the inner city.

"I attend a church Jesus would go to," was my typical response.

As the neighbors paused and their brows furrowed, I could see the gears working. Though the knowledge people have about the Bible may be limited, what they know of Jesus is enough of a key to solve the equation. When you think of the kinds of people Jesus attracted, you can envision what his church would look like; a church of people that nobody else knows what to do with.

Tony Campolo told the story of flying from Chicago to Hawaii. Because his clock changed time, but his body didn't, he ended up at the counter of a greasy spoon diner at 3:30 a.m. As he sat on the bar stool, a group of eight or nine boisterous women came through the doors after a night's work, and sat on the stools on either side of him. Campolo recounts the conversation he overheard:

> Their talk was loud and crude. I felt completely out of place and was just about to make my getaway when I overheard the woman beside me say, "Tomorrow's my birthday. I'm going to be 39."

Her "friend" responded in a nasty tone, "So what do you want from me? A birthday party? What do you want? Ya want me to get you a cake and sing 'Happy Birthday'?"

"Come on," said the woman sitting next to me. "Why do you have to be so mean? I was just telling you, that's all. Why do you have to put me down? I was just telling you it was my birthday. I don't want anything from you. I mean, why should you give me a birthday party? I've never had a birthday party in my whole life. Why should I have one now?"

Campolo said as soon as he heard that, he'd made a decision. He motioned for the guy that ran the diner, whose name was Harry, and asked him if those girls came in every night. When Harry said yes, Campolo asked if he could throw a party the next night by decorating the diner and getting a cake. Harry's wife came out from the back and said that the woman's name was Agnes. She said that although Agnes was nice, and always helped people out, people never did anything nice for her in return. Harry said he'd bake the cake, and at 2:30 a.m. the next morning, Campolo returned to the diner to decorate. At 3:30 on the dot the diner doors swung open and the parade of prostitutes rushed in as usual. Agnes was stunned and shaken. As they all sang Happy Birthday to her, her friend had to steady her so she didn't faint. They asked her to cut the cake, but she just stared at it, unsure what to do. Campolo continues, "Agnes looked down at the cake. Then without taking her eyes off it, she slowly and softly said, 'Look, Harry, is it all right with you if I . . . I mean is it okay if I kind of . . . what I want to ask you is . . . is it O.K. if I keep the cake a little while? I mean, is it all right if we don't eat it right away?'"

When she left, there was a stunned silence, and Campolo suggested they pray for her on her birthday. Campolo prayed God would bless her, save her, and change her life. When he was finished, Harry sneered that he didn't know Campolo was a preacher, and then asked what kind of church he went to. Campolo's answer is classic,

"I belong to a church that throws birthday parties for whores at 3:30 in the morning."

Harry waited a moment and then almost sneered as he answered, "No you don't. There's no church like that. If there was, I'd join it. I'd join a church like that!"

Wouldn't we all? Wouldn't we all like to join a church that throws birthday parties for whores at 3:30 in the morning?[4]

That's the type of church Jesus would go to, and I think it's the kind of church he came to create. Anywhere Jesus went he threw parties for sinners. Well, Matthew did anyway (Matt. 9:10).

In the short time I was at Refuge, a.k.a. "the last stop before hell," we had more funerals because of overdoses on relapse, people murdered, AIDs, or death by some other hardcore lifestyle taking its toll on the body. Churches may tend to follow the white, middle-class trajectory and plant in those neighborhoods, complaining of how tough it is to reach people, but they're ignorant of the low hanging fruit that exists in the neighborhoods where they're afraid to go. Jesus said, "The harvest is plentiful but the workers are few" (Matt. 9:37). Perhaps the workers just weren't willing to go where the harvest was.

Spend enough time on the front lines of mission work and you'll come out feeling like part firefighter scraping body parts off the road with a shovel, part combat veteran fighting for your own life and those around you, part RN administering CPR, and part cop being called to murder scenes where the blood is still fresh and the brown paper bag you brought is for the lunch you've already eaten. Being on the front lines of ministry will expose you to things that will twist up your mind, and send you reeling from the depths of depravity. You'll conduct funerals for addicts who knelt before Jesus, but lost the fight with addiction, or for a reformed gang member shot to death by police crossfire when the gang member they're ministering to resists arrest. You'll be called to the scene of a teenage suicide where the body is still hanging but the family is falling apart. Nothing prepares you for the carnage of lives that have been stolen, killed, and destroyed. Although there is often more weeping in tears then there is rejoicing in the sheaves, nothing can extinguish the joy from baptizing a member of the Aryan Brotherhood next to a member of the Mexican Mafia. But if we don't do it, who will?

I've seen it time and again: today's lost are tomorrow's disciple makers. From the ashes, God will begin to resurrect a fiery phoenix from divorcees, former racists, abortionists, prostitutes, ex-cons, and all of society's second-class citizens. It's what made up the core of the crowd that followed Jesus. People who live in No Man's Land are the kinds of people who mess your church up, but are precisely the type of people who make a church the type that Jesus would actually go to. If we're going to see people the way Jesus sees them, then we need to see them through his eyes. Have you ever noticed the way Jesus dealt with people in sin? He saw the whole person. He didn't just see the woman at the well as a filthy, man-eating whore. She says, "Come, see a man who told me everything I ever did" (John 4:29). Ironically, that statement had always meant shame when she'd uttered it in the past about any other man whom she had entrusted her heart to, but not with this man. This time, her very statement is reborn, as her heart was reborn. The shame was buried in the baptism of forgiveness. There is no trace of shame but relief. It was as if the sin that emptied out of her had created a vacuum, and the fresh air of liberation and freedom rushed in and filled the void. Instead of seeing a tart, Jesus saw a little girl with dreams and aspirations, who all her life dreamed of her future wedding day. Jesus knew something had happened to that little girl along the way.

Similarly, there was the woman caught in adultery. As the sound of her exposed flesh hitting pavement fills the air, along with the rabble of men's heavy steps, a sneering challenge cuts the air, tinged with violence. "The law requires we stone her; what do you say, Rabbi?" Rather than telling her that "the fire that burns in ye loins shall reach full combustion in the fires of hell!" Jesus appears to trace the journey that led her to this harsh, cold stone pavement.

Perhaps he knows about the uncle who molested her, or the neighbor who whispered unfulfilled promises as he took advantage of her body through her young and naive romantic vulnerabilities as she dreamed of someone to love her. On the other side of soppy fantasies strangled by lust, it isn't just her heart that has been broken. It is her dignity, her sense of worth, and along with it, her life, that are the casualties of war.

EAT THE UNCLEAN

We all have been guilty of being the priest or Levite passing the broken and bleeding man on the side of the road. We've all been shocked to find that the Samaritan of the story is the hero. God is using the "trash" of the world to show where the treasure is. There was a subtle switch on my computer a few years ago. It was so subtle that I still don't remember exactly when it happened, but I remember thinking how strange that my "trash" bin had been renamed "recycle" bin. This is how Jesus sees people. Whereas some only see trash, Jesus sees something that he can recycle for his own glory. A prostitute can be so transformed by Jesus that a year after her conversion, nobody would suspect that she first came to you asking if God would forgive her for turning tricks again when she couldn't pay the rent. A homosexual used to be scandalous, but now the most scandalous thing that a homosexual can do is to repent. That's still too scandalous for the world. They're not ready for it. Yet Jesus is still breaking society's taboos, and he will continue to do so until he returns. He will prioritize the rescue of the down-and-outs. Will you?

This is how Jesus calls us to love the unlovable. We come away from ministry smelling like pot because the people we minister to reek of it. We learn to fist bump instead of shake hands because hepatitis infects the unwashed hands of the people we feed. We all eventually learn to touch the unclean. We all begin to resemble Jesus who left the immaculate throne room of a sin-sterile heaven, and waded up to his eyes in our human sewage until it pulled him under and drowned him at the cross. God touched lepers. Jesus ate with tax collectors. The Spirit filled prostitutes. Paul ingested pork. Peter ate with gentiles. Eventually, we all hear his voice saying, "Rise up. Kill and eat." We can only resist for so long, but a world that is sick with sin and in desperate need of mission awaits those who are willing to rise up. Will you be one of them?

There are Samaritans out there who need saving, so that they can go and do some saving. Think about it. What if the church is merely frustrated because it's exhausted the opportunities to save the middle class? What if it's time to cast the nets to the other side of the boat? The other side of the tracks? If the apostles could tell you one thing—no, scratch that—if Jesus could tell you one thing, it'd be, "Make your church a church I'd actually go to." A scandalous church. A church where the cross-dressing prostitute using the ladies room isn't even your biggest problem on a Sunday; cleaning up the barf on aisle twelve from the guy withdrawing from heroin is. Listen, if families aren't concerned for their children because of the types of people they're being exposed to at church, then you're probably not reaching the unreached.

UNROLLING THE SCROLL

When Jesus unrolled the scroll in the synagogue at Nazareth, he said, "The Spirit of the Lord is on me, because he has anointed me to proclaim good news to the poor" (Luke 4:18). The poor are another marginalized people, and God moves stronger within the poor communities than we realize. Like the apostles reminding Paul as he set out for Asia Minor that he should not forget the poor, church planters need reminding that they shouldn't build the church merely with middle class Americans. The gospel travels in middle class white people channels because middle class white people like reaching out to middle class white people. The church in America is largely within the middle class strata. This isn't a problem in and of itself, but we keep reaching the people just like us. The problem is, we don't tend to go beyond our socio-economic boundaries and reach the people who are different than us. The beauty of the early church was that it brought people from Caesar's household to worship next to slaves.

An abundance of monetary success easily replaces dependence upon God. Even King Agur knew that too much of the green stuff makes you forget God (Prov. 30:9). But our priorities get misplaced so easily. During the sixties, the hippies were cutting edge of non-materialism in society, and they brought that dynamic into the church. Ten years after the height of the hippy movement however, the idealistic hippies morphed into yuppies, as did the churches they founded. I witnessed this at the church where I started my Christian pilgrimage. Other churches felt sorry for the small organic movement known as Calvary Chapel that couldn't afford their own buildings, met in schools, and attracted non-ordained "blue jean preachers" who had never gone to seminary. Rumored to be a cult, we lacked big buildings, respect, and money, but we experienced the presence and power of God. I witnessed miraculous healings, supernatural occurrences, and unexplainable exorcisms in the eighties. In the nineties we exploded numerically, but traded in all of the supernatural power for renovated warehouses with more seats. The parking lot was fuller, but the church somehow seemed emptier. It felt as if we experienced God less, only with more people now. Instead of seeking God in prayer together, we were entertained by the worship. There had been a subtle, yet perceptible shift. We hardly noticed.

We filled the seats, outgrew our warehouses, signed bigger leases, and got rich. Our movement seemed like it had finally "arrived." Former draft-card-burning hippies climbed into bed with mainstream American culture, unaware they were sacrificing the dynamic and attractive power that came with being a radical, underground, countercultural movement in the first place. People vaguely remembered the days of old when crazy things happened, crazier stories were told. As one born out of that time, I listened to the same stories for twenty years, wondering why it didn't happen like that anymore, but nobody seemed to be asking that question. We were too "successful" to care.

Over a century ago, E. M. Bounds warned:

> This is the day of great wealth in the Church and of wonderful material resources. But unfortunately the affluence of material resources is a great enemy and a severe hindrance of strong spiritual forces. It is an invariable law that the presence of attractive and potent material forces creates a trust in them, and by the same inevitable law, creates distrust in the spiritual forces of the Gospel. They are two masters which cannot be served at one and the same time. For just in proportion as the mind is fixed on one, will it be drawn away from the other. The days of great financial prosperity in the Church have not been days of religious prosperity.[5]

We have merely to go to the poor to be where Jesus is, on mission to preach the gospel to them. His ministry hasn't changed. The Lord is still near to the poor, and he pleads their cause. When you give a homeless person money you become an extension of the gospel itself. You embody grace. People are quick to point out, like most rich people do, that the money will be used for drugs, or that we're acting as enablers for people's irresponsibility. I like to ask those people how many homeless people they've seen get off the streets. The answer is always zero. That's not my answer, so I stand by my results more than their words. When D. L. Moody was told by a listener that his methods of bringing the lost to faith were wrong, Moody replied, "Oh? How do you do it?" The critic stammered that he didn't. "That settles it then," said Moody. "I like the way I do it better than the way you don't."

One thing we're careful *not* to do is belittle people that have less than we do. At Refuge Long Beach, we found out the kids who attended the school where we met generally only ate one meal a day at home. The school was the only one in the district that served breakfast to ensure the kids got two meals a day. We decided to eat breakfast as a church before doing anything else on Sundays. First time attenders frequently come to the church wanting to join us in "serving the poor." We always remind them it's not like the *Time Bandits* depiction of John Cleese's "Jolly Good" Robin Hood, where he's so upper class that the poor are a project to him. He introduces the poor: "The poor are going to be absolutely thrilled. Have you met them at all? The poor. Oh you must meet them. I'm sure you'll like them. Of course they haven't got two pennies to rub together, but that's because they're poor (laughter)."

It's insulting. Here's the truth. Everybody has pride, and if you make people feel like your Eagle Scout benevolence project, they'll resent you for it. When you reach out to people, you need to help them maintain their dignity in the process. You let them know God values them. We tell the newcomers to our church that we don't feed the poor. We eat breakfast together as a family before church. See the difference? We've helped a number of people off the streets, but the big turning point came when we started announcing to the homeless, "The only thing separating you from the rest of us is you have no place to lay your head down at night. You're in good company. Jesus was also homeless. Welcome to the family." Right now, we've even got a home study running in the park, taught by a formerly homeless person, because for some of our peeps, that's their living room, and Jesus is meeting them right where they're at.

THE ROAD TO JERICHO

The gentile world was ready for the gospel. It was Peter who wasn't ready for the gentiles. We probably don't think of the apostles as racists when they started, but it's all there in the text. Can you imagine how great the prejudice was in Peter's heart towards the gentiles if it required Jesus appearing to him in a vision, not once, but three times to go and reach them? A lifetime of prejudice is not easily broken. It's also not helped by radio talk shows or your news station of choice. Each side of the cultural divide talks about the other like sheer lunatics and morons as they pump out their propaganda that fuels hatred, brings advertisers, and keeps the machine running. If you've been imbibing on that kind of division, it's a demonic ploy to keep you from reaching others with the gospel. Jesus tackled racism frequently because it was just another division that keeps us from the unity he created us for. The Road to Jericho was a story that intended to make the marginalized pagan half-breed the hero. Jesus masterfully contrasted the godly behavior of the despised Samaritan against the Pharisees and priests, or those who should have known better. The point in all of these scriptural examples was that the gospel motivated people to launch out of their own group. What are you doing to cross cultural barriers, showing Jesus as the reconciler of all things?

Jesus was way ahead of his time in reaching homosexuals, people of other races, and the poor. But the world has been ahead of the church. We should have had a two thousand year head start on these issues after seeing how Jesus interacted with people from all walks of life. But like Peter, it's not too late for us.

There is no formula for this. If you're reading this, taking notes, I'd suggest doing something very simple. Put the notebook down. Lay your pen to rest. Get on your knees, and ask God to give you his heart. When he writes the law on your heart with his Spirit, there's no more need for the letter of the law written in a notebook. When you actually roll up your sleeves and start working with people, God will give you the wisdom to deal with those situations. Experience is God's best classroom. Get out there, to the people you don't want to hang out with, in the places you don't want to go. Samaria is waiting.

Discussion Questions

(For Dr. Jones, the Princeton Professor in you)

1. Who are the people you don't want God to send you to?
2. What would it look like to become "all things" to that particular people group?
3. Who do you think God is using to reach them today?
4. How can you be a part of reaching them?
5. Do you think God uses people who naturally find it hard to share the gospel? Why or why not?

Adventurous Actions

(For Indiana, the Temple Raider in you)

1. Go to "the other side of the tracks" this week and reach out to somebody who is *not* like you and get together with them.
2. Ask them what barriers they have to becoming a Christian. Ask them how the church could overcome those barriers.
3. Ask them if you were to start something like that, if they'd be interested in coming along.
4. With a small team of partners, start a group and invite those from "the other side of the tracks."

CHAPTER 10

TO THE ENDS OF THE EARTH

Enough talk. Go live this.

You will be my witnesses . . . to the ends of the earth.
JESUS (ACTS 1:8)

*Men of Galilee, why do you stand
here looking into the sky?*
CHEEKY ANGELS (ACTS 1:11)

*What a fitting end to your career Dr. Jones.
You're about to become a permanent part of this
archaeological find. Who knows? Maybe in a thousand
years, you might actually be worth something.*
BELLAQ TO INDIANA JONES WHEN IT SEEMED IT WAS ALL OVER

When I was a kid, I had a Sesame Street book called *The Monster at the End of This Book*, featuring the furry, blue monster Grover, begging you not to turn the pages. He warned of a monster at the end of the book. As each page turned, the tension mounted until the end, when Grover realized he was the monster. Well, there's no monster at the end of this book, but I can assure you there is danger when you're done reading it. It's the danger of doing nothing, and just reading another book. Reading a book about evangelism doesn't make you a temple-raiding gospel adventurer any more than retweeting a Greenpeace tweet makes you a Rainbow Warrior. But if you're hungry enough, bored enough, or fed up enough, that holy discontent that can be created from reading will serve as a catalyst. But it's going to cost you. All valuable things do.

Know why most people don't write a book? It's hard.

Climb Kilimanjaro? It's hard.

Live the mission of Jesus? It's hard.

Chesterton said, "Christianity isn't tried and found wanting. It's been found difficult and not tried."[1]

Remember, at the beginning of Acts, the Apostles wanted something easy. But in the end, they greased their elbows and got down to business. Jesus found a guy working hard. True, he was working hard killing Christians, but he had the necessary work ethic. He had been used to doing hard things. Studying hard, obeying hard, being a Pharisee, hard. Killing hard. But then he found Jesus and did something harder for him. And it wrecked him. Paul felt the weight lift off his shoulders, and it turned him from being a weighed down power lifter into a light-footed marathon sprinter.

Jesus always does the heavy lifting. In our salvation, he did it all, but on mission he says, I'll share the yoke with you. My burden is light. I'll do all the heavy lifting.

TALK IS CHEAP

Words may be powerful, but talk is cheap.

Words cost nothing and unfortunately you usually get what you pay for. I was at a church recently where an individual spoke to me about how he'd been studying discipleship for a decade and really felt burdened to teach the church about discipleship. I asked him if he'd discipled anybody during the last ten years. I don't have to tell you the answer. The inherent pitfall of a movement where the leaders are paid to talk is that talking becomes the end, not the means to one. When talking becomes the end, then the end is at hand. Words can spark a revolution, but they're not the active flame. Every revolution that ever wrought change in a country, marriage, or heart was fueled by the fires of action; not the mere spark of a thought. If the pen is mightier than the sword it's only because words drive men to action. Words are only as powerful as they are lived out. Even God's Word itself effects no change if we become hearers only.

Perhaps the scariest thing about talking is that it all too easily becomes a substitute for doing. There is a scientific reason for this. The part of your brain that controls the sensation of pleasure and reward is known as the medial prefrontal cortex. It releases a chemical called dopamine that increases a satisfied feeling when you accomplish something.[2] That means it's possible to get satisfaction after talking about something that you have no real intention of doing. This is because although you've not done the activity, you've imagined it by talking about it and dopamine was released, causing the feeling of satisfaction. But it's not the same. There are others who can only experience the endorphin rush from taking action and accept no substitutes for it.

The risk of action-less talk is compounded in the age of social media. We enjoy posting a clever word, turn of phrase, or pithy quote, zipping through cyberspace. Knowing that your tweet thundered like a truth bomb, causing somebody out there to reply "boom" makes us feel warm and gooey inside. Digital posts can have a "boom" factor, but if they don't lead to action, they're only as effective as a water balloon. In your momentary explosion, somebody got splashed, but nothing got damaged in the process. Like Keats' famous epitaph, our words are writ in water, and are quickly covered back over and drowned forever in an endless sea of more words. Don't worry. No animals were actually harmed during this process. In fact, nothing really happened at all. When I tweet something clever, people may say, "Boom." When I actually live out the words of my social media posts, heaven says, "Boom." And that's a thunder worth hearing. On the banks of the Jordan at Jesus's baptism, God's voice thundered, "This is my Son, whom I love" (Matt. 3:17). Boom. Jesus wasn't all talk. He could say, "I always *do* what pleases him" (John 8:29, emphasis mine).

DON'T EXPECT PEOPLE TO UNDERSTAND

When Paul visited the disciples, he communicated the five-year plan for reaching the pagan gentile world on a whiteboard. Because Peter hadn't yet had his vision about eating deep fried alligator wrapped with bacon, the other apostles exchanged bemused glances, and raised their eyebrows as if Paul was using a non-erase marker on their whiteboard. Because they didn't get it, I can imagine them shifting uncomfortably, and moving on to the next agenda item. Have you ever laid out the vision of the ages, and everybody in the room looks at you like you just farted and stunk up the room?

This is what happened to William Carey, the Father of the modern missions movement, when he shared the necessity to reach the Orient with the gospel. At a church meeting he shared "whether the command given to the apostles to teach all nations was not binding on all succeeding ministers to the end of the world, seeing that the accompanying promise was of equal extent."[3] The minister convening the meeting shouted him down, "Young man, sit down! You are an enthusiast. When God pleases to converse with the heathen He'll do it without consulting you or me."[4] Undeterred, Carey preached at the local association meeting on May 30, 1792 about the necessity to go to the ends of the earth with the gospel. After finishing business matters, the meeting was about to adjourn when Carey turned to his minister friend Andrew Fuller in distress. "Turning to Fuller he asked tragically, 'Is there nothing again going to be done, sir?' The heartbreak in Carey's voice, the fire which pierced through the words, stabbed Fuller awake."[5] He asked for the meeting to reopen and by the end of it, they'd made an action plan to make a plan. It was a start, and thus the start of the modern missions movement, simply because one person wasn't content to just keep talking about the action that should be taken.

Years of hiding behind theological platitudes were enough to make Paul ask how people would believe unless somebody was sent (Rom. 10:14–15). That's a man of action trying to get people of words to get moving. It is a choice that starts by making a decision.

Paul had been ignored* by the apostles and everyone else, and for eleven long years, he worked his calloused hands making tents in Tarsus, wondering if he'd gotten it wrong, if everybody else was crazy, or just him. Finally, Peter had his vision of the unclean animals. About that same time, reports returned to Jerusalem about some crazy Jesus parties up in Antioch. That thar was Gentile country, and those apache savages weren't supposed to be Jesus followers! So they sent Barnabas up to investigate. Barnabas decided to head over to Tarsus and ask for Paul's help. Once he recruited Paul, Paul got started and never stopped. He was like a bull out of the gate; a tireless, indefatigable gospel animal. God pulled him back for long enough to make him like a slingshot, and once God let him go, Paul was propelled outward with a force that didn't stop until they removed his head from his body. That'll stop pretty much anybody, but *that's what it took* to stop Paul once he got going.

WHY YOU WOULDN'T LIKE PAUL

Paul did boast a lot. You probably wouldn't have liked him. Most people didn't like Wesley for the same reason either. Hardly anyone in church history matched his efforts as a gospel preacher, and he regarded his fellow contemporary ministers as helpful to the lost as "ropes of sand." One man said that by the time Wesley's detractors had gotten out of bed, he'd already ridden horseback one hundred miles and preached

---

* Approximately nine years had passed from Paul's first visit to Jerusalem, recounted in Galatians 2 and his first missionary journey.

to two crowds. The truth is, Paul also did more than anybody, and he let us know. Consider what Paul said to the Corinthians. Whatever they were boasting about, Paul was saying he had more reason to, even though he sarcastically said, "we were too weak for that!" (2 Cor. 11:21). In 2 Corinthians 11:23, Paul asked "Are they servants of Christ? (I am out of my mind to talk like this.) I am more. I have worked much harder." We catch him boasting again in Romans 15:17–18, "Therefore I glory in Christ Jesus in my service to God. I will not venture to speak of anything *except* what Christ has accomplished *through me* in leading the Gentiles to obey God by what I have said and *done*" (italics mine). Boom. Paul could say, "For the kingdom of God is not a matter of talk but of power" (1 Cor. 4:20). Not just words.

Boom.

He told the Galatians that they had no more right to give him guff because his back, unlike theirs, was scarred to the extent it resembled a walnut shell, and Paul proudly bore his scars like badges of honor. In nearly every epistle, Paul wrote a variation of "imitate me," using his lifestyle as a guide. We make the mistake of reducing Paul's life to a representation of a minister, forgetting that according to his own urging to be imitated, Paul saw himself as a model of how every believer should live.

Did Paul brag? Sure he did, but he'd earned his bragging rights. He wasn't so much elevating boasting, as much as making fun of it. Paul simply showed what it looked like when somebody actually did the stuff they talked about, in contrast with his opponents who talked much and did little. Paul was really mocking the boasting of his opponents by calling them do-nothing leaders. They boasted when they had nothing to boast about. The Corinthians were lapping up the brain drippings of these "talkers" as Paul calls them. They didn't *do* anything. Paul's boasting was a way of showing that actions speak louder than words. Paul's mic drop came when he told them pointedly, that they were his credentials or letters of commendation. You're saved because *I did something.* Let that sink in a bit.

Paul had done things worth bragging about, which always irritates those who don't do much. Like Morpheus said, "I'm trying to free your mind, but I can only show you the door. You're the one that has to walk through it. Neo, sooner or later you're going to realize just as I did that there's a difference between knowing the path and walking the path."[6]

DO SOMETHING . . . ANYTHING

You've probably heard the saying, "To fail to plan is to plan to fail." That's clever. Here's one that doesn't sound as clever but is probably more truthful, "To fail to act is to act out failure." People who like words will probably not internalize it, but for those who take action, it doesn't need to be put into words. They live it.

At my last inner-city church plant, Refuge Long Beach, Christmas loomed ever nearer. With our most recent neighborhood move, we knew we couldn't just repeat our Christmas Party outreach in the school with a gift drive, pictures with Santa, and a raging cookie party (yeah, it's a thing). None of us seemed to have the white hot bat phone to heaven either. The commissioner wasn't lighting the bat signal in the sky telling us where we were needed. We didn't know what we were doing. We didn't know what our strategy should look like. Our leadership team knew just one thing. We had to keep moving forward on mission.

Our new plan sucked. We scraped together a plan to do a toy drive with the Starbucks across the street. We started making plans to meet with the principal of Wilson High School, notorious for its depiction in the Hillary Swank film, *Freedom Writers*, to enlist youth volunteers. We all knew it probably wasn't going to work, but as each day came closer, people weren't thinking about the fact that it was going to fail. When the chips are down and imminent failure is looming, you start getting serious. We were acting out of the conviction that to do nothing would be irresponsible. Heartless. Possibly even sinful.

Suddenly, we got a call putting us in touch with a local women and children's shelter, and recognizing it as divine providence decided our toy drive would serve the local shelter, and Starbucks jumped in with both feet. The relationship with the local manager of the Starbucks on the corner received a boon as we were now serving the community in local causes rather than just trying to suck people into our machine. Yeah, people see through that. Believe me.

The lesson? At some point, you have to take action. It felt as if God were taking action in response to ours. Perhaps God doesn't move often until we do. Here's the cool part. Pastors don't typically go to women's shelters. They're busy doing their churchy church things. Yet ministry like this can have an exponential impact on a city.

It was taking action that made the difference.

That's why Peter said to prepare your minds for action (1 Pet. 1:13). This is why I've been asking you to act every week. To do something. Anything. A major shift happens when we make that choice. A. W. Tozer, at the end of preaching, once said, "Don't come down here to the altar and cry about it—go home and live it!"[7]

LASTING IMPACT

By the time you read this, I may not be training church planting trainers anymore. More than likely, I'll be working some secular job again, living out what I've written, just like I have since 1998. Then again, maybe I'm in a lock up phase so I could get writing. Every time I get held back from being around lost people, I start to get a little twitch. I get funky, but not in a Lenny Kravitz kind of way. It's more like a gym sock in your locker kind of way.

Like Gandhi never said, but is nonetheless true, you will need to become the change you want to see in the world to truly impact it. There is simply no other way. What Gandhi actually said was, "If we could change ourselves, the tendencies in the world would also change. As a man changes his own nature, so does the attitude of the world change towards him. . . . We need not wait to see what others do."[8] Make no mistake, this has not been a book about making a huge splash and becoming famous. It's not about making an impact measured by Twitter followers, Facebook friends, or YouTube views. It's a book about reaching the unreached, and that starts with God reaching us. For the world around the church to change, the church must change first, for judgment begins with the house of God. If this book did nothing but change you, it would be the first step to making world changers.

Perhaps a major change in this social-media fueled age would be to choose between being popular or being effective. The two don't often don't go together. They didn't for Jesus anyway. Or Paul. Or any of the apostles. Even A. W. Tozer once remarked to Lloyd-Jones that he'd preached himself out of nearly every conference he'd been invited to because he'd desired to be a mouthpiece for God rather than build his own reputation. You can hide behind the enemy lines and put on a great United Service Organizations show for the troops, or you can penetrate No Man's Land, behind enemy lines where there is little recognition, but maximum impact.

I leave you with one penetrating question to help get you going in the right direction. If God appeared to you as he did to Solomon, and offered to give you something, what would you ask for? What if he asked you to make a choice between having a medium impact here, where people knew your name, and admired you, asked you to speak, interviewed you, and wrote articles about what you were doing, versus having a ministry that blessed millions in a country where you lived in obscurity, worked in the underground church, and nobody ever knew your name. Which would you choose?

How you answer that question will largely determine the course of your life, and possibly the degree of reward in the afterlife. As the Grail Knight said at the end of *Indiana Jones and the Last Crusade,*

"Choose wisely, for while the true grail will bring you life, the false grail will take it from you." Fame, being liked, and having people applaud you is a life-sucking-false grail. Jesus said that recognition here was often the full reward, whereas the Father rewards that which is done in secret (Matt. 6:2–4). I'm convinced that the ordinary everyday ministry of believers who work with their hands, keep their day jobs, and serve Jesus simply to hear him say, "Well done, good and faithful servant," are the force that will change the world, and have the most impact in the world around them.

In the words of Evel Knievel, "I decided to fly through the air and live in the sunshine and enjoy life as much as I could." That might sound strange coming from a man who suffered more fractures than you have bones in your body, but I think he was on to something. Enjoying life isn't about a peaceful existence with no alarms and no surprises. It's in the ups and downs on mission with the Holy Spirit, like the wind at your back and the rev of power in the engine. It's in leaving earth momentarily, in the grips of the Holy Spirit as he revs you, watching the ground beneath you dropping, and rising back up to you again, feeling alive because you survived the jump. Freefalling into the hands of God is something that only a few brave souls know how to do. You see, it's not the jumping, it's the falling. Gravity can be a harsh mistress. But the ups and downs balance out with the risk and reward. The crashes and flashes of God's glory. The soaring and the falling. The things you can control, and the things that are left to his control. In that balance comes the exhilaration of making an eternal impact and being a part of the legend of Jesus Christ's mission on earth.

John Wesley and some of his followers, such as Asbury, may have been the closest thing we've had to the apostle Paul in the history of the church, and the Evel Knievel of church history. Until you've had people peeing on you from a tree while you're trying to preach the gospel, you've not really lived. It wasn't just that his life was impressive, but that he, like Paul, inspired an entire generation to burn up, and blaze out like comets for Jesus, radiating his glory across the black backdrop of the night. Here's to you leaving behind the life as you knew it, and blazing your own path before him.

"Commencing countdown.

Engines on.

Check ignition and may God's love be with you."[9]

Daredevils John and Charles Wesley penned the Methodist covenant prayer for his circuit riders* to be declared together once each year. It would serve any well who were brave enough to pray it. And many, many did, leading to the Great Awakening.

> *I am no longer my own, but thine.*
> *Put me to what thou wilt, rank me with whom thou wilt.*
> *Put me to doing, put me to suffering.*
> *Let me be employed for thee or laid aside for thee,*
> *exalted for thee or brought low for thee.*
> *Let me be full, let me be empty.*
> *Let me have all things, let me have nothing.*
> *I freely and heartily yield all things to thy pleasure and disposal.*
> *And now, O glorious and blessed God, Father, Son and Holy Spirit,*
> *thou art mine, and I am thine.*
> *So be it.*
> *And the covenant which I have made on earth,*
> *let it be ratified in heaven.*
> *Amen.*

Remember those cheeky angels after Jesus said his final words to the apostles and ascended into heaven? "Why do you stand looking into heaven?" (Acts 1:11). I'd pose the same question to you now. We've got work to do. Don the fedora. Grab the whip and get cracking. Adventure beckons.

---

* Had they lived in the age of Evel, they would have totally had motorcycles, white pantsuits with stars and stripes, a cape, and a helmet with a big star on it. Okay . . . That's too far. Maybe not the cape.

Discussion Questions

(For Dr. Jones, the Princeton Professor in you)

1. What in this book has stood out to you the most?
2. What has been the greatest change you've experienced since starting this book?
3. How has God started to take you on a journey to reach the unreached?
4. What advice would you give to someone just starting this journey?

Adventurous Actions

(For Indiana, the Temple Raider in you)

1. Buy another copy of this book, and give it to a friend. (Haha . . . a joke. But erm . . . really, buy another copy.)
2. Write your own covenant and put it somewhere you will see it every day.
3. Ask the Holy Spirit to fill you daily, step out in faith regularly, and be prepared for surprises!
4. Do something. Anything.

AFTERWORD

Let's face it. What used to work in church just doesn't anymore. You know it. I know it.

If you've been in ministry for a decade or more, you know the old methods (which were new when you started . . . because you were one of those mavericks back then) only bring diminishing results.

And you're stumped.

If you're just starting out in ministry, you've chosen a brave path . . . one strewn with many problems but not nearly as many solutions. And you're looking around for "models" or "formulas," only to discover it's harder than you thought to find something that connects with the unchurched. I know.

That's why I love what Peyton Jones does in this powerful book.

Maybe our model's not broken. Maybe we are.

Let me rephrase that. Maybe we *need* to be broken.

Peyton sums it up so well: "Despite what you may have been led to believe, the church services you attend are *not* the key to reaching the unreached. You are."

He's so right. And this book takes you on that journey. If you don't get punched in the gut more than a dozen times, your reading comprehension is poor. This book made me cry (not figuratively . . . literally). It also broke my heart. Which is exactly what my heart needed.

Like you, I'm not 100 percent sure what the answer to the future church is. I *am* confident there's a bright future, because the church is Jesus's idea, not ours.

As much as we'd love to find five things that would solve everything, or ten ways to bullet-proof your leadership (who writes blogs like that anyway?), we all know it's not that simple.

One thing I do believe that will make a difference is passion. I've noticed that churches whose leaders have a white-hot passion for Christ and for the mission tend to reach far more people than churches led by leaders whose passion glows less.

In this book, Peyton pokes and prods the souls of leaders until they start to bleed.

You can't read this book without becoming uncomfortable or convicted. Every time you think you're off the hook, Peyton launches into another chapter where he pushes you into an encounter with the God who moves mountains and (hopefully) the callous hearts of church leaders.

This book is a unique blend of the inspired leadership of the past, the pain of the present, and the promise of the future. It will both challenge you deeply and inspire you greatly, until your walk with God becomes so uncomfortable you either throw yourself at Christ's feet or you decide to walk away—both of which could be good things because the church is no longer at the point where mediocrity is helping anyone.

If you want an easy ride, this book isn't for you.

If you're looking for simple formulas and easy solutions, put this book back on the shelf.

But if you're ready to go on a soul journey that can kindle within you the kind of white-hot passion that will help lead a new generation to Jesus . . . read on and lead on.

That's what I'm doing.

CAREY NIEUWHOF
Founding Pastor, Connexus Church

NOTES

Chapter 1: A Butt-Kicking is a Terrible Thing to Waste

1. Luther's letter to Pope Leo, May 30, 1518.
2. This is not a translation, but my paraphrase.
3. Carey Nieuwhof, "A Response To Christians Who Are Done With Church." June 12, 2015. http://careynieuwhof.com/2015/06/a-response-to-christians-who-are-done-with-church.
4. Sutton, Robert I. *Weird Ideas That Work* (New York: The Free Press, 2002), 23.
5. Addison, Steve. *What Jesus Started* (Downers Grove, IL: IVP Books), 15.
6. Lewis, C. S. *Christian Reflections* (Grand Rapids, MI: William B. Eerdmans Publishing Company, 2014), 33.
7. *Raiders of the Lost Ark.*
8. Dr. Martin Luther King, Jr. "Letter from a Birmingham Jail" April 16, 1963. https://www.africa.upenn.edu/Articles_Gen/Letter_Birmingham.html.
9. Stetzer, Ed. *Planting Missional Churches* (Nashville: B&H Academic, 2016), 9.
10. Ibid.
11. Ibid.
12. Stearns, Richard. *Unfinished: Filling the Hole in Our Gospel* (Nashville: W Publishing Group, 2013), 175.
13. Tozer, A. W. *The Pursuit of God: The Definitive Classic* (Ventura, CA: Regal, 2013), 43.
14. Lewis, C. S. *Mere Christianity* (New York: Macmillan, 1952), 190.
15. Baker, S. *Life of Evel: Evel Knievel* (New York: St. Martin's Press, 2008), 56.

Chapter 2: Wait

1. Snyder, James, L. *The Life of A.W. Tozer* (Ventura, CA: Regal, 2009), 50.
2. Belmonte, Kevin. *D. L. Moody: A Life* (Chicago: Moody Press, 2014), 106.

3. Lloyd-Jones, Martyn. *Revival* (Westchester, IL: Crossway Books, 1987), 158.

4. Torrey R. A. *The Person and Work of the Holy Spirit* (Zeeland, MI: Reformed Church Publications, 2015), 117.

5. A sermon delivered in 1982 and available on YouTube. I highly suggest you watch it. https://www.youtube.com/watch?v=pQKc6MMNYnI.

6. C. H. Spurgeon. "The Former and the Latter Rain" July 11, 1869. http://www.biblia.work/sermons/the-former-and-the-latter-rain/.

7. Piper, John. *Let the Nations Be Glad! The Supremacy of God in Missions* (Grand Rapids: Baker, 2003), 17.

8. Quote famously attributed to Oswald J. Smith.

Chapter 3: Not Many Days from Now

1. Cameron, Kirk, and Ray Comfort. *The World's Greatest Preachers* (New Kensington, PA: Whitaker House, 2003). Google Books ed.

2. Tozer, A. W. *Jesus, Our Man in Glory* (Camp Hill, PA: Christian Publications, 2009), 16.

3. *Indiana Jones and the Crystal Skull.*

4. My paraphrase of John 21:18.

5. Tolkien, J. R. R. *The Hobbit* (New York: Houghton Mifflin, 1994), 2.

6. Ibid., 4.

7. Ibid., 15.

8. Tolkien, J. R. R. *The Lord of the Rings* (Boston: Houghton Mifflin Harcourt, 1993), 87.

9. Tolkien, J. R. R. *The Hobbit* (New York: Random House, 1982), 223.

10. Dwight Eisenhower speaking to the National Defense Executive Reserve Conference in Washington D.C. on November 14, 1957.

11. Hebrews 12:1–4.

12. Unsourced, but well-known quote.

13. Carmichael, Amy. "Make Me Thy Fuel" in *Toward Jerusalem* (Fort Washington, PA: CLC Publications, 2013) Google Books ed.

14. Addison, Steve. *Movements that Change the World* (Downers Grove, IL: IVP Books, 2011), 93.

15. Spurgeon, Charles. *Lectures to My Students* (London: Passmore and Alabaster, 1897), 160.

16. Spurgeon, C. H. *An All-Round Ministry* (London: Banner of Truth, 1960), 55.

17. Franklin, Benjamin. *Poor Richard's almanac for 1850–52* (New York: John Doggett Jr., 1849). Google Books ed.

18. Spurgeon, Charles. *Lectures to My Students* (London: Passmoor and Alabaster, 1887), 13–14.

19. Tolkien, J. R. R. *The Hobbit* (New York: Random House, 1982), 302.

Chapter 4: You Will Receive Power

1. Melville, Herman. *Moby Dick* (New York: Barnes and Noble Books, 1994), 1.
2. Lewis, C. S. *The Weight of Glory* (New York: Harper One, 1976), 160.
3. "Facing a Task Unfinished" by Frank Houghton, 1930.
4. Popular quote often attributed to A. W. Tozer.
5. Judges 6:13.

Chapter 5: When the Holy Spirit Has Come upon You

1. Roxburgh, Alan. *Joining God, Remaking the Church, Changing the World.* (New York: Morehouse Publishing, 2015). Kindle edition.
2. Torrey, R. A. *The Person and Work of the Holy Spirit* (Zeeland, MI: Reformed Church Publications, 2015), 118.
3. John 12:32.
4. John 16:14.
5. Lloyd Jones, Martin. *Revival* (Wheaton, IL: Crossway, 1987), 160.
6. Snyder, J. *The Life of A. W. Tozer* (Ventura, CA: Regal Books, 2009), 160.
7. Hutson, C. *Great Preaching on the Holy Spirit* (Murfreesboro, TN: Sword Of The Lord Publishers, 2000), 98.
8. Whitefield, George. *The First Two Parts of His Life, with His Journals* (London: W. Strahan), 33.
9. Carmichael, Amy. "Flame of God" in *Toward Jerusalem* (Fort Washington, PA: CLC Publications, 2013). Google Books ed.
10. Newell, M. J. *Expect Great Things* (Pasadena: William Carey Library, 2013), 211.
11. Matthew 11:19.
12. Spurgeon, Charles. *Lectures to My Students* (London: Passmore and Alabaster, 1887), 14.
13. Lewis C. S. *The Great Divorce* (New York: Macmillan, 1946), 101.
14. Newell, M. J. *Expect Great Things* (Pasadena: William Carey Library, 2013), 213.
15. Stadtmiller, Adam. *Praying for Your Elephant* (Colorado Springs, CO: David C Cook, 2014), 142.
16. Anonymous, but quoted by E. M. Bounds.

Chapter 6: You Will Be My Witnesses

1. Lewis C. S. *The Weight of Glory* (New York: HarperOne, 2015), 15.
2. Pastor, Paul. *The Face of the Deep* (Colorado Springs, CO: David C Cook, 2016). Google Books ed.
3. Snyder, J. *The Life of A. W. Tozer* (Ventura, CA: Regal Books, 2009), 128.
4. "Dwight L. Moody" *Christianity Today*. http://www.christianitytoday.com/history/people/evangelistsandapologists/dwight-l-moody.html.
5. Bounds, E. M. *The Works of E. M. Bounds* (Zeeland, MI: Reformed Church Publications, 2015), 566.
6. Guinness, Os. *The Call* (Nashville: Thomas Nelson, 1998), 46.

Chapter 7: In Jerusalem

1. Nieuwhof, Carey. *Lasting Impact* (Cumming: GA: The reThink Group, Inc., 2015), 88.
2. Chesterton, G. K. *Heretics and Orthodoxy* (Nashville: Thomas Nelson, 2000), 228.
3. Colson, Charles. *Who Speaks for God?* (Carol Stream, IL: Tyndale House Publishers, Inc., 1994), 85.
4. An unspecified platform appeal, as quoted in *The Musical Salvationist* (September 1927). Several variants of this exist, some of them credited to his speech at the Royal Albert Hall on May 9, 1912, as researched "While Women Weep-I'll Fight" by Gordon Taylor at the International Heritage Centre (19 July 1996).
5. Edwards, Darren. *Chav Christianity* (London: New Generation Publishing, 2013), 87.
6. Spurgeon, C. H. "Baptism Essential to Obedience." Spurgeon's Sermons Volume 39: 1893 http://www.ccel.org/ccel/spurgeon/sermons39.li.html.

Chapter 8: In Judea

1. Jones, Peyton. *Church Zero* (Colorado Springs, CO: David C Cook, 2013), 24–25.
2. Anonymous again . . . man, that guy has all the best quotes!
3. Grubb, Norman. *C. T. Studd: Cricketer & Pioneer* (Fort Washington, PA: CLC Publications, 1982), 120.
4. Cameron, Kirk, and Ray Comfort. *The World's Greatest Preachers* (New Kensington, PA: Whitaker House, 2003). Google Books ed.
5. From the TV sitcom *WKRP in Cincinnati* . . . ah, the seventies.

6. "Charles Studd," *Wikipedia*, last modified October 12, 2016, https://en .wikipedia.org/wiki/Charles_Studd.

7. Spurgeon, Charles. *Lectures to My Students* (London: Passmore and Alabaster, 1897), 254.

Chapter 9: To Samaria

1. Diaz, Maria Carrillo, Antonio Crego Diaz and Martin Romero Maroto. *Mission America: A Wesleyan Perspective* (Nacogdoches, Texas: Gospel Outpost Network, 2012), 71.

2. Spurgeon C. H. *The Sword and the Trowel* (Nabu Press, 2010), 464.

3. Bonhoeffer, Dietrich. *Life Together: The Classic Exploration of Christian Community* (New York: HarperOne, 1978), 110.

4. Tony Campolo. "Tony Campolo Throws a Party for a Prostitute" Excerpted from *The Kingdom of God Is a Party: God's Radical Plan for His Family* June 2008. *PreachingToday.com:* http://www.preachingtoday.com/ illustrations/2008/june/15742.html.

5. Bounds, E. M. *The Weapon of Prayer: A Study in Christian Warfare* (Woodstock, Ontario: Devoted Publishing, 2015), 16.

Chapter 10: To the Ends of the Earth

1. Zuck, Roy B. *The Speaker's Quote Book* (Grand Rapids, MI: Kregel, 2009), 80.

2. Victoria Woollaston, "Why Talking about Yourself with Friends Can be as Pleasurable as Sex," July 18, 2013. *DailyMail:* http://www.dailymail.co.uk/ sciencetech/article-2368451/Why-talking-friends-pleasurable-SEX.html.

3. Miller, Basil. *William Carey: The Father of Modern Missions* (Minneapolis: Bethany House, 1980), 31.

4. Ibid., 32.

5. Ibid., 37.

6. Morpheus to Neo, *The Matrix*.

7. Snyder, James L. *The Life of A. W. Tozer: In Pursuit of God* (Ventura, California: Regal, 2009), 152.

8. Gandhi, Mahatma. *The Collected Works of M. K. Gandhi, Volume 13* (New Delhi: Publications Division Ministry of Information and Broadcasting Government of India, 2000), 241.

9. David Bowie, *Space Oddity*.

WANT TO BE A PART OF A CHURCH PLANTING NETWORK THAT FUNCTIONS LIKE PAUL DID IN THE BOOK OF ACTS?

If you actually like what you read in this book, the New Breed Network will scratch where you itch.

And now New Breed Network is offering a FREE webinar

REACHING THE UNREACHED:
What They Didn't Teach You in Seminary
(but should have)

You'll learn stuff like:
- How to get involved with a network of like-minded church planters
- How to take the Church Zero philosophy and reinvent your church
- How to setup and maintain a gift-driven ministry that conforms to standards of the early church
- How to make sure you don't waste valuable time and money on the wrong training... and start training with church planters in the field
- How to start a church based on team ministry the way it's modeled in Acts
- And MORE!

PASTORS:
Get your church out of the current rut and revitalize it into a dangerous, dynamic force to reach the unreached!

CHURCH PLANTERS:
Find out if seminary is going to prep you for the real world of church planting!

Register now for this FREE webinar! New Breed loves doing stuff for free, but due to time constraints, there are a limited number of times Peyton Jones will give this webinar and the number of attendees is capped by the webinar provider.

To register, visit: **www.NewBreedCP.org**